Dialogues in a Dream

Dialogues in a Dream

THE LIFE AND ZEN TEACHINGS OF MUSŌ SOSEKI

TRANSLATED AND ANNOTATED BY THOMAS YŪHŌ KIRCHNER

Wisdom

Wisdom Publications
199 Elm Street
Somerville, MA 02144 USA
wisdompubs.org

Library of Congress Cataloging-in-Publication Data
Musō Soseki, 1275–1351, author.
 [Muchu mondoshu. English]
 Dialogues in a dream / translated and annotated by Thomas Yūhō Kirchner, Associate Researcher, International Research Institute for Zen Buddhism, Hanazono University, Kyoto, Japan.
   pages cm
 Includes bibliographical references and index.
 ISBN 1-61429-253-1 (pbk. : alk. paper)
  1. Zen Buddhism—Doctrines—Early works to 1800. I. Kirchner, Thomas Yūhō, translator, writer of added commentary. II. Title.
 BQ9268.M8513 2015
 294.3'927—dc23

                      2014041852

ISBN 978-1-61429-253-1   ebook ISBN 978-1-61429-268-5

19 18 17 16 15   5 4 3 2 1

Cover image by Kawase Hasui, "Moonlit Night at Miyajima." Used with permission from the Art Institute of Chicago. Cover and interior design by Gopa&Ted2, typeset by LC. Set in Diacritical Garamond Pro 12/15.54.

Wisdom Publications' books are printed on acid-free paper and meet the guidelines for permanence and durability of the Production Guidelines for Book Longevity of the Council on Library Resources.

This book was produced with environmental mindfulness. We have elected to print this title on 30% PCW recycled paper. As a result, we have saved the following resources: 12 trees, 6 million BTUs of energy, 1,039 lbs. of greenhouse gases, 5,638 gallons of water, and 377 lbs. of solid waste. For more information, please visit our website, wisdompubs.org.

Printed in the United States of America.

Please visit fscus.org.

Table of Contents

PART II

PART III

PUBLISHER'S ACKNOWLEDGMENT

THE PUBLISHER gratefully acknowledges the generous contribution of the Hershey Family Foundation toward the publication of this book.

ZEN MASTERS have never been averse to using language as a means of conveying their message, even as they stress the ineffability of the experience that their message attempts to describe. The masters active during Zen's early years in Japan in the thirteenth and fourteenth centuries were no exception, leaving numerous writings in the form of recorded sayings, Dharma talks, and poetry collections. Among these works, the one that has perhaps best stood the test of time, as judged by its enduring popularity throughout the ensuing years, is a moderately sized publication known as *Dialogues in a Dream* (*Muchū Mondō 夢中問答). This three-fascicle work consists of ninety-three chapters, each chapter being a question-and-answer exchange between Musō Soseki 夢窓疎石 (1275–1351), one of the most influential Japanese Zen masters of his time, and Ashikaga Tadayoshi 足利直義 (1306–1352), a founder and leader of the Muromachi Shogunate that governed Japan between 1336 and 1568.

Compiled in 1342 and first published in 1344, *Dialogues in a Dream* appeared at a seminal time in the history of Japanese Zen. Zen was originally introduced to Japan at the end of the twelfth century by Myōan Eisai[1] and nurtured through the following years by a succession of Japanese masters who had trained in China and Chinese masters who had immigrated to Japan. With the generation of Musō

Soseki, however, a growing number of the school's leaders were native-born and native-trained, and the tradition was making the transition from a foreign import to a naturalized expression of Japanese spirituality. Musō himself was deeply involved not only in teaching Zen but also in shaping its cultural manifestation in such areas as poetry and garden design.

As a work that has been consistently available throughout the centuries since its original publication, *Dialogues in a Dream* has been one of Musō's most enduring contributions to Zen teaching in Japan. Written in the Japanese language rather than the Classical Chinese that most Buddhist works were composed in at the time, it has always been more approachable to the literate public than most Zen literature. It is, in addition, expressed in a relatively straightforward expository style that testifies to Musō's clear, systematic thought, refined through the years he spent studying the doctrines and rituals of exoteric and esoteric Buddhism prior to his practice of Zen meditation. His solid background in these traditions was to serve him well in his career of proselytizing not only to the ordained clergy but also to the Buddhist laity.

Given the importance of this background in Musō's career as a teacher, as well as in the thought that found expression in the exchanges that comprise *Dialogues in a Dream*, a brief account of the master's life provides an appropriate starting point for understanding this text.

THE ZEN MASTER MUSŌ SOSEKI

Many factors—including Musō's high profile as a teacher of emperors and shoguns, his large following of well-educated disciples, and his own willingness to discuss the events of his career—combined to make Musō's life one of the best-documented among the early Japanese Zen masters. The primary source for Musō's life is the *Chronological Biography of National Teacher Musō Shōkaku Shinshū Fusai, Founder of Tenryū-ji* (*Tenryū kaisan Musō Shōkaku Shinshū Fusai*

Kokushi nenpu 天龍開山夢窓正覺心宗普濟國師年譜), compiled by Shun'oku Myōha,[2] Musō's nephew and Dharma successor, and published in 1353, just over a year after Musō's death. The *Biography* is an invaluable resource, as Shun'oku's proximity to Musō left him eminently positioned to give an accurate account of the master's life, probably based on reports heard from Musō himself. A limited amount of additional information is found here and there in the master's poems and other writings, including *Night Talks on West Mountain* (*Seizan yawa* 西山夜話)[3] and *Dialogues in a Dream.*

Owing to the subsequent prominence of Musō's Dharma lineage in medieval Rinzai Zen, a number of additional biographical texts were compiled in the centuries following Musō's death, but much of the material in these texts that is not found in Shun'oku's account (such as information relating to Musō's ancestry) appears to be based less on verifiable historical fact than on attempts to burnish Musō's image.

In the present biographical overview I have relied primarily on Shun'oku's *Biography*, as translated into modern Japanese and supplemented with other historical materials by the Japanese scholar Nishiyama Mika 西山美香 in an appendix to her PhD thesis entitled "The Life of Musō Soseki" 夢窓疎石の生涯. Another especially helpful reference was Martin Collcutt's chapter on Musō Soseki in *The Origins of Japan's Medieval World.*[4] Collcutt's treatment takes full account of the information in the *Biography* as it contextualizes Musō's contributions within the historical framework of fourteenth-century Japan.

The *Biography* provides only a sketchy picture of Musō's earliest years, saying that he was born in the year 1275 in the province of Ise (the central portion of present-day Mie Prefecture), that his father was of the Minamoto clan and his mother of the Taira clan,[5] and that Musō himself was a ninth-generation descendant of Emperor Uda 宇多 (867–931). It adds that his mother prayed to the bodhisattva Kannon (Avalokiteśvara) for the birth of a son, and that one night she had a dream in which a golden light streamed from the west and entered her mouth. Thirteen months later Musō was born. Musō himself was later known for his devotion to Avalokiteśvara, constructing shrines dedicated to the bodhisattva at most of the temples he founded and often performing Kannon Purification rituals during the course of his Zen training.

The *Biography* gives the year but not the date of Musō's birth (though later materials suggest that it was on the first day of the eleventh month), and his exact birthplace remains unidentified. Regarding the latter there are two rival claims, advanced, respectively, by Tenryū-ji and Shōkoku-ji, the two largest temples associated with Musō. Tenryū-ji proposes the village of Miyake 三宅, located in the southwestern environs of the present city of Suzuka, while Shōkoku-ji's candidate is the village of Katada Ido 片田井戸, about fourteen kilometers south of Miyake on the western outskirts of the city of Tsu.

In 1278, owing to an unexplained disturbance in Musō's mother's family, the family left Ise and moved to Kai (present-day Yamanashi Prefecture) in the mountains of eastern Japan. The family's move to Kai may have been motivated in part by the fact that it was the seat of the Takeda family, a powerful branch of the Minamoto clan.

In the eighth month of 1278 Musō's mother died. Although it is unlikely that Musō, just three years old at the time, was turned toward the religious life by this early loss, the *Biography* reports that there were already signs that the boy was temperamentally inclined in that direction. He is said to have been quiet and gentle, intelligent and studious. By the time he was five he was already able to write characters and demonstrated comprehension of the sutras he recited.

In 1283, at the age of eight, Musō was taken by his father to the nearby temple Heien-ji 平塩寺 and placed under the tutelage of the eminent priest Kūa 空阿 (n.d.). Although the *Biography* reports that Musō's father did so out of a strong desire to have his son become a monk (Musō, according to the account, had already shown his spiritual fervor by chanting the *Lotus Sutra* for seven full days to mark the anniversary of his mother's death), residence at a temple may simply have been the most effective way at the time to further the education of an obviously precocious and sensitive child.

There is some question regarding what branch of Buddhism Heien-ji was associated with. Founded in 755 as a Hossō school[6] temple, it soon reaffiliated itself with the Tendai school,[7] then—either while Musō was there or shortly thereafter—with the Shingon school.[8] In any event, a shift from Tendai to Shingon would have meant little with regard to the content of Musō's studies, which in either case would have focused on esoteric ritual and exoteric doctrine. Musō's early education would also have included extensive readings in the classics of Chinese literature and philosophy as well as training in the secular accomplishments.

In 1286 Musō's father remarried. His new wife, a woman of Minamoto ancestry, became like a second mother to Musō and was warmly remembered by him in later life. He paid visits to the family home every ten days, often bringing a number of young friends for a good meal. At the same time, his awareness of the ephemeral nature of life appears to have been deepening. The *Biography* reports that in 1288, at age thirteen, Musō completed the considerable task of painting the "Nine Images for Contemplation," a series of illustrations showing the stages of decay a corpse undergoes until nothing is left but scattered bones. Musō meditated on these images until he came to perceive his own body as nothing but lifeless flesh, and he subsequently spent much time sitting in contemplation under trees and in quiet places.

In 1292, at the age of seventeen, Musō journeyed to the ancient capital of Nara, several hundred kilometers to the west of Kai, to take the formal precepts at Tōdai-ji 東大寺 under a precept master named Jikan 慈観 (n.d.). Following his return that year to Heien-ji, Musō abandoned all non-Buddhist pursuits and focused upon deepening his understanding of Buddhist doctrine and ritual. Musō's spiritual life took a decisive turn in 1293, when one of the priests teaching Tendai doctrine at Heien-ji became ill and shortly thereafter died in a state of great suffering. This painful death caused Musō to question the entire direction of his education. According to the *Biography*, Musō reflected that

> Buddhism has many paths, but all are directed toward
> leaving the world's dust behind and gaining the Way. This
> lecture master was famous for his knowledge, but at the
> time of his death it benefited him nothing. The Buddha-
> dharma is beyond the reach of learning and intellect. Is it
> not for this reason that the Zen school speaks of "a sepa-
> rate transmission outside the teachings"?

In an effort to clarify his own future course, Musō embarked upon a hundred-day solitary retreat devoted to prayer and medita-tion. Where this occurred is uncertain, but Nishiyama notes that the historical records of Mitomi-mura 三富村, a village in the vicinity of present-day Yamanashi City, mention a ninety-nine-day period of meditation by the nineteen-year-old Musō in a hillside cave near the community.

Three days before the end of the retreat Musō had a dream in which a guide led him deep into the mountains to a solitary temple. The place was decorated in a dignified manner, though no one was there. When Musō asked the name of the temple his guide answered, "Sozan." They then continued on to another temple, identified by the guide as "Sekitō," where an elderly priest greeted them. Musō's guide said to the priest, "This monk has traveled here in search of a sacred image. Please, Reverend, be so kind as to present him with one." Thereupon the old priest picked up a scroll and handed it to Musō. Upon unrolling it Musō saw that it was a portrait of Bodhidharma,[9] the Indian monk traditionally honored as the transmitter of Zen to China. Musō rolled up the scroll and placed it in the folds of his robe, at which point he awoke from his dream.

Sozan and Sekitō were two well-known Tang-dynasty Zen masters: "Sozan" refers to Sushan Guangren (J., Sozan Kōnin),[10] while "Sekitō" refers to Shitou Xiqian (J., Sekitō Kisen).[11] While their exact signifi-cance for Musō is not explained in the texts, both were important fig-ures who played significant roles in the development of Chinese Zen.

Musō's dream settled for him the course of his future practice.

Seeing it as a sign of a deep connection with the Zen school, he took the new name "Soseki" (combining the "so" of "Sozan" with the "seki" of "Sekitō") and "Musō" (meaning "Dream Window," his dream having provided the window through which he could perceive his future course; although I have been using the name Musō for him as a matter of convenience, until this point in his life he had been known by his novice name Chikaku 智曜). He then commenced a training pilgrimage that was to last, off and on, for nearly forty years.

In 1294 Musō left Kai to visit Shinchi Kakushin,[12] a Shingon priest who, like Musō, had turned to the practice of Zen, and who in the late thirteenth century was priest of the temple Saihō-ji 西方寺 in Yura, a town on the mountainous shore of present-day Wakayama Prefecture. On his way to Yura, however, Musō called upon a Zen monk named Tokushō 徳照, an old friend then living in Kyoto, who advised him that before setting off for a retreat at a remote temple like Saihō-ji it would be best to learn the basics of Zen practice at a large monastic community. Musō therefore changed plans and entered Kennin-ji, the oldest Zen monastery in Kyoto, to study under the master Muin Enban.[13] Practice at Kennin-ji had originally consisted of the syncretic mix of Zen meditation and Tendai ritual introduced by its founder, Myōan Eisai, but Muin Enban's teacher, Lanxi Daolong,[14] had reformed life at the temple according to the strict monastic regulations of Song-dynasty Zen. It was in this style of Zen that Musō began his training.

In the tenth month of 1295 Musō traveled to Kamakura to continue his practice at Tōshō-ji 東勝寺 under the Lanxi-line master Mukyū Tokusen.[15] Following a major fire at Tōshō-ji, Musō moved nearby to the great monastery of Kenchō-ji 建長寺 to study under another Lanxi successor, Ikō Dōnen.[16] While at Kenchō-ji, an older monk encouraged Musō to read the Zen records. According to *Night Talks on West Mountain*, the monk spoke as follows:

The enlightened words of the ancient masters are published and read so that young monks may study them and receive guidance in their quest for awakening.... In the Latter Age of the Dharma it is hard to find true teachers. If we arouse our aspiration and read the Zen records, we will see that the enlightenment of the ancient masters is itself our enlightenment today. Why should past and present differ?

Hearing these words, Musō, who since turning to Zen had devoted himself almost entirely to meditation, started spending what time he could on examining the old records.

In 1296 Musō continued his instruction in Lanxi-line Zen from Chōkei Tokugo[17] at Engaku-ji 圓覺寺, a large monastery located a ten-minute walk northwest of Kenchō-ji. When yet another Lanxi successor, Chidon Kūshō,[18] became abbot of Kenchō-ji, Musō sought instruction from him at Chōkei's urging.

Musō returned to Kyoto following the end of the 1297 training season and reentered Kennin-ji to continue his study under Muin Enban. In the summer of 1299, however, he encountered the Chinese Zen master Yishan Yining,[19] soon after the latter's arrival from China. Yishan appears to have impressed him very favorably, since, not long afterward, Musō traveled to Kamakura to join him at Kenchō-ji, where Yishan had just been installed as abbot. So many monks flocked to the monastery to practice under him that Yishan, in order to narrow the field, devised an entrance examination ascertaining the applicants' literary abilities. Musō was one of the two monks who received top marks for the test.

Musō remained at Kenchō-ji for two training periods, then, in the autumn of 1300, set out for the province of Dewa 出羽 (present Yamagata and Akita prefectures) in the northern reaches of Japan to visit an old friend. When news reached him that his friend was no longer alive, he instead made his way to the temple Shōtō-ji 松島寺 (present Zuigan-ji 瑞巖寺), a large Kenchō-ji affiliate located near what is now the city of Sendai. While there, the *Biography* reports, he was deeply inspired by a certain monk's discourse on Tendai meditation. Sitting in *zazen* (Zen meditation) through the night, he had a sudden insight into the distinctions between the teachings of the various Buddhist schools, and he subsequently noticed that his thought was clearer, his speech more fluent, and his mind much freer of fear.

Although he didn't regard this experience as true enlightenment, Musō was nevertheless interested in knowing what it signified, so late in the year he departed Shōtō-ji for the temple Ungan-ji 雲巖寺 in Nasu, about two hundred kilometers to the south, to check his understanding with the noted master Kōhō Kennichi.[20] As chance would have it, when Musō arrived Kōhō had just departed for Kamakura. Musō decided to remain at the temple anyway, as he was suffering from a leg affliction. The *Biography* reports that while there he performed a Kannon Purification Ceremony during which he experienced a *makyō*—an illusory event that occasionally arises out of states of deep concentration—where the faded image of Avalokiteśvara suddenly appeared as if newly painted. Avalokiteśvara herself smiled and appeared vibrantly alive, then took on the form of monks, nuns, demons, and countless other beings. Realizing that all of these phenomena were nothing more than creations of his mind, Musō paid them no heed.

In February 1301 Musō returned to Kenchō-ji to resume his training under Yishan. The following year, when Yishan agreed to serve concurrently as abbot of both Kenchō-ji and Engaku-ji, Musō accompanied him to the latter temple in order to continue his studies.

By 1303, however, Musō was beginning to question the direction his practice had taken ever since he spoke with the old monk at Kenchō-ji in 1295 and occupied himself with investigating the traditional Zen records. *Night Talks on West Mountain* records Musō as saying:

> Yishan at the time was serving as abbot of both Kenchō-ji and Engaku-ji. I had been with him for several years and received his teaching morning and evening as I continued studying the writings of the Five Houses.[21] By that time I felt thoroughly confident in my understanding of the

principles of Zen. Then one day, upon examining my own heart, I realized how uneasy I still felt. For the first time I understood the saying, "That which comes from outside the gate is not the house treasure."[22] As an ancient master said, "Never obscure the light of the spirit—this is the eternal way; having entered the gate, do not tarry in intellectual understanding."[23] I had left the school of doctrine and entered the school of Zen, yet my studies, although different in content, were equally based on conceptual knowledge. If I go on like this, I thought, I'm simply obscuring the light of my spirit. I therefore took the bag filled with the notes I had accumulated over the years and threw it into the fire.

Musō then went to Yishan and said, "I still have not clarified the matter of self.[24] Master, please, directly point the way." Yishan answered, "Our school has no words or phrases, and nothing to transmit to anyone." "That may be so," responded Musō, "but be compassionate and at least teach me an expedient means." "There are no expedient means," declared Yishan, "nor is there any compassion." From then on this is all that Yishan would say to Musō.

The *Biography* reports that Musō, though recognizing the profound lesson that Yishan was attempting to convey, felt frustrated by his inability to communicate with the master in a more effective way. He decided to call upon Kōhō Kennichi, then serving as abbot at Manju-ji in Kamakura. At their first meeting Musō told him of his conversation with Yishan. Kōhō laughed and responded, "Why didn't you say to him, 'Master, aren't you getting a bit confused?'" Kōhō then spoke as follows:

When I was sixteen I was ordained at Tōfuku-ji and placed under the tutelage of an old monk. The monk directed me to read the Zen records. Every time I read a line I would ask him the meaning, until he said, "The writings of Zen are unlike those of other Buddhist schools—they are not to be explained."

"But how can they be understood," I asked, "if they are not explained?" "Only with enlightenment does one understand the meaning," he replied. "If I persevere in my reading, will I naturally enlighten?"

"If you wish to attain enlightenment," he replied, "you must directly investigate the self."

Upon hearing this I read no more, devoting myself instead to *zazen* in the meditation hall. Many monks advised me, saying, "Young people should devote themselves to study. A momentary zeal for enlightenment won't carry you through to the end. You will regret this when you are old."

I simply practiced meditation even more than before. I'm now more than sixty years old, and to this day I have no regrets."

Musō, deeply moved by Kōhō's words, dedicated himself with renewed resolve to meditation. *Night Talks on West Mountain* continues as follows:

I sensed some progress, but was still unable to apply myself single-mindedly to the practice. Finally, desiring to seclude myself deep in the mountains so that I could thoroughly investigate the self, I departed Engaku-ji for Okushū.[25] There I built a hut and vowed to myself that I would either clarify this matter or molder away with the grasses and trees. As a spur to training I laid on the table the *Essential Teachings of Meditation Master Foguo Yuanwu Zhenjue*,[26] the *Letters of Meditation Master Dahui*,[27] and the *Zen Forest Records* of Meditation Master Juefan Huihong;[28] these were the only possessions I had.

This marked the beginning of a new phase in Musō's practice, quite different in character from what had gone before. Whereas previously he had always stayed at temples or monasteries under the direct guidance of a teacher, for the next several decades he was to spend long periods meditating alone and away from established centers. During the times when he did live in communities it was often in remote areas.

Musō's determination to meditate in the mountains and "molder away with the grasses and trees" if he failed to reach enlightenment echoes in many ways the stories of the two Chinese Zen masters Liang Zuozhu 亮座主 (J., Ryō Zasu, n.d.) and Nanyang Huizhong 南陽慧忠 (J., Nan'yō Echū, 675–775), and indeed his new direction may have been inspired in part by their example. Both of these masters would have been familiar to Musō from his extensive study of Zen literature, and both were in fact mentioned by him in his subsequent writings as men whose lives helped shape his ideals for spiritual training.

Liang Zuozhu, whom Musō mentions several times in the *Biography, Dialogues in a Dream*, and other works, was a semilegendary Chinese Buddhist scholar ("Liang Zuozhu" means, literally, "Eminent Scholar Liang") who abandoned his studies to become a religious anchorite in the mountains. In the Zen classics Liang's story appears in two parts. A representative example of the first part is found in the *Compendium of the Five Lamps*:

> Eminent Scholar Liang visited Mazu.[29] Mazu said to him, "I have heard that the master lectures on the sutras and śāstras. Is this true?" "Yes," replied Liang.
>
> Mazu then asked, "What do you lecture with?" Liang said, "I lecture with my mind."
>
> Mazu replied, "'The mind is like an actor, consciousness is like an assistant.' How can they explain the sutras?"
>
> Liang said in a loud voice, "If the mind cannot lecture, can empty space lecture?"
>
> Mazu said, "Yes, indeed, empty space can lecture."

Liang disagreed and got up to leave. When he was about to step down the stairs, Mazu called to him, "Eminent Scholar!" When Liang turned his head, Mazu said, "What is *that*?" Liang had a great awakening. He bowed to Mazu, who said, "This stupid monk! What are you bowing for?"

Liang said, "I used to think that no one could lecture on the sutras as well as I. Today at a single question by Great Master Mazu my whole life's work has melted away." He then entered the West Mountains and was never heard from again.[30]

It was, however, the second part of Liang's story that most deeply affected Musō. This part, which appears most notably in Dahui Zonggao's *Zen Arsenal*,[31] tells of two twelfth-century travelers who were journeying deep in the West Mountains one rainy day when they caught sight of an ancient monk meditating on a rock. The monk, who radiated an air of exceptional purity, had long white hair and wore a robe of woven leaves. One of the travelers, marveling that such a monk still lived in the West Mountains, suddenly remembered that they were in the area where Liang had secluded himself over three hundred years before. Approaching the monk, he asked, "Are you Eminent Scholar Liang?" The ancient monk raised his hand and pointed toward the east, and the travelers turned their gaze in that direction. When they looked back to where Liang had been a moment before, no one was there, although the spot on the rock where the monk had been sitting was still dry.[32]

Musō's admiration of Liang is evident from his prominent mention of the hermit in chapter 46 of *Dialogues in a Dream*, as well as his use of Liang's story in naming certain design features in the gardens he later created (such as the "Pointing-East Hut" at Saihō-ji 西芳寺, the Moss Temple). The image of the ancient monk sitting deep in the mountains and in full harmony with his natural surroundings epitomized for Musō one aspect of the religious ideal, one that, as we shall see, formed a continuing theme in his life.

As we will also see, however, Musō's attraction to the life of solitude in nature was balanced by another dynamic that increasingly expressed itself in his later life: the call to leave the life of solitude and live and teach in the midst of society. The person who for Musō best served as an example of this pattern of practice—long years of postenlightenment cultivation in the mountains followed by a busy teaching career in the capital—was the above-mentioned master Nanyang Huizhong. Nanyang lived in the early Tang dynasty, when Zen was first taking form as a distinct tradition in China. He began his training at the age of sixteen under Huineng, the Sixth Patriarch.[33] After succeeding to Huineng's Dharma he left on a pilgrimage to various Buddhist sites, eventually settling in the Dangzi Valley 党子谷 on Mount Baiya 白崖 in present-day Henan, where he dwelt as a hermit for forty years. He finally departed only in 761 at the age of eighty-six, when Emperor Suzong 肅宗 called him to Chang'an, the capital of the Tang dynasty. There Nanyang resided at Guangzhai si 光宅寺, a temple established for him by Emperor Daizong 代宗, who conferred upon him the title National Teacher Liangdi 兩帝國師, "National Teacher of Two Emperors."

The symbolic importance that Nanyang held for Musō is reflected in the fact that when, decades later, Musō was in Kyoto teaching, he bestowed upon Nanyang the same honor he had upon Eminent Scholar Liang by assigning names based on elements of Nanyang's story to various features in the famous garden he designed at Saihō-ji.

Musō's call to service in the world was foreshadowed in Kōhō Kennichi's final advice to him as he prepared to leave Kamakura for his retreat in Okushū to the north, so let us return at this point to Musō's spiritual journey. Kōhō said to his departing student, "If a follower of the Way separates the mundane and the supramundane by even so much as a hairbreadth, he cannot attain satori." The true significance of these words struck Musō only some time later. In *Night Talks* Musō recalls:

> I had spent three years in seclusion without yet reaching
> the stage of insight. Then one day I happened to remember

Kōhō's parting words.... I realized that although there was nothing I desired with regard to the secular world, thoughts of the Dharma may well have become obstacles to enlightenment. Having seen my error, my seeking mind vanished of itself and from then on I passed my time in stillness. Then one night I kicked over the age-old nest of delusion and finally realized that Kōhō's words were true.

Although this passage gives the impression that Musō spent the next few years in a single solitary retreat leading to the experience of "kicking over delusion," the *Biography* speaks of several shorter retreats interspersed with periods of wandering. After his departure from Kamakura, the *Biography* tells us, Musō first headed north for Shiratori 白鳥, an area located near the present city of Iwaki, where he made a grass hut for himself and passed the winter. A wealthy believer, seeing Musō's simple quarters, offered to build a temple for him, but Musō demurred, realizing that such a project would simply distract him from his search.

Seeking perhaps to further distance himself from such hindrances, Musō left Shiratori in the second month of 1304 and moved to Mount Uchinokusa 内草, where he made another hut and resumed his meditation. The location of Mount Uchinokusa is uncertain; Nishiyama believes that it corresponds to a hill in what is now the northwestern part of the city of Iwaki. Musō spent about a year there, in the course of which he gave away the three texts he had brought with him for inspiration. From that point on he communed only with his natural surroundings.

The *Biography* reports that one night as he was sitting by the fireside a bright flame suddenly leapt into the air. The instant Musō saw the flash his mind opened and was filled with a shining clarity. The following day when he saw the shadows of the breeze-blown bamboos moving against his paper window he no longer felt hindered by the activities of daily life. At that time he reflected to himself:

Even the buddhas and the patriarchs cannot explain Original Nature, but if one perseveres in clarifying it one cannot fail to understand. Thus one must take every opportunity to practice. Still, desire for the Way cannot overcome the feelings. When the mind moves one loses oneself in the surrounding circumstances. Thus from today I will make no distinction between self and circumstances. As the Buddha said, "Waking and sleeping are the same; remembering and forgetting are one."[34]

Starting on New Year's Day 1305, Musō conducted a week-long Kannon Purification Ceremony, promising himself that after finishing he would never again rest his side against his bed. Not long after the end of the ceremony, however, he was sitting on the floor when sleep suddenly overcame him, and it wasn't until he felt the afternoon sun shining through the window that he awoke. Realizing what had happened, he first felt a deep sense of shame. Then he thought, "If it is true that 'waking and sleeping are the same; remembering and forgetting are one,' then there is nothing to be ashamed of even if one were to sleep through Maitreya's coming."[35]

Wishing to discuss this insight with Kōhō, Musō left Mount Uchinokusa and set out for Kamakura in the second month of 1305. His reputation appears to have preceded him, however. As Musō passed through Usuba,[36] near the present city of Kitaibaraki, a layman named Hisa 比佐 received him and implored him to stay for a time, saying that he owned a hermitage where Musō could meditate in peace. At first Musō declined the offer, citing his desire to meet with Kōhō as soon as possible. That evening, however, he remembered Kōhō's parting words, "If a follower of the Way separates the mundane and the supramundane by even so much as a hairbreadth, he cannot attain satori," and decided that the small rural town might be the best place to continue his retreat.

One day in the early summer Musō was meditating in the cool shade of a tree in front of Hisa's hermitage. The sun went down, and soon the night had deepened. Feeling tired, he stood up and entered the pitch-dark building. Intending to rest for a moment against a wall that, in the darkness, turned out not to be there, Musō lost his balance and fell over, precipitating a profound enlightenment experience. Musō broke out in sudden laughter. Later he described the moment in a poem:

> For many years I dug the earth in search of the blue sky,
> Piling useless obstructions layer upon layer.
> One night in the darkness I kicked a tile
> And no-mindedly smashed the bones of the void.

Musō continued his retreat in Usuba until the early winter, then walked the remaining distance to Kamakura. There he met Kōhō at the large temple Jōchi-ji 淨智寺, where Kōhō was abbot at the time. His teacher immediately noticed the change in Musō, and, after a lively exchange of questions and answers, recognized him as his successor. Musō was just thirty-one years old.

Musō's awakening in the hermitage was the pivotal experience that resolved his spiritual questions, but it did not mark the end of his training. Following satori, Zen traditionally demands a period of postenlightenment training known as "long cultivation of the sacred embryo" (*shōtai chōyō* 聖胎長養). The classic literature is filled with stories of masters who, after their awakening, retreated to the mountains and spent twenty, thirty, or (like Nanyang) forty years cultivating their understanding. It is a time of integrating spiritual realization into everyday life and removing the "smell" of enlightenment, so that one can live the truth of the teaching that "ordinary mind is the Way." In chapter 35 of *Dialogues in a Dream* Musō provides a succinct description of this stage of practice and its results:

> The beginning student should first of all thoroughly grasp the intent of the Patriarch, and not dwell, lifeless, amid the words. The ancient masters, after awakening to the

Patriarch's intent, would spend thirty to fifty years in intensive refinement, eliminating their remaining karma and residual hindrances.[37] This type of training is known as "nourishing the sacred embryo." When the process fully matures everything is united into one, and there naturally appears the lucid eloquence and appropriate functioning that enables complete freedom in helping other people.

The *Biography's* account of the next few decades of Musō's life makes it clear that Musō, too, attempted to follow the classical pattern of *shōtai chōyō*. Circumstances in Kamakura-era Japan, however, rendered postenlightenment training considerably more challenging than in Tang-dynasty China. Almost from the start Musō was in demand as a teacher and abbot, and his efforts to postpone such responsibilities until he felt spiritually mature enough to guide students sometimes bordered on the extreme.

After his meeting in Kamakura with Kōhō, Musō immediately set out for Kai. There he met his parents for the first time in many years and, at the invitation of the head of the Nikaidō clan (an influential branch of the Minamotos),[38] took up residence at Jōko-ji 淨居寺, a temple newly established for him. He remained there throughout 1306 and into 1307, attracting many believers as well as Zen students eager to receive his instruction.

Sometime in 1307 he commissioned a portrait of Kōhō, which he took to Kamakura to be inscribed by Kōhō himself. Kōhō, who in the meantime had returned to Manju-ji, willingly wrote the inscription, then asked his attendant to bring a robe. He handed the garment to Musō, saying, "This is the robe worn by my teacher, Wuxue Zuyuan,[39] when he delivered his lectures. I now present it to you as a sign of my trust." He then asked Musō to remain with him at Manju-ji for a time. Musō acceded, serving as Kōhō's head monk through the end of the training period of 1308.

At the end of the training period Musō took his leave of Kōhō and his former teacher Yishan (then abbot of the subtemple Gyoku'un-an

玉雲庵 of Kenchō-ji), saying that he wished to further cultivate his understanding in the rural surroundings of Kai. Both masters presented him with farewell gifts, Kōhō giving him a written sermon and Yishan a long formal poem. When Musō reached Kai and called upon "the doctrinal temple he had trained at previously" (presumably Heien-ji, although the *Biography* does not mention the temple's name), his teacher, referred to as "the Venerable Jōtatsu 静達上人," entreated him to receive transmission in the esoteric teachings. Musō's association with the Zen school was irrelevant, Jōtatsu said, arguing that "even Nāgārjuna[40] mastered both the exoteric and esoteric teachings, and was simultaneously a patriarch in the Zen lineage." Musō, the *Biography* reports, simply nodded his head noncommittally. Later he said to a disciple, "The doctrinal schools and the Zen school are as incompatible as charcoal and ice. Even if Nāgārjuna were to reappear and combine the practice of the various traditions, it would benefit the world nothing."

The following year, 1309, Musō paid a visit to Kōhō, who in the meantime had retired from his position as abbot of Manju-ji and returned to Ungan-ji in the mountains north of the Kantō Plain. During the period of his stay Musō was appointed secretary of the monastery. As Kōhō was in poor health at the time, the monks in training started going to Musō for instruction, a development that Kōhō heartily approved of. The *Biography*, however, reports that Musō himself was not naturally inclined to the constant interaction of teaching and desired to withdraw to quieter surroundings. Finally, before the completion of the training period, he went to Kōhō and announced his intention to leave. Kōhō produced a letter from his own teacher, Wuxue Zuyuan, in which Wuxue, concerned about Kōhō's taste for solitude and isolation, urged him to keep company with like-minded seekers and warned him that his duty to "repay the benevolence of the Buddha" by transmitting the Way is not something that can be accomplished alone.

Musō accepted the letter and returned to Jōko-ji. This was the last time he saw Kōhō, but in the twelfth month of 1309 he wrote a letter to his old teacher informing him of his activities and promising that if his own attainments in the Dharma fell short of Kōhō's he would not go forth into the world but remain secluded and "molder away with the grasses and trees." Kōhō, worried perhaps that Musō intended to do precisely that, wrote back saying:

> You must never think of remaining in seclusion and "moldering away with the grasses and trees." Even the trees and the grasses turn the wheel of the Dharma.... Who will address the evils of the Latter Age? You must...scold the buddhas and revile the patriarchs, and restore the Buddha-dharma to its former vigor.

Musō, the *Biography* says, accepted this as Kōhō's sincere attempt to cure his disciple's hidden faults, and told himself, "I must remember Baizhang's warning not to cling to petty gains and merits."[41]

Musō remained at Jōkō-ji throughout 1310. In light of the 1306 *Biography* entry reporting the presence at the temple of numerous Zen monks already seeking his teaching, it must be assumed that by 1310 a large community had gathered. In order to further the cultivation of his own enlightenment in more tranquil surroundings, Musō left Jōkō-ji in the spring of 1311 and moved to a hut he built for himself in the mountains of Kai. The hut, to which he gave the name Ryōzan-an 龍山庵 (Dragon Mountain Hermitage), was located on the upper reaches of the Fuefuki River about twenty kilometers from the nearest settlement. Once again, however, it was not long before fellow monks started to gather around him, seeking his instruction and making huts of their own.

In its entry for the following year, 1312, the *Biography* reports a small incident at Ryōzan-an that is interesting for what it says of Musō's character. In the early spring a wildfire broke out on the mountain and threatened the collection of huts. Musō, taking with him only the robe he had received from Kōhō, went to the top of a nearby rocky precipice together with his students to wait out the conflagration. Suddenly the wind reversed direction, blowing the fire back on itself and extinguishing the flames. The onlooking monks all attributed this to divine intervention, but Musō simply laughed and said, "In the mountains the winds change direction all the time. That saved us from misfortune this time, but why call it a miracle?"

Despite Ryōzan-an's remoteness, the number of monks living around Musō steadily increased until huts covered the nearby hills and lined the banks of the local streams. Looking around, Musō reflected to himself that he had come to the mountain intending to live like the Chinese Zen recluse Yinshan,[42] yet now was surrounded by what had become for all intents and purposes a sizeable village. Deciding that he needed even remoter surroundings, he walked down the mountain one day at the end of 1312, leaving the Dragon Mountain Hermitage behind.

It appears from the *Biography* account that at first Musō had no clear idea of where to go. He returned for a time to Jōkō-ji, where friends suggested that he might find the peaceful environment he sought in the provinces of Enshū (present-day Shizuoka Prefecture) or Nōshū (the southern part of present Gifu Prefecture). He remained undecided, however, until his teacher Kōhō encouraged him to take the position of abbot of Chōraku-ji 長樂寺, an important temple in what is presently Gumma Prefecture. According to Nishiyama's research, Chōraku-ji had long been associated with the lineage of Kōhō's teacher Wuxue Zuyuan, and thus Kōhō was no doubt desirous of continuing this tie by installing Musō, his top disciple, as the new abbot. Chōraku-ji, moreover, had suffered a serious fire shortly before, and Kōhō likely recognized in Musō the administrative skills necessary to complete the task of reconstruction.

Musō, however, did not feel ready at that point to assume such responsibilities, so in 1313 he quietly left Jōkō-ji and made his way west to Enshū together with another monk, Gen'ō Hongen,[43] and six or seven others. From there they continued to Mikawa, Gen'ō's birthplace, and then north through Nōshū until they reached the area of Mount Nagase. There, where the valley of the Toki River wound its way through the range of low mountains just northeast of present-day Nagoya, they found what they were looking for: an area of outstanding natural beauty located far from their nearest neighbors. They received permission from the local landowner to build a small temple, which they called Kokei-an 古谿庵 (Old Valley Hermitage). The characters were later changed to 虎谿庵, pronounced the same but meaning Tiger Valley Hermitage, an allusion to Tiger Valley on Mount Lu, one of the most famous, and secluded, places of Buddhist practice in China.

During their first two months there not a single visitor disturbed the peace of their mountain retreat. By 1314, however, word of Musō's presence had spread, and a growing stream of people was calling upon the temple. Within a year, the *Biography* tells us, Kokei-an had become every bit as busy as the Dragon Mountain Hermitage. Musō, tired of dealing with guests, put up a sign in front of the gate entreating callers not to disturb the tranquility of the temple and advising them that fine Zen teachers and quiet surroundings could be found elsewhere throughout Japan. This appeal, however, did nothing to slow the ever-increasing number of visitors. Musō finally reflected, "This land is not my private property, so it is unfair to try to keep it for myself and prevent others from coming. It is I who ought to leave." At just this time believers at the nearby temple Seisui-ji 清水寺, knowing of Musō's desire for a more peaceful location to continue his training, offered to build a hermitage for him in the nearby mountains. Musō, delighted by this proposal, promised to accept their offer the following year.

In the spring of 1316 Musō and two companions went to live at the new hermitage, which in later years became the temple Tōkō-ji 東香寺. Here again the peace of their new surroundings did not last for long—already by summertime monks eager for instruction were coming from Seisui-ji and elsewhere. Meanwhile the news reached Musō that the assembly at Kokei-an had dispersed, leaving only the monks who had originally accompanied him there. Now that the new hermitage was nearly as busy as Kokei-an had ever been, Musō decided to return to his old temple, saying that it wasn't Kokei-an itself he had disliked but the crowds of visitors it had attracted. Once back at Kokei-an he attempted to maintain some sense of solitude by leaving the main temple in the care of Gen'ō and taking up residence in a nearby hermitage.

In the winter of 1316 Musō, receiving word of his teacher Kōhō's death, performed a memorial service with all due ceremony.

The *Biography* account tells us that in the ninth month of 1317 Musō left Kokei-an and resided for a time in the Kitayama area of northern Kyoto. No reason for this move is given, leaving several modern commentators free to conjecture political considerations on Musō's part. Nishiyama, however, offers a more commonsense scenario. Since it is known that Musō's former teacher Yishan had fallen ill at Nanzen-ji just before Musō arrived and died soon afterward, Nishiyama hypothesizes that Musō's move to the capital was prompted by a desire to pay his last respects to the teacher under whom he had studied for so long. That he had so recently heard of Kōhō's death only after the fact would have undoubtedly strengthened that desire.

The location of the *Biography*'s "Kitayama" is uncertain; Nishiyama suggests the area just east of Ninna-ji 仁和寺 in northwestern Kyoto, in the neighborhood of a hermitage, Shōmyaku-an 正脈庵, honoring the remains of Kōhō's teacher Wuxue Zuyuan. In a poem Musō describes his life in Kitayama:

> Staying a while in the busy town,
> I keep my gate shut even during the day;
> In the midst of the city I have the mountains of Wozhou.
> This mouth I was born with is free of blood,
> Suspended for a time between heaven and earth.

The poem portrays an atmosphere of silent serenity. Even in the vicinity of the capital Musō maintained his solitude, keeping his gate closed to casual visitors. The mountains of Wozhou were renowned for their quiet beauty; a mouth that is "free of blood" is one that is not being used. "Suspended for a time between heaven and earth" suggests stillness and tranquility.

Once again, however, it was not long before Musō's reputation cut short his retreat. This time the intrusion came in the form of an invitation from Kakukai Enjō-ni 覺海圓成尼 (d. 1345), the cloistered widow of the regent Hōjō Sadatoki 北条貞時 (1271–1311), to come to Kamakura to continue Kōhō's work. Hearing of the approach of Kakukai's messenger, Musō left his Kitayama hermitage at the beginning of 1318, crossed the Inland Sea to the island of Shikoku, traversed several rugged ranges of mountains, and made his way to the province of Tosa on the island's southern coast. Hoping perhaps that this time the remoteness of the location would allow him to practice in peace, he settled on a hillside overlooking a large estuary in the area of the present-day city of Kōchi. There, near an established temple named Chikurin-ji 竹林寺, he built himself a hut that he called Kyūkō-an 吸江庵.[44] Musō was clearly quite taken by the beauty of the area's natural surroundings, which he extolled in a collection of thirty *waka* poems.

Even the isolation of Shikoku did not protect Musō for long, however. In the fourth month of 1319, Kakukai, having learned of the master's whereabouts, dispatched another messenger whom she warned either to return with Musō or not to return at all. Musō, again hearing of the messenger's approach, attempted to conceal himself in the nearby countryside, but when the messenger threatened to prosecute anyone who hid the master he finally bowed to the inevitable. Stating, "One cannot escape one's karmic obligations," he made the long trip to Kamakura and was warmly received by Kakukai.

It would appear, however, that Musō proved a match for the determined widow. Though placed temporarily in the temple Shōei-ji 勝榮寺, he kept the gate firmly shut and refused to meet even old monastic friends who had studied with him under Kōhō. When a short time later he was offered the position of abbot at Ungan-ji, Kōhō's temple in the mountains, he firmly declined. Finally, at the end of the summer he departed Shōei-ji and traveled east across the neck of the nearby Miura Peninsula to the vicinity of present-day Yokosuka City, where, on the side of a low mountain facing the bay, he established the hermitage Hakusen-an 泊船庵.[45] Located no more than a few hours' walk from Kamakura, Hakusen-an was near enough, apparently, to satisfy Kakukai's demand that he reside close by, yet far enough to afford Musō the solitude he desired.

Visitors here, too, were many, but the *Biography* tells us that Musō protected his privacy with a gate he did not feel compelled to open to everyone. To those who felt it strange that he would not receive them, he laughed and said, "I can't understand why you think it so. Those with eyes to see understand me and my situation. As for those without eyes to see, what benefit would it be to meet them?" On his gate he posted a poem:

> My thatched reed roof is vast as the heavens;
> The surrounding mountains are my fence, the sea is my
>   garden.
> I conceal not what happens in my hut, yet those who come
>   still say my bamboo door is shut.

Musō was not a hermit, however, and actually seems to have had a fair amount of interaction with his friends and neighbors. The *Biography* reports invitations to dinner from Kakukai as well as friendly exchanges with Lingshan Daoyin,[46] the abbot of Kenchō-ji at the time. Lingshan visited Hakusen-an on at least one occasion and regarded Musō's Zen attainments so highly that he sent his Japanese students to Musō for instruction, explaining that he himself was not sufficiently skilled in Japanese to teach them.

Musō was active in other ways as well. In its entry for 1321, the *Biography* mentions that he built a pagoda, called the Kai'in Futo 海印浮圖 (Ocean-Imprint Pagoda), on top of Mount Hakusen as an object of devotion for the seafarers on the bay below. He also hoped, the account adds, that the sea creatures sensing the form of the pagoda through the clear waters of the bay would thereby form subtle connections with the Ocean-Imprint Samādhi of Buddhism.[47]

Musō remained at Hakusen-an until 1323, when he moved to the rural area of Isumi in the central section of Bōsō Hantō, the large peninsula lying directly east across the bay from Yokosuka. There he built another hermitage, which he named Taikō-an 退耕庵 (Hermitage for Secluded Cultivation). The biographical materials offer no reason for this move, but the possibility that it was simply the next step in Musō's "long cultivation of the sacred embryo" is supported by the fact that, cut into the cliffside to the rear of the site of Taikō-an (presently occupied by the temple Taikō-ji 太高寺), there is a meditation cave dating back to the time of Musō.

Since his move to Ryōzan-an in 1311 Musō had for the most part managed to reside in remote hermitages and deflect attempts to appoint him to important temples. Even Kakukai's persistent invitations had been skillfully parried. In the spring of 1325, however, Emperor Go-Daigo dispatched a close retainer to Kamakura requesting Musō to come to the capital and accept the abbacy of Nanzen-ji, the preeminent Zen temple in Japan. When Musō demurred on grounds of illness the emperor sent a formal invitation written in verse, to which Musō responded with a matching verse expressing contentment with his simple lifestyle. Go-Daigo then dispatched an imperial messenger to the Kamakura regent, Hōjō Takatoki 北条高時 (1303–1333), directing him to order Musō's compliance with the imperial summons. Left with little choice, Musō set out for the capital in the seventh month of the year. He followed a rather roundabout route that took him through Kai and the mountains of central Japan to Kokei-an in Nōshū. From there his old friend Gen'ō Hongen accompanied him the rest of the way to Kyoto.

His first meeting with Go-Daigo went well, according to the *Biography*, with the emperor listening to Musō's explanation of the essentials of Zen with such great interest that he forgot the passage of time. When, upon finishing his lecture, Musō was once again asked by Go-Daigo to accept the abbacy of Nanzen-ji, Musō responded that he had no desire for status in the world and wished only to remain hidden deep in the mountains. Go-Daigo responded that Musō could use Nanzen-ji as his hermitage, since his sole duty there would be to instruct the emperor occasionally in Zen; no administration would be required of him. Acceding to the emperor's wish, Musō entered Nanzen-ji in midsummer and received Go-Daigo for instruction three times a month.

Musō's assumption of the abbacy of Nanzen-ji was the occasion of one of the best-known criticisms directed against him. One month after Musō's investiture, the retired emperor Hanazono 花園 (1297–1348) criticized both Musō and Go-Daigo in his journal, the *Hanazono Tennō Shinki* 花園天皇宸記:

> Everyone says that His Majesty [Go-Daigo] earnestly desires the Buddhadharma to flourish. So I do not understand why he tries to make a secret of his reliance [on Musō]. To treat this man as a venerable abbot is to destroy the patriarchal succession of the Zen school. One cannot help but grieve.[48]

The full story behind this critique is impossible to know, but it should be noted that it occurred in the context of a strong rivalry between Hanazono and Go-Daigo, members of the competing branches of the imperial family known as the Jimyōin and Daikakuji lines. The Jimyōin line, which descended from Emperor Go-Fukakusa 後深草 (1243–1304; r. 1246–1259), and the Daikakuji line, which descended from Go-Fukakusa's brother Emperor Kameyama 亀山 (1249–1305; r. 1259–1274), each asserted its sole right to the imperial throne. In order to resolve the impasse an agreement was worked out under the authority of the Shogunate in which the imperial succession would alternate between the two lines at roughly ten-year intervals. Hanazono, a Jimyōin-line emperor, duly abdicated in 1318 after a ten-year reign, but his successor, the Daikakuji line Go-Daigo, soon showed signs that he intended to assert the supremacy of his branch over the Jimyōin line (and, indeed, over the Shogunate itself, as later became apparent). Not long after assuming the throne,

Go-Daigo began issuing imperial edicts and judicial rulings that were clearly intended to undercut the economic position of the Jimyōin line and thus relegate it to a subordinate position. Prior to 1325 Hanazono protested several times to the Shogunate regarding Go-Daigo's actions and in several passages in his diary, the aforementioned *Hanazono Tennō Shinki*, lamented his successor's highhanded behavior.[49]

Hanazono thus had ample reason to resent Go-Daigo by 1325, and part of the tension between the two played out in rivalry over the patronage of Shūhō Myōchō,[50] the founding priest of the great Zen temple Daitoku-ji. Although no specific written comments or other historical data exist, Shūhō is believed to have held Musō in less than the highest regard, perhaps because Shūhō, like Musō, had received Dharma recognition from Kōhō Kennichi and yet remained unsatisfied, prompting him to train further under the master Nanpo Jōmyō.[51] It is interesting that Hanazono's aforementioned diary entry regarding Musō was written immediately after a conversation with Shūhō and may therefore have simply reflected Shūhō's sentiments. In any event, Hanazono's reservations regarding Musō appear to have been short-lived, since a number of Hanazono's immediate successors in the Jimyōin line, such as Kōgon 光嚴 (1313–1364), Kōmyō 光明 (1321–1380), and Sukō 崇光 (1334–1398), went on to ordain in Musō's lineage.[52]

Musō taught at Nanzen-ji through the autumn of 1325 and until the end of the summer training session of 1326, spending exactly one year there. So many monks came to study under him, the *Biography* reports, that he was hard-pressed to keep them supplied with food. In the seventh month of 1326 he turned down an invitation from Hōjō Takatoki to assume the abbacy of the important temple Jufuku-ji 壽福寺 in Kamakura, but he nevertheless departed for the eastern capital in the eighth month. He stopped on the way to visit Ise, the province of his birth, where he established the now-defunct temple Zen'ō-ji 善應寺. After another side trip to the Kumano Shrines and the scenic area of Mount Nachi with its famous waterfall, he continued his journey east. By the ninth month Musō had reached Kamakura and taken up residence in the hermitage Nanpō-an 南芳庵, located next to Yōfuku-ji 永福寺, an important temple built by Minamoto Yoritomo 源頼朝 (1147–1199), founder of the Kamakura Shogunate. He remained there until the second month of 1327, when he was asked by Hōjō Takatoki to become abbot of Jōchi-ji. Reluctantly accepting, he served in the position for only a single training period, after which he returned to Nanpō-an. In the eighth month of the year he moved into the new temple Zuisen-in 瑞泉院, built for him in the northeast corner of the city by Nikaidō Sadafuji 二階堂貞藤 (1267–1335), the head of the Nikaidō branch of the Minamoto clan and an important official in the Shogunate.

Although Musō was at Zuisen-in for only about two years, he appears to have developed a special affection for the place. At the foot of the cliff that rose behind the temple he designed a small landscape garden, the first garden known to have been specifically laid out by him. In 1228, a year after assuming the abbacy, Musō constructed a Kannon Hall and built the Henkai Ichirantei 遍界一覧亭 (Pavilion with a View of the World) on top of the steep hill in back of Zuisen-in. The Henkai Ichirantei, with its panoramic views of Mount Fuji and the rugged hills surrounding Kamakura, became the site of frequent poetry gatherings attended by Musō and his friends, among them Chinese émigré masters such as Mingji Chujun[53] and Qingzhuo Zhengcheng,[54] both of whom served as abbot of Kenchō-ji and other important temples in Kamakura and Kyoto. It was a fitting beginning for Zuisen-in, which later became the Kamakura base of the Five Mountain literary movement,[55] a cultural tradition centering on the lineage of masters descending from Musō.

At the end of 1328 Hōjō Takatoki asked Musō to become abbot of Engaku-ji, but the master refused both this and a second request by Takatoki in the summer of 1329. He was equally resistant to similar appeals, made at Takatoki's behest, from senior prelates and from fellow students of Kōhō. Finally, the *Biography* reports, the Engaku-ji monks themselves, "with tears in their eyes," beseeched Musō to accede to Takatoki's request in order that the lineage of Wuxue

Zuyuan, so carefully maintained by Kōhō, might continue. With this, Musō finally agreed to become abbot.

Nevertheless, in the ninth month of 1330 the fifty-four-year-old Musō, still feeling unready as a master, secretly departed Engaku-ji and returned to Zuisen-in, refusing to meet the monks who soon sought him out. Early the following morning he left for Kai. There, once again supported by Nikaidō Sadafuji, then living at the Nikaidō home estate, he established the temple Erin-ji 惠林寺 in what is presently the city of Enzan. He stayed there until the second month of 1331, when he returned for a year to Zuisen-in. While at Zuisen-in he was invited by Takatoki to become abbot of Kenchō-ji, but he declined, instead nominating the master Kengai Kōan[56] for the post.

After returning to Kai in the spring of 1332 Musō continued his quiet residence at Erin-ji; the only event for this year noted in the *Biography* is that Musō at some point established the temple Zuikō-ji 瑞光寺 in Banshū (present Hyōgo Prefecture), several hundred kilometers to the west of Kai. Despite the relatively peaceful picture of his existence conveyed in the *Biography*, Musō's comings and goings between Kamakura and Kai may have been related to the fact that the early 1330s were years when Go-Daigo's increasing ambitions to restore control of the government to the emperor had finally resulted in the outbreak of military conflict between the Shogunate and the imperial household.

Already in 1324 a plot by Go-Daigo's subordinates to overthrow the warrior rulers in Kamakura had been discovered by the Shogunate; Hino Tsuketomo 日野資朝 (1290–1332) and Hino Toshimoto 日野俊基 (d. 1332), leaders of the plot and close associates of the emperor, had been exiled to the island of Sado. Although Go-Daigo, too, had almost certainly been involved, the Hōjō accepted his claim of innocence. By the early 1330s, however, Emperor Go-Daigo's ambitions had progressed from political intrigue to military action.

Go-Daigo's struggle to overthrow the Shogunate, known as the Genkō War (1331–1333) after the name of the imperial era in which it occurred,[57] started inauspiciously when his initial attack in 1331 ended in failure. The Shogunate counterattacked, and soon afterward the emperor's stronghold on Kasagiyama was taken. Go-Daigo was exiled to the remote island of Oki and a new emperor, Kōgon 光嚴 (1313–1364) of the Jimyōin lineage, was enthroned in his place. However, two of Go-Daigo's best generals, Kusunoki Masashige 楠木正成 (1294–1336) and Prince Morinaga 護良 (1308–1335), remained at large and continued to harass the Shogunate's armies, joined by growing numbers of disaffected samurai. When Go-Daigo escaped Oki in 1333, events quickly turned against the Hōjō. Two of the Shogunate's most powerful generals, Ashikaga Takauji 足利尊氏 (1305–1358) and Nitta Yoshisada 新田義貞 (1301–1338), both members of branch families of the Minamoto, decided to side with the emperor, and with their defection the Hōjō cause was lost. Ashikaga seized Kyoto while Nitta overran Kamakura, marking the end of the Kamakura Shogunate.

There are good reasons to believe that Musō kept his distance from these events and was desirous of maintaining good relations with both the Hōjō and the Minamoto: he was by birth both a Minamoto and a Taira (of which the Hōjō were originally a branch family), and he had benefited from the support of patrons on both sides. Moreover, he seems by nature to have been little inclined to political activism. Certain Japanese biographers have argued otherwise, asserting that Musō was a proponent of Go-Daigo's cause and adversary of the Hōjō, but Martin Collcutt's analysis seems far more in keeping with the known facts of Musō's life:

> [Musō does not] seem to have had the strong antipathy to the Hōjō as patrons that Tamamura Takeji asserts in his biography of Musō. If anti-Hōjō and pro-Go-Daigo sentiments were motivating factors in his decisions, he would hardly have returned from Kyoto to Kamakura or accepted, however reluctantly, the headship of Jōchi-ji and Engaku-ji. I would prefer to argue that Musō, after years of semiretirement and outright reclusion, was shy of all authority figures and large institutional monasteries. He

was, however, being tugged steadily and somewhat reluctantly out of obscurity and into the mainstream of Rinzai
Zen by powerful would-be patrons who were unwilling to
take no for an answer.[58]

In any event, Musō once again left Kai for Kamakura in the third
month of 1333 to resume residence at Zuisen-in, even though earlier
the same year he had declined, on grounds of illness, yet another invitation from Hōjō Takatoki to head Kenchō-ji. Two months later, in
the fifth month of the year, the imperial armies under Nitta attacked
Kamakura, and by mid-month the city had fallen. The entire Hōjō
clan, including Takatoki and nearly nine hundred others, committed
suicide at the family temple Tōshō-ji 東勝寺. The *Biography* reports
that, with the city burning, "countless warriors' lives were spared"
owing to Musō's intervention.

Go-Daigo entered Kyoto at the beginning of the sixth month of
1333 and assumed control of the government. The following month
he asked Ashikaga Takauji to dispatch an imperial messenger to
Zuisen-in conveying the emperor's request that Musō come to the
capital. Musō consented, arriving there during the seventh month.
He received an imperial audience the day after reaching the city, and
within a few weeks he was appointed priest of the temple Rinsen-ji
臨川寺, located on the grounds of the Kameyama-dono 龜山殿, Go-
Daigo's summer palace on the western outskirts of the city.

Rinsen-ji was situated on the site of a subpalace within the
Kameyama-dono precincts, occupied by Shōkei Mon'in 昭慶門院
(n.d.), the widowed empress of Kameyama, and Prince Tokinaga 世良
(1306–1330), one of Go-Daigo's sons. Tokinaga, perhaps because of ill
health, had become deeply interested in Zen and taken up meditation
under Musō's longtime friend Gen'ō Hongen. The prince hoped to
remodel his residence as a Zen temple and have Gen'ō live there, but
he passed away before his plans could be realized. Go-Daigo established the temple in his memory, naming Gen'ō as founder. Gen'ō
himself died in 1332 at Kokei-an, however, leaving the post of abbot

empty. Go-Daigo thus requested Musō to take the temple over and two years later, in 1335, issued an imperial edict officially designating Musō as founder.

From the time he called Musō to the capital Go-Daigo almost certainly had it in mind to install the master once again as abbot of Nanzen-ji, but there were sound reasons to place him in Rinsen-ji first, as explained by Collcutt:

> Go-Daigo would have been aware that Nanzen-ji was regarded as an official, or public, monastery and that its abbacy frequently changed. Even if Musō wished to remain in Kyoto, he would not have been able to stay indefinitely as abbot of Nanzen-ji. A private temple would have to be made available for him. In the seventh month of 1333 (twenty-third day) Go-Daigo issued an edict addressed to Musō offering him "oversight" (*kanryō*) of Rinsen-ji and granting more landholdings to the temple.[59]

In any event, the *Biography* reports that in the ninth month of 1334 the emperor invited Musō to the palace, received a robe, and became the master's disciple. Later, overcoming the master's protestations of age and infirmity, Go-Daigo prevailed upon him to accept the abbacy of Nanzen-ji, saying, "Whether the Buddhadharma prospers depends entirely upon the quality of the teacher. To whom can I turn if you refuse me?"

Musō, inviting Mukyoku Shigen[60] of Engaku-ji to serve as his head monk, headed Nanzen-ji until the end of 1335. During his tenure he obtained an imperial edict to have Shōzoku-an 正續庵, a subtemple honoring the memory of Wuxue Zuyuan, moved to Engaku-ji (where Wuxue had served as founder) from its previous location in Kenchō-ji (where Wuxue had been abbot for a time but not founder). It was also at this time that Musō was first referred to by his honorary title, Musō Kokushi 夢窓國師 (National Teacher Musō), in the aforementioned imperial edict designating him founding abbot of Rinsen-ji.

Meanwhile, the Kenmu Restoration—Go-Daigo's effort, as leader of the Japanese government, to initiate various reforms—was already encountering difficulties. One of Go-Daigo's errors was his failure to sufficiently recognize the importance of support from the warrior class. When the new imperial government set out to reform land policies and distribute properties to its backers, the disproportionate amount of attention paid to aristocrats and religious institutions left significant segments of the warrior class dissatisfied. Major samurai supporters such as Ashikaga Takauji and his brother Ashikaga Tadayoshi did indeed receive suitable rewards but were alienated when Go-Daigo made it clear that they would not receive positions of real power in the new government. Takauji's discontent increased when Prince Morinaga was designated Sei'i Daishōgun 征夷大將軍 (Great Barbarian-Quelling General), a title that Takauji felt he had earned with his contributions to Go-Daigo's victory in the Genkō War.

Matters reached a head in 1335 when Takauji, fresh from quelling a rebellion in Kamakura by Hōjō Takatoki's son Tokiyuki 時行 (1322–1353), decided to turn on Go-Daigo. As he marched on Kyoto he defeated the forces of Nitta Yoshisada, sent by Go-Daigo to stop him. He reached Kyoto at the beginning of 1336 but was unable to capture the emperor, who had taken refuge with the soldier monks of Mount Hiei. Takauji was soon driven from the capital by the imperial armies under Yoshisada and Kitabatake Akiie 北畠顯家 (1318–1338) and forced to retreat to the island of Kyūshū. He managed to regroup there, however, and within a few months resumed his attack, defeating the imperial army near what is presently the city of Kobe and entering Kyoto in the seventh month of 1336. Go-Daigo once again escaped to the confines of Mount Hiei as Takauji took over the capital. Takauji proceeded to enthrone Emperor Kōmyō 光明 (1322–1380) of the Jimyōin line in the eighth month and, in the eleventh month, declared himself shogun on Kōmyō's authority. Go-Daigo, after several failed counterattacks, retreated to Mount Yoshino deep in the mountain fastnesses to the south of Nara and there established the Southern Court, in opposition to Kōmyō's

Northern Court. The period of the Northern and Southern Courts was to continue until 1392.

Musō, seeing the tumultuous events unfolding in the capital, had left Nanzen-ji in the first month of 1336 and returned to Rinsen-ji. Following the establishment of the new Muromachi Shogunate by Ashikaga Takauji and his brother Tadayoshi, the new authorities—apparently unconcerned by Musō's previous ties with the Kamakura Shogunate and Emperor Go-Daigo—looked to the respected and charismatic prelate as a potential ally. Rinsen-ji records show that already in the ninth month of 1336 Emperor Kōmyō had confirmed Rinsen-ji's lands, recognized Musō's honorary title of National Teacher, and designated the temple first among the important *shozan* class of the Five Mountain system of Zen temples.[61] Later, the *Biography* reports, Takauji invited him to his headquarters and asked to become a disciple.

In 1337 Musō, then sixty-two, turned over Rinsen-ji's abbacy to his disciple Mukyoku and entered the subtemple San'e-in 三會院, which from that point became the de facto center of the Rinsen-ji complex. Musō, in marked contrast to his earlier penchant for solitude, became increasingly involved in activities related to teaching and administration, cooperating on several major projects with both the Northern Court and the new Muromachi Shogunate. One such project, conceived in 1338 and carried out during the following decade, was the establishment of a network of temples and pagodas in the sixty-six provinces of Japan. The temples, called Peace-in-the-Land Temples (Ankoku-ji 安國寺), belonged to the Zen school, and the pagodas, known as Benefiting-Life Pagodas (Rishō-tō 利生塔), were associated with existing Tendai and Shingon institutions. The new system, completed by about 1350, served both the religious purpose of honoring those who had died in the warfare that brought the Ashikagas to power and the political purpose of strengthening the Ashikagas' oversight of outlying districts.

By this time Rinsen-ji was a growing center of Zen practice. In order to regulate the temple's affairs and provide guidelines for the students' practice, Musō wrote two sets of regulations. The first, issued in the third month of 1339, was the *House Rules of Rinsen-ji* (*Rinsen-ji Kakun* 臨川寺家訓), a code regulating the property, layout, and administration of the monastery; the organization and responsibilities of the community; and the conduct of everyday monastic life. The second, released in the fifth month of 1339, was the *San'e-in Admonitions* (*San'e-in ikai* 三會院遺戒), a shorter document in which Musō described the duties of the abbot and the makeup and activities of the assembly. In a famous passage he describes three types of disciples:

> I have three kinds of disciples. The first group is made up of students who energetically try to remove all attachments and concentrate on investigating the self. The middle group are those whose practice is not pure and who are distracted by intellectual pursuits. The bottom group is made up of those who cloud their minds and only lick the spittle of the Buddha and patriarchs. As for those who shave their heads and poison their minds with foreign literature, aspiring to be authors, they are lay people with shaven heads, not even worthy to be placed below the lowest group. Even less worthy of being called monks are those who indulge in lavish meals, long hours of sleep, and unbridled pleasures.[62]

It was also in the spring of 1339 that Musō started on a project that enabled him to fully indulge his love of nature and garden design: the restoration of Saihō-ji 西芳寺, now popularly known as the Moss Temple. Saihō-ji, said to have been founded by the Buddhist holy man Gyōki,[63] is located in Kyoto's West Mountains about a thirty-minute walk south of Rinsen-ji. Although by the fourteenth century the temple had fallen into a state of complete disrepair, Musō was delighted when invited to restore it by Nakahara Chikahide 仲原親秀 (n.d.), an important vassal of the Shogunate and priest of the nearby Matsuo

Shrine. The *Biography* quotes Musō as saying, "I have always yearned to live like Eminent Scholar Liang. How wonderful that I, too, can now dwell in the West Mountains!" When Musō rebuilt the temple structures and gardens he obviously kept Liang in mind—as noted earlier, several features of the upper garden, such as the Shitō-an 指東庵 (Pointing-East Hut) and the *zazen seki* 坐禪石 (meditation stone), recall elements in Liang's story.

The place-names associated with the other master Musō honored in this way, National Teacher Nanyang Huizhong, were drawn from the following koan:

> Emperor Taizong asked National Teacher Nanyang Huizhong, "What will you need after your life is finished?" The teacher said, "Build me a seamless tower." The emperor said, "Tell me, what would the monument look like?"
>
> Nanyang was silent. After a while the teacher asked, "Do you understand?" The emperor said, "I don't understand." The teacher said, "I have a successor, Danyuan, who knows all about this. Please summon him and ask."
>
> After the National Teacher passed on, the emperor summoned Danyuan and asked him the meaning of the master's statement. Danyuan said: "South of Xiang, north of Tan; in between, gold fills the entire land. Beneath the shadowless tree, ferry boats; in the crystal palace there is no knowing."[64]

From this koan Musō drew the names of several features in the Saihō-ji garden: the Tanhoku-tei 潭北亭 (North-of-Tan Pavilion), Shōnan-tei 湘南亭 (South-of-Xiang Pavilion), and Ōgon-chi 黄金池 (Golden Pond). Atop one of the buildings was a crystal spire that Musō called the Muhō-tō 無縫塔 (Seamless Tower). Around these features Musō laid out a beautiful garden with trees, watercourses, white-sand beaches, and pine-studded islands. This became a well-known sightseeing destination in Kyoto, famed for its beautiful views.

Regarding his garden-making efforts Musō wrote:

> The benevolent naturally love the silence of mountains;
> The wise naturally delight in the purity of water.
> So do not disdain the pleasure I take in landscape gardens;
> I'm simply attempting through them to refine my mind.

Not long after Musō began work on Saihō-ji, however, the death of Emperor Go-Daigo involved Musō in a far larger project, one that has remained one of his major legacies: the establishment of the great Zen temple Tenryū-ji 天龍寺.

The *Biography* reports that Musō foresaw Go-Daigo's death when, in the sixth month of 1339, he had a dream in which the emperor rode a phoenix carriage into Kameyama-dono, his summer palace near Rinsen-ji. When Go-Daigo died two months later at the Southern Court, Musō suggested to the Ashikaga brothers that Kameyama-dono would be an appropriate location for a temple to honor Go-Daigo's memory and pray for the peace of his spirit.

The Ashikagas acted quickly on the suggestion. Their interest was undoubtedly influenced in part by the popular spirituality of the time, which regarded the aggrieved spirits (*goryō* 御靈 or *onryō* 怨靈) of powerful people as capable of visiting misfortune upon those toward whom their resentment was directed. The classical example was the vengeance believed to have been wreaked upon the Fujiwara family by the angry spirit of Sugawara no Michizane.[65] Moreover, the Ashikagas would certainly have perceived the political expediency of the move. The Southern Court retained a considerable amount of support, and in the years since their assumption of power the Ashikagas had been forced to fight periodic battles with Go-Daigo's backers. Construction of a major temple complex in Go-Daigo's honor would not only placate the emperor's supporters but would also constitute an important demonstration of the new Shogunate's authority in the capital.

The Ashikaga brothers nominated Musō as founding priest of the proposed temple, but the master resisted the appointment on the grounds that imperial prayer temples were traditionally associated with the Tendai and Shingon schools. The decision was thus referred to Kōgon, the cloistered emperor of the Northern Court, who on the fifth day of the tenth month of 1339 designated Musō founder by imperial decree. A week later Kōgon announced that the new temple would be called Reikizan Ryakuō Shisei Zenji 靈龜山曆應資聖禪寺, making it known by use of the appellation "Zenji" that it was to be associated with the Zen school, and by use of "Ryakuō" that it was to be honored with the name of the imperial era of the time, Ryakuō 曆應 (1338–1342).

Both moves gave rise to so much resentment from the established schools in Kyoto that Musō resigned as abbot just a month after Kōgon's edict. The Zen master Kosen Ingen,[66] Ashikaga Tadayoshi's Zen teacher, replaced him, an arrangement that continued until Musō reassumed the abbacy in 1341. The year 1341 was also when the temple's name was changed to Tenryū-ji (Temple of the Heavenly Dragon) because of a dream Tadayoshi had in which a golden dragon flew out of the river immediately south of the temple property.

Musō oversaw affairs at Tenryū-ji even as he continued his activities at Rinsen-ji and Saihō-ji, since all three temples were within easy commuting distance. Work on the Tenryū-ji complex began in 1340 with the construction of a hall honoring the memory of Emperor Go-Daigo; the hall, known as Tahō-in 多寶院, was consecrated in the fourth month of the year. A year later, in the summer of 1341, construction of the main temple formally commenced when Musō, soon after reassuming responsibilities as abbot, performed the dedication ceremony for Tenryū-ji's building site.

In the twelfth month of 1341 Musō and Tadayoshi devised a plan to send two ships—known ever since as the "Tenryū-ji ships" 天龍寺舟—on a trade mission to China to help finance the construction work. Musō proposed that the mission be managed by Shihon 至本, a trader in the Kyūshū port city of Hakata, who guaranteed Tenryū-ji a return of five thousand *kan*[67] regardless of the success or failure of the mission. The ships finally set sail in the fall of 1342, taking with them not only merchandise for trade but also Zen monks wishing to train in the monasteries of Yuan China. The mission, which returned in the summer of 1343, realized a profit of one hundred times its original investment, according to the *Taiheiki* 太平記 (although "one hundred times" in this usage can be interpreted to mean simply "many times"), and also brought back to Japan a set of the Buddhist Canon.

The year 1342 was marked by several other significant events. According to the *Biography* account, on the eighth day of the fourth month, not long after the foundations were laid for Tenryū-ji, Cloistered Emperor Kōgon visited Saihō-ji and received a robe from Musō to mark his formal acceptance as a disciple. The temple Mannenzan Shinnyo-ji 萬年山眞如寺 was constructed on the site of Shōmyaku-an, the hermitage in Kitayama honoring Kōhō Kennichi's teacher, Wuxue Zuyuan (see p. 23 above); Wuxue was designated founder and Musō named second abbot. The Rishō-tō pagoda project also got a concrete start with the rebuilding of the five-storied pagoda of Hōkan-ji 法觀寺 not far from Kennin-ji in the southeastern section of Kyoto; Hōkan-ji had been destroyed by fire in the fighting between Emperor Go-Daigo and the Ashikagas during 1336.

Meanwhile the construction of Tenryū-ji continued apace, with work on the framework beginning on the third day of the eighth month and the ridgepole-raising ceremony—attended by Emperor Kōmyō, Ashikaga Takauji, and Ashikaga Tadayoshi—being celebrated on the fifth day of the twelfth month. Shortly thereafter, on the twenty-third day of the month, Kōgon reorganized the Five Mountain Zen temple system, placing Tenryū-ji in the number two position together with Engaku-ji in Kamakura (in the number one positions were Nanzen-ji in Kyoto and Kenchō-ji in Kamakura).

One important development from the point of view of the present book was the first compilation of *Dialogues in a Dream* in an edition with a postscript by the Chinese Zen master Zhuxian Fanxian.[68]

The eighth month of 1343 saw the completion at Tenryū-ji of the Butsuden (Buddha Hall), one of the seven major buildings in every top-class Zen monastic complex. By the end of the year the Sanmon

(Mountain Gate), another of the major buildings, had been finished. At Rinsen-ji, meanwhile, Musō oversaw construction of a sutra library.

In the tenth month of 1344 an edition of *Dialogues*, revised by Musō and with a second postscript by Zhuxian, was published under the sponsorship of Ōtaka Shigenari 大高重成 (d. 1362), lord of Wakasa Province.

By early 1345 Tenryū-ji was approaching completion. An opening ceremony for the Hattō (Dharma Hall) was held on the eighth day of the fourth month, with the Ashikaga brothers in attendance and Musō delivering the keynote sermon. The opening ceremony for the main temple was scheduled to coincide with the seventh annual observance of Go-Daigo's death on the sixteenth day of the eighth month, but when the authorities on Mount Hiei heard that Cloistered Emperor Kōgon was to attend they demanded the destruction of Tenryū-ji and the exile of Musō. After weeks of escalating tensions, Kōgon, two days before the scheduled events, announced that he would not be present. A small ritual in honor of Go-Daigo, with the Ashikaga brothers attending, was held on the sixteenth, while the main ceremonies were postponed until the twenty-ninth.

As it was, these ceremonies, with an imperial representative present (though not Kōgon himself), went off without interference by Mount Hiei, its success no doubt aided by a major display of military force in the streets of the capital by the Ashikagas. Kōgon visited Tenryū-ji the following day to pay his respects, and Musō delivered a commemorative sermon in his presence.

Soon after the opening ceremonies, Musō, now sixty-nine years old, designated his nephew Shun'oku Myōha as acting abbot of Tenryū-ji; six months later, in the third month of 1346, he retired as abbot entirely, entrusting operation of the temple to his student Mukyoku Shigen. Although Musō remained active, the rest of his years marked something of a return to the quieter days of his life prior to his arrival in Kyoto in 1333. The *Biography* and other historical materials record little more than visits to Tenryū-ji and Saihō-ji by the imperial family, the Ashikagas, and other important guests; poetic and other leisurely pursuits by Musō; and ceremonies honoring Go-Daigo, Kōhō Kennichi, and other figures close to the master.

Among the events noted in the *Biography* for these years were a visit by Musō to the imperial palace on the twenty-fifth day of the eleventh month of 1346 to receive a robe from Emperor Kōmyō; the following day he was granted the honorary title Shōkaku Kokushi 正覺國師 (National Teacher True Awakening). On the twelfth day of the eighth month of 1347 Musō held a ritual for Emperor Go-Daigo at Tenryū-ji, attended by Ashikaga Tadayoshi. A year later, on the twentieth day of the tenth month of 1348, he presided over the memorial service marking the thirty-third anniversary of Kōhō Kennichi's death; the occasion was commemorated by a large dedication ceremony for a recently completed revolving sutra repository.

An event of greater political significance is recorded for early in the year 1349, when Ashikaga Tadayoshi became a formal disciple of Musō. Tadayoshi had long maintained an ongoing communication with Musō but had avoided a closer master-disciple relationship, preferring to take instruction from Zhuxian Fanxian and Kosen Ingen. However, in the third month of 1349 he called upon Musō and asked to become a student, though only after first ascertaining the propriety of such a relationship, since a number of years before he had "received the robe" from Wuxue Zuyuan, the teacher of Kōhō Kennichi. Replying that it was all in the same family, Musō accepted Tadayoshi's request and presented him with a robe and bowl.

Meanwhile the political situation around Musō had taken a disquieting turn for the worse. Since 1338 Tadayoshi and Takauji had ruled as joint shoguns, with Tadayoshi responsible for administration and Takauji for military affairs. Tensions between the two emerged, however, when Tadayoshi became disaffected with Kō no Moronao 高師直 (d. 1351), a warlord who served as Takauji's *shitsuji* 執事 (chief deputy). In the summer of 1349 Tadayoshi's faction managed to have Kō removed as *shitsuji*; Kō's faction, in turn, attacked Tadayoshi and forced him to take refuge in Takauji's compound, which the

Kō warriors then proceeded to surround. The siege was only lifted when Tadayoshi agreed to leave the government and enter the priesthood. In the eighth month, however, Musō mediated a settlement between Tadayoshi and Kō in which Tadayoshi retained administrative authority and Kō was restored to his position as *shitsuji*.

By late 1350, however, the tensions between Takauji and Tadayoshi had boiled over again. On the twenty-sixth day of the tenth month Tadayoshi fled Kyoto by night and joined the forces of the Southern Court, which at that time was headed by Emperor Go-Murakami 後村上 (1328–1368), one of Go-Daigo's sons. Appointed general of Go-Murakami's forces, Tadayoshi and his allies quickly dealt the Shogunate a series of defeats and occupied Kyoto. In the second month of 1351 Takauji and Tadayoshi reached another agreement, also negotiated by Musō, but this reconciliation lasted only a short time. At the end of the seventh month Tadayoshi left the capital and hostilities between the two brothers resumed. In early 1352 Takauji's troops defeated Tadayoshi at Sattayama, in present-day Shizuoka Prefecture. Tadayoshi accepted Takauji's peace offer and was taken to Kamakura, only to die there suddenly on the twenty-sixth day of the second month—the victim, most historians agree, of poisoning.

This final denouement would no doubt have been deeply distressing to Musō, but by the time of Tadayoshi's end several months had passed since Musō's own death. After accepting Tadayoshi as his disciple in 1349, the seventy-four-year-old Musō appears to have increasingly confined his activities to his three Arashiyama temples: Tenryū-ji, Rinsen-ji, and Saihō-ji. Following its entry on Tadayoshi's lay ordination, the *Biography* mentions only an imperial visit in the second month of 1350 before describing Musō's final major project, the construction of a meditation hall for Tenryū-ji in 1351. The seventy-six-year-old master told his disciples, "This year I will surely depart. Tenryū-ji was established by the present cloistered emperor in honor of the memory of Emperor Go-Daigo. Although the thirteenth anniversary of Go-Daigo's passing is now drawing near, the meditation hall has yet to be built. If I do not complete it, who will?"

In order to expedite work on the project Musō once again assumed the abbacy of Tenryū-ji. Construction commenced in the fourth month and was completed in just one hundred days. Dedicated on the twentieth day of the seventh month, the meditation hall, as described in the *Biography*, was spacious and bright, with the capacity to seat a thousand people. A special training season followed the opening ceremony, and for the next month Musō disregarded old age and infirmity to teach the Dharma to the assembly. On the sixteenth day of the eighth month Musō presided at the large memorial service marking the thirteenth anniversary of Go-Daigo's death. Two days later he retired as abbot, installing in his place the Chinese monk Dongling Yongyu.[69]

On the first day of the ninth month Musō announced to his students that his departure was near and requested that anyone who had remaining questions on the Dharma confer with him soon. The *Biography* reports that he devoted several days to the host of seekers who responded, all the while showing no signs of fatigue. Nevertheless, his obviously weakening condition prompted the court to proffer the services of the imperial doctor. Musō declined, saying, "Old age and death are in the natural course of things. There is nothing a doctor can do about them."

During his remaining days he continued meeting with well-wishers, including the reigning emperor and the cloistered emperor, and set to paper his final admonitions for his disciples. On the thirtieth day of the month, three days after designating Mukyoku Shigen as his successor at San'e-in, he bid farewell to those assembled at the temple and passed away at ten o'clock in the morning.

Musō was honored both before and after his death with seven imperially bestowed *Kokushi* (Teacher of the Nation) titles: Musō Kokushi 夢窓國師 (National Teacher Dream Window), Shōkaku Kokushi 正覺國師 (True Awakening), Shinshū Kokushi 心宗國師 (Mind Source), Fusai Kokushi 普濟國師 (Universal Salvation), Genyū Kokushi 玄猷國師 (Mysterious Path), Buttō Kokushi 佛統國師 (Buddha Lineage), and Daien Kokushi 大圓國師 (Great Perfection).

Musō's Legacy

Among Musō's many accomplishments, the most influential from the perspective of Japanese Zen history relate to the Zen school's development as an institution. When Musō began his training in the late thirteenth century the Zen school was still centered in Kamakura and was, to a significant degree, dependent upon the protection of the Shogunate. When the great shift of political power from Kamakura to Kyoto occurred at the time of the Kenmu Restoration, Musō, with his ties to both the imperial family and the warrior clans, was able to oversee a parallel transfer of Zen influence to the capital. With the subsequent rise of the Muromachi Shogunate, Musō maintained the momentum of the Zen school's growth through his promotion of the Ankokuji temple system and his foundation of important Five Mountain institutions like Rinsen-ji, Tenryū-ji, and Tōji-in 等持院. By the time Musō died in 1351, Rinzai Zen had the solid support of the imperial and feudal authorities in the capital and of increasing numbers of local leaders throughout the country.

With this as a basis the Five Mountain system developed during the medieval period into one of the most influential forces in Japanese Buddhism, occupying a privileged position among the various Buddhist schools and serving, in effect, as a bureaucracy through which the Shogunate countered the political and military power of the established Buddhist sects and strengthened its political influence. Musō's successors dominated the system through their control of the post of *sōroku* 僧錄 (Registrar General of Monks), which had authority over the entire Five Mountain organization and was always filled by a member of Musō's lineage.

Although it is likely that Zen would have continued its growth in the capital even without Musō, given the prominence of established Zen temples such as Nanzen-ji and Tōfuku-ji, the Northern Court's patronage of eminent masters like Shūhō Myōchō of Daitoku-ji, and Ashikaga Tadayoshi's commitment to Zen practice under Zhuxian Fanxian and Kosen Ingen, it is unquestionable that this growth was facilitated by Musō, with his quiet charisma, cultural sensitivity, and wide popularity among the governing classes. Indeed, Musō's success at working with the succession of rulers during the tumultuous period between the Kamakura and Muromachi Shogunates has led several biographers to characterize him as a master of political maneuver. The way in which he lived the first fifty years of his life does not support this view, however. Although Musō obviously possessed administrative talents, it is hard to imagine anyone drawn to secular intrigue spending what was in those days the span of an average lifetime meditating in remote areas of the country and deliberately avoiding rank and privilege. I personally find it far more likely that Musō so readily won the respect and cooperation of regents, emperors, and shoguns precisely because his motivations were obviously spiritual and not political. Certainly *Dialogues in a Dream*, far from attempting to advance the secular fortunes of the Zen school, urges upon the government authorities an even-handed approach toward all Buddhist traditions:

> Because of their duty to support the Dharma, those of the ruling classes who receive it should not limit themselves to faith in a single school and reject all others. Nor, if one's faith does extend to all traditions, should one utilize those traditions to offer prayers directed toward secular goals. In this degenerate age, is it not a privilege to receive the teaching of the Tathāgata? Vowing deeply never to betray this trust, support Buddhism externally by building temples large and small and support it internally by fostering the true spirit of the Way, supporting all schools and forming whatever connections might help in guiding all living beings to the realization of enlightenment. This is the truest of prayer rituals and the most boundless of meritorious acts. (Chapter 10)

Musō's influence on Japanese literary culture was perhaps not as direct as his influence on the Zen institution, but it was quite significant nevertheless, particularly through the association of his direct descendants—Shun'oku Myōha, Gidō Shūshin,[70] and Zekkai Chūshin[71] chief among them—with the Five Mountain literary movement. Although Musō's *San'e-in Admonitions* make it clear that the proper vocation of the Zen monk is "removing all attachments and concentrating on investigation of the self," and although they severely condemn those students who "shave their heads and poison their minds with foreign literature, aspiring to be authors," Musō himself obviously loved verse and was fond of poetry gatherings like the ones he hosted at Zuisen-in and Saihō-ji. Indeed, his taste for such activities was unquestionably part of his appeal to the ruling classes, particularly the court nobility. Although his statements in the *Admonitions* suggest that Musō regarded literary pursuits as proper only for monks who had completed their training, his enthusiasm for them would have inevitably set the stage for his descendants to make such pursuits a more central part of Zen temple culture.

Musō's love of poetry was equaled by his affection for landscape gardens, an affection undoubtedly rooted in the appreciation of natural beauty so often seen both in Musō's verse and in expository writings like *Dialogues in a Dream* (see, for example, his descriptions of Ise Shrine in chapter 7 and West Lake in chapter 76). Musō designed gardens in most of the monasteries he lived in for any length of time and obviously considered them an important part of the ambiance; in the case of Saihō-ji the garden was for all intents and purposes the soul of the temple. Musō was also unusual in that he expressed in writing his ideas on the spiritual significance of these man-made landscapes that obviously gave him so much pleasure. In chapter 57 of *Dialogues*, for example, we find the following remarkable passage:

[Some people] use landscape gardens to ward off sleepiness and boredom as an aid in their practice of the Way. This is something truly noble and is not at all the same as the delight ordinary people take in gardens. However, since such people still make a distinction between gardens and the practice of the Way, they cannot be called true Way-followers.

Then there are those who regard mountains, rivers, grass, trees, tiles, and stones to be their own Original Nature. Their love for gardens may resemble worldly affection, but they employ that affection in their aspiration for the Way, using as part of their practice the changing scenery of the grasses and trees throughout the four seasons. One who can do this is truly an exemplar of how a follower of the Way should consider a garden.

Therefore it cannot be said that a love of gardens is necessarily a bad thing, or necessarily a good thing. In gardens themselves there is no gain or loss—such judgments occur only in the human mind.

Although the connection between Zen practice and temple gardens is occasionally exaggerated (I have, for example, heard nothing in my many years at Japanese Zen temples to suggest that the stone garden at Ryōan-ji constitutes in itself a koan, a belief held by a number of Western Zen followers I have met), Musō's words should remove any doubt that in traditional Japanese Zen the creation and enjoyment of landscape gardens has always been considered part of the practice of the Way. Musō states his own position quite unequivocally in the verse cited above (page 38), "Do not disdain the pleasure I take in landscape gardens; I'm simply attempting through them to refine my mind."

Musō's legacy as a Zen master is a bit less clear. His own Zen practice was plainly the central theme of his adult life, and he became without question one of the most influential teachers of his time. It may still be asked, however, whether Emperor Hanazono was justified in his claim that Musō's inner awakening did not match that of his contemporary Shūhō Myōchō. To be sure, it could be pointed out that Musō's influence as a master owed much to the prominence of his followers and was notable more for its breadth than its depth.

Although Musō is said to have had more than 13,000 students and 127 Dharma successors,[72] none of these followers (even those, like Gidō Shūshin, remembered for the simplicity and piety of their lives) left a lasting legacy with regard to the transmission of the Dharma. Those in his lineage who earned places in Zen history generally did so as a result of their political or cultural accomplishments.

Nevertheless, it would be rash to dismiss the importance of Musō as a Zen master. His personal practice was held in high regard by as strict and astute a Zen adept as Hakuin Ekaku,[73] and his wide influence as a teacher helped cement the acceptance of Zen in Japanese society. Though he may not have produced successors matching those of Shūhō Myōchō, it might equally be said that Shūhō was incapable of reaching ordinary people and spreading the teaching in the way that Musō was.

Indeed, I find Musō's human side to be one of his most appealing qualities. Although he spent much of his life practicing in remote places far from the centers of influence and power, he was by no means a recluse or misanthrope. As indicated in the *Biography*, his pilgrimage wanderings were often directed to the residences of friends or to temples associated with people he knew. Even during his periodic escapes from the ties of temple life, as when he left Jōko-ji in 1313 and made his way to Nōshū, comrades often accompanied him. During his more solitary periods, such as his sojourn on the Miura Peninsula, his gate was open to kindred spirits, and he appears to have maintained good relations with the local people. He seems, in short, to have been a man who appreciated the company of others, despite the simultaneous taste for solitude that formed an enduring part of his spiritual search.

Musō's views on the Buddhist teachings were fully in line with this accepting spirit. Even on those occasions when he criticized other traditions he was careful to balance his statements by contextualizing them in a broader outlook. One example is his critique of popular contemporary Pure Land teachings, which tended to privilege the *nenbutsu* as superior to all other Mahayana practices. In chapter 85 of

Dialogues in a Dream Musō writes:

> Among ordinary *nenbutsu* devotees there are some who
> insist that calling the Name is the only correct practice
> and that all other practices are useless. This viewpoint goes
> against the true principles of the Mahayana and cannot be
> said to agree with the central teaching of the patriarchs.
>
> It would be equally mistaken for followers of the Zen
> school to declare that the only true practice is *zazen* and
> that all other practices are a waste of time. Nevertheless, it is
> helpful for beginning Zen students to set aside other meth-
> ods for a time and concentrate solely on *zazen*, singling out
> this practice though fundamentally nothing is rejected. It
> is in this sense that the eminent priests who established the
> Pure Land school set aside the "other practices" and aspired
> to "the samādhi of the single practice [of *nenbutsu*]"; it was
> not that they condemned the other methods. Similarly, the
> intent of clear-eyed Zen masters when they criticize *nen-*
> *butsu* is never to condemn this practice.

This evenhanded approach is typical of Musō's attitude toward all
of the non-Zen schools of Buddhism. He follows his words on *nen-*
butsu in the statement quoted above with the comment:

> This is the case not only with criticisms directed toward
> the Pure Land school but also with those directed toward
> all other traditions. Even when non-Buddhists and celes-
> tial demons engage enlightened masters in discussion, the
> masters do not regard themselves as superior and their
> adversaries as inferior. Rather, they criticize their chal-
> lengers only in order to disabuse them of their biased
> notion that "our views are better than the teachings of
> the Buddha"—a notion based on their failure to see that
> there is not a hairbreadth of difference between a sage and

an ordinary person. The *Sutra of Complete Enlightenment* says, "The Dharma attained by bodhisattvas and by non-Buddhist practicers is the same bodhi".... Anyone speaking of right and wrong who still has strong attachments to self and objects is not a true disciple of the Buddha. How could such behavior be in accord with the truth?

Because of such statements, and perhaps also because of the intimate knowledge of the sacred texts that he displayed in his writings on Zen, Musō's teaching is often described as a synthesis of the doctrinal and meditative traditions, suggesting that his approach as a Zen master accorded equal value to *zazen* and textual study. The facts of his life and teaching suggest otherwise, however. Although Musō never disparaged the doctrinal teachings and consistently recognized them as an authentic expression of the Buddha's original message, and although, as noted above, he urged the nation's rulers to support all traditions equally, Musō, once committed to Zen practice, devoted himself almost exclusively to meditation. Even his study of the classical Zen records during his time in Kamakura ultimately left him more convinced than ever of the futility of focusing on the written word if one desired to realize the "separate transmission outside the teachings." It is worth repeating here the passage, quoted earlier, from his *Night Talks on West Mountain*:

> One day, upon examining my own heart, I realized how uneasy I still felt. For the first time I understood the saying, "That which comes from outside the gate is not the house treasure." As an ancient master said, "Never obscure the light of the spirit—this is the eternal way; having entered the gate, do not tarry in intellectual understanding." I had left the school of doctrine and entered the school of Zen, yet my studies, although different in content, were equally based on conceptual knowledge. If I go on like this, I thought, I'm simply obscuring the light of my spirit. I

therefore took the bag filled with all the notes I had accumulated over the years and threw it into the fire.

Musō, moreover, clearly identified the Zen path as one distinct from the paths of ritual and scholarship, as in the above-mentioned *Biography* passage (see p. 19) where he commented that "the doctrinal schools and the Zen school are as incompatible as charcoal and ice." Musō also devoted considerable space to this matter in *Dialogues in a Dream*, with a particularly clear statement occurring in chapter 46:

> Although he had long since mastered the teachings of the sutras and commentaries, [Eminent Scholar] Liang had yet to experience enlightenment. Why did he suddenly attain a great awakening at Mazu's single phrase, "What is *that*?" You must realize that that which Liang awakened to is not found in the teachings of the sutras and commentaries. Those who devote their entire lives to intellectual understanding would more profitably have spent their time directly observing the arising and passing of thoughts, whether walking, standing, sitting, or reclining. Practicing in this way, how could anyone fail to experience enlightenment, like Nanyue or Scholar Liang? How unfortunate to spend all of one's time in intellectual pursuits.

However, Musō, while he plainly saw enlightenment-oriented practice as the highest ideal, nevertheless regarded sutra study as far superior to the lazy type of practice that remained mired in delusion. With proper study, he asserted in chapter 66, "even if you have not attained enlightenment you will at least never mistake a fish eye for a pearl." In the same chapter he continues:

> Those born in the Latter Age have shallow karmic roots, so those who follow the scholarly path believe that the ultimate goal consists of mastering the various doctrines

expounding the principle of mind-nature, and thus they fail to realize the source of mind-nature itself. People who enter the path of Zen tend to regard such doctrines as something for scholars to discuss, and nothing for Zen practicers to bother about. Sincerely abandoning both mundane delusions and supermundane teachings and wholeheartedly striving toward Supreme Enlightenment—this is truly what the Zen school encourages. But is it not a great error to avoid studying the doctrinal meaning of the sutras and treatises and indulge instead in false thinking based on your own mental biases, thereby confusing the thinking consciousness for the Original Mind?

Chapter 76 presents a clear discussion of the original unity from which both the Zen and doctrinal schools emerged, even as it explains Musō's view of the differences between the two.

The ancient masters asserted that Bodhidharma came from the West, not in order to transmit a particular teaching, but simply to point out that which everyone already possesses in complete perfection. If it is already possessed by everyone, how can it be said to be limited to followers of Zen and to be lacking in followers of the doctrinal schools? Nor is it perfectly present only in the followers of Zen and the doctrinal traditions—it may be discerned in the labors of the farmer cultivating his fields and in the blacksmith and carpenter exercising their crafts. The essential point is that everything living beings do—seeing, hearing, thinking, knowing, walking, standing, sitting, reclining, playing, and talking—is without exception an expression of the Mysterious Principle of the Coming from the West. How much more so does this apply to the actions of those who, following the Buddha's teachings, perform all manner of meritorious deeds?

However, not being aware of this Mysterious Principle, most people are deceived by the illusions of the world and squander their existence in the cycle of birth and death. The Buddha expounded various teachings intended to help people escape from this deluded thinking, but people then became attached to these teachings and again obscured the Mysterious Principle. Therefore the Patriarch came from the West and revealed Original Nature. This revelation is called "the Mysterious Principle outside the teachings that is transmitted by mind to mind." This Mysterious Principle is not simply another type of Dharma gate transmitted in the same way as the various doctrinal traditions. If it were just another teaching passed on through words, then it would be no more than an unusual teaching method and could not be called "a separate transmission outside the teachings."

The broadness of outlook revealed in this passage is typical of Musō's manner of expression throughout *Dialogues in a Dream*. One is left with the impression of Musō as a clear, balanced thinker for whom discursive exposition, though ultimately inadequate for conveying "the separate transmission outside the teachings," was an important means of instruction. This approach contrasts with the better-known Zen tactic of shocking the questioner out of conceptual thinking, a famous example of which involves Musō's eminent peer Shūhō Myōchō, the founder of Daitoku-ji.

When, during a public debate between the Zen school and the older established schools of Buddhism, the Tendai prelate Gen'e 玄慧 (1279–1350) asked Shūhō to explain the separate transmission outside the teachings, Shūhō responded, "An eight-sided millstone flies through the air!" Gen'e is said not to have understood. Next a Tendai monk presented Shūhō with a box, telling him it represented the universe. Shūhō immediately broke the box with his stick and asked, "What about when the universe is shattered to bits!" The questioner was again bewildered.

Shūhō's responses were unquestionably effective—the Zen school was judged winner of the debate, and Gen'e was impressed enough to later take up Zen practice under Shūhō's instruction. And it should be noted that on occasion Musō, too, used methods similar to Shūhō's. When Ashikaga Tadayoshi asks him, in the final chapter of *Dialogues in a Dream*, "Master, what, truly, is the Dharma that you teach people?" Musō's response comes in the form of a koan as cryptic as Shūhō's: "At midnight in Silla the sun shines bright!"

Yet it is interesting that this exchange comes at the very end of the book, after Musō has devoted thousands of words to explanation. Musō obviously recognized that the final destination of Zen lies in the ineffable, but also, and just as importantly, that there is a place for a clear understanding of the nature of the path. *Dialogues in a Dream* may be seen as his attempt to provide a comprehensive guide to such understanding.

DIALOGUES IN A DREAM

Dialogues in a Dream, the best-known and most influential of Musō's writings, has remained available ever since its original publication in 1344. Originally compiled in the year Kōei 1 (1342), it was revised and published with a new postscript in Kōei 3 (1344), then reprinted in, to name only the editions for which records remain, Genna 8 (1622), Kan'ei 11 (1634), Shōhō 4 (1647), Jōkyō 3 (1687), Bunsei 2 (1819), and Tenpō 4 (1833). In postfeudal Japan it has seen numerous reprints, both in its original form and in modern Japanese translation.

Dialogues in a Dream is remarkable for the fact that it is the first book in Japanese publishing history to have been printed in *kana-majiri*, a type of text that mixes Chinese characters (*kanji*) and the Japanese *kana* syllabary, with the *kanji* indicating the root elements of words and the kana indicating articles, conjunctions, and grammatical forms. *Kanamajiri*, as the most logical and accessible approach to rendering Japanese in textual form, is now the standard way of writing the language.

As mentioned above, the main text of *Dialogues in a Dream* consists of three sections containing a total of ninety-three chapters, with each chapter comprising a question posed by Ashikaga Tadayoshi to Musō, followed by Musō's answer. The present text concludes with two short postscripts by the Chinese Zen master Zhuxian Fanxian.

Tadayoshi's questions deal at the start with relatively down-to-earth issues relating to the religious life, and over the course of the text gradually take up topics that are increasingly abstract. Thus in Part 1 of the book Tadayoshi asks about such matters as the need for moderation in the pursuit of wealth; the purpose of reciting the sutras and dhāraṇīs; the true meaning of prayer, ritual, and offerings; and the nature of demonic obstructions, both inner and outer. Part 2 takes up issues like the difference between knowledge, wisdom, and enlightenment; the nature of true practice and meditation; and the difference between "words" and "intent" in the Zen teachings. Part 3 devotes several chapters to topics like the Ground of Original Nature, the true mind, and the use of language in the various Zen schools, and also discusses the meaning of meditation, the true Dharma, and Zen's "separate transmission outside the teachings."

Although *Dialogues in a Dream* is in many ways a product of its era, with several of its chapters devoted to celestial demons and other subjects that may seem quaint to modern readers, it has stood the test of time precisely because its concerns are for the most part timeless in nature. Topics like the true meaning of prayer, compassion, and wisdom are as relevant today as they were in the fourteenth century. It was partly owing to this enduring relevance that *Dialogues in a Dream* was selected as the Tenryū-ji Institute for Philosophy and Religion's next translation, following the publication of *Entangling Vines* in 2004. Also pertinent to the decision, of course, was the fact that Musō Soseki is the founder of Tenryū-ji.

The present translation had its origins in a trial rendition by Fukazawa Yukio 深沢幸雄, professor emeritus of Tokiwakai Gakuen University, made at the request of the late Rev. Hirata Seikō, former chief abbot of Tenryū-ji. The resulting translation, based on a modern Japanese translation by Kawase Kazuma entitled the *Muchū Mondō shū*,[74] provided valuable reference material regarding vocabulary and meaning even as it motivated me to forge ahead with my own version.

The translator of *Dialogues in a Dream*, as of any Classical Japanese text, faces a number of challenges. The first, needless to say, is the language itself. Classical Japanese, in addition to its frequent ambiguity regarding the subject of sentences, is more limited in vocabulary than modern Japanese, enriched as the latter has been with many new Sino-Japanese compounds inspired by the Western languages, as well as with numerous loanwords taken directly from those languages. Lacking such vocabulary, the Japanese of Musō's time was forced to employ what words it had in multiple meanings. As a result Musō's prose, though quite poetic, is occasionally lacking in precision, a quality aggravated by a paucity of conjunctions that often leaves the reader guessing as to the relationship between one idea and the next.

Reference to Kawase Kazuma's *Muchū Mondō shū* and Nakamura Bunpō's *Gendaigo yaku Muchū Mondō*,[75] the two modern Japanese editions of *Dialogues in a Dream*, greatly eased the challenges of parsing Musō's classical grammar, flawed though both works are by misreadings and a tendency to leave the really difficult passages virtually unchanged from the original Classical Japanese. More helpful in this regard were the modern versions by Karaki Junzō[76] and Nishimura Eshin;[77] unfortunately, both works include only selected chapters.

Partial translations also exist in English. The longest of these is Thomas Cleary's *Dream Conversations on Buddhism and Zen*,[78] which covers perhaps a third of the original text. Kenneth L. Kraft translated nine chapters of the text in an article for *The Eastern Buddhist*,[79] and W. S. Merwin, with Sōiku Shigematsu, translated sections of three chapters in *Sun at Midnight*.[80] All of these translations are of high quality, often bettering the modern Japanese versions in conveying the sense of especially obscure passages in the original.

There were, nevertheless, a number of sections whose meaning remained unclear even after repeated readings. Ueda Shizuteru, professor emeritus of philosophy at Kyoto University, generously agreed to look over these passages with me. Prof. Ueda, who has been conducting a monthly seminar on *Dialogues in a Dream* for several years, was in every case able to reveal the logic of Musō's thought and clarify how it fit into the larger context of his argument. Without Prof. Ueda's help my translations of these passages would have remained tentative at best.

I would also like to thank Nishiyama Mika for the use of her aforementioned essay, "The Life of Musō Soseki," which presented in a well-organized manner the major events in Musō's life. Nishiyama's research uncovered important clues, missed by other researchers, which help to explain certain developments in Musō's life (his move to Kitayama in Kyoto in 1317 being a notable example). Her explanations also clarified several difficult passages in the *Biography* and the *Dialogues*.

The present translation, although it attempts to be academically responsible, is not intended as a strictly academic work. I have therefore felt free to employ certain conventions that are no longer followed in most academic writing, such as the capitalization of religiously significant terms like Original Nature.

I have also stressed readability when deciding how to render the many Buddhist terms in the text, keeping in mind that Musō himself envisioned it as a popular work.

Sanskrit and Japanese terms are rendered with the appropriate diacritical marks, except in the case of words that have long since passed into common English usage, such as "sutra," "koan," "Mahayana," "samsara," and "nirvana." Although Japanese terms are generally italicized, I have followed the convention used by certain scholars of romanizing Sanskrit terminology. Names are rendered in their original languages; thus Chinese names are used even for Chinese masters known primarily for their work in Japan (e.g., Lanxi Daolong rather than Rankei Dōryū, as he is known in Japan). Sanskrit names are used even for bodhisattvas best known by their East Asian names (thus Avalokiteśvara rather than Guanyin or Kannon), except in the case of obscure bodhisattvas, whose names are translated into English.

Rev. Fukita Takamichi, the priest of Shōzen-ji in Kyoto and an instructor at Bukkyō University, offered much useful information on simplifying the onerous task of indexing the volume.

The completed manuscript was examined by Edmund Skrzypczak, former editor of *Monumenta Nipponica* at Sophia University in Tokyo, whose sharp eye for errors and inconsistencies greatly improved the overall quality of the text.

Finally, I owe a debt of gratitude to Prof. Yoshizawa Katsuhiro of the International Research Institute for Zen Buddhism at Hanazono University and Rev. Toga Masataka of the Institute for Zen Studies, without whose constant support this project would not have been possible.

Dialogues in a Dream

PART I

PROSPERITY IN THE PRESENT LIFE

Question: The Buddha, in his great compassion, alleviates the suffering of sentient beings and seeks to give them comfort. Why, then, do the Buddhist teachings urge restraint in our desire for prosperity?

Answer: Those who seek worldly wealth engage in farming or trade, devise moneymaking schemes, or sell their skills, knowledge, or services to others. Their activities differ, but the goal is the same. Observing them, we see that such people suffer lifelong hardship in body and mind while gaining none of the true prosperity they seek. Even when they do acquire some measure of wealth, there is always the danger that it may be lost to fire, swept away by floods, stolen by thieves, or confiscated by the authorities. Those lucky enough to avoid such misfortunes still cannot retain their property once their allotted years have passed.

Furthermore, great wealth commonly involves great wrongdoing, so that the rich often fall into the evil realms[81] in their next existence. This is what is meant by "small gains bring great losses." Poverty in this existence is retribution for avarice in past lives. Unaware of this basic principle, people often assume that poverty stems from a lack of worldly wisdom. They fail to realize that unless the karmic seeds for prosperity have been sown in past existences it is impossible to gain wealth in the present life regardless of what practical skills one may possess. Rather than blaming poverty on a lack of worldly wisdom, people should recognize that a lack of worldly wisdom is the result of not having planted the karmic seeds for success.

Other people blame their poverty on their superiors, whom they accuse of refusing to grant them land due to them or wrongfully seizing their property.[82] Here again, the situation of these individuals is the result, not of their superiors' lack of generosity or their own loss of property, but rather of their having sown the karmic seeds for poverty. If people simply abandoned their craving for prosperity they would feel quite satisfied with the share of good fortune that comes their way in the natural course of things. It is for these reasons that the Buddhist teachings urge us to restrain our desire for prosperity. It is not because they expect people to renounce all wealth and live in destitution.

In ancient India, Śākyamuni's great patron Sudatta[83] lost his fortune during his old age and was left without any means of livelihood. Sudatta and his wife were utterly alone in their household, abandoned by everyone whom they had supported for so many years. Sudatta's wealth was gone, and the storehouses that had once held his possessions stood empty.

One day, searching through his storehouses once again in the hope that something might still remain, Sudatta came across a rice-measure made of fragrant sandalwood. This he was able to trade for four *shō* of rice.[84] Delighted, he calculated that this would be enough to keep him and his wife alive for a number of days. Soon afterward, however, while Sudatta was out on an errand, the Buddha's disciple Śāriputra[85] called upon the household during his begging rounds. Sudatta's wife gave him one *shō* of the rice. Next came Maudgalyāyana[86] and Mahākāśyapa,[87] and to each of them, too, she donated a *shō* of rice, so that finally only a single *shō* remained. This, she thought, will at least suffice to keep us alive for today. Just then, however, the Tathāgata appeared. Unable to refuse him, she immediately offered the final *shō* of rice.

Afterward, though, she sadly pondered on what she would do when her husband returned, exhausted from his errand. Surely, she thought, he would be angry with her, saying that there's a proper time and place even for dāna[88] to the Buddha and Sangha, and that, at this critical moment when they were hard pressed simply to stay alive, it was absurd to donate their last four measures of rice. Heartsick, she fell to the ground and wept.

Just then Sudatta returned from his errand. When he asked why she was crying, she related everything that had happened. Hearing this, Sudatta said, "For the sake of the Three Treasures[89] one mustn't begrudge even one's very life. Though we stand on the brink of starvation, how could we, out of our own personal concerns, refuse to make donations? How admirable that you understand this!"

Later Sudatta decided to search his storehouses again, thinking that something like the rice-measure might still be there. When he tried to enter, however, he found that every door was jammed and couldn't be opened. Thinking this strange, he broke through the doors and found that each and every storehouse was filled with grain, money, silk, gold, silver, and various other treasures, just as they had been before. With this all the members of his household returned, and Sudatta was once again a wealthy man.

The restoration of Sudatta's wealth was not a reward from the Buddha for the four measures of rice. Rather, it came forth from the pure, generous hearts of Sudatta and his wife. Even in this Latter Age of the Dharma,[90] anyone as free from avarice as they were is sure to have happiness and prosperity to his or her full satisfaction. Though you may by nature lack such a spirit, if you renounce the mind that seeks after small gains and aspire to the spirit of Sudatta and his wife, how could you not but profit greatly? If you fail to emulate Sudatta's freedom from avarice and, desiring only a comfortable lifestyle, seek after prosperity with a covetous mind, then you not only fail to gain any true benefit in the present life but invariably fall into the realm of the pretas[91] in the next.

THE WAY OF THE BUDDHA,
THE WAY OF THE WORLD

Question: Since the pursuit of prosperity through worldly activities results in sinful karma, it is only natural that it should be prohibited. However, by praying for prosperity we show reverence for and faith in the gods and the buddhas, and by reciting the sutras and dhāraṇīs[92] we deepen our connections with the Buddha Way. Therefore, shouldn't these activities be permitted?

Answer: If the prayers are offered in order to deepen one's connection with the Way, then what you suggest is indeed superior to seeking worldly wealth through secular activities. But then, those so foolish as to focus solely on worldly wealth are hardly worthy of mention. How much more foolish are those who—having received a human body (so hard to obtain!) and heard the Dharma (so rarely encountered!)—spurn the supreme teaching of enlightenment in order to chant sutras and dhāraṇīs for the sake of secular success.

A man of old said, "To forget the passions while in the secular realm—this is the realm of Buddhadharma. To arouse the passions while in the realm of Buddhadharma—this is the secular realm." Though one practices the Buddhadharma, attains enlightenment, and takes the great vow to liberate all sentient beings, should one then become attached to the Buddhadharma one will benefit neither oneself nor others. How, then, could it possibly be in accord with the enlightened will to worship the gods and buddhas and recite the sutras and dhāraṇīs, not for the sake of one's own liberation or the welfare of other beings, but merely to gain worldly fame and profit?

Even secular activities create good karmic roots if done in order to further the practice of the Buddhadharma and guide other sentient beings. And if in performing these activities you come to awakening, then not only does your prior work in the world serve for the benefit of all beings and contribute to the practice of the Buddhadharma, but it also becomes itself the mysterious functioning of ineffable liberation. This is what the *Lotus Sutra* means when it says that "earning a living and producing things never transgresses the True Law."[93]

THE TRUE MEANING OF PROSPERITY

3

Question: It is said that actions resulting in prosperity can be divided into those that are defiled and those that are undefiled.[94] What does this mean?

Answer: Actions form causes that can lead to either good or evil results. Performing good deeds produces causes that result in good fortune. Good cultivated for the sake of rewards in the human or heavenly realms is defiled, since it is moved by a spirit of greed. But good acts are undefiled if done, not in the hope of worldly gain, but out of devotion to the supreme teaching. Thus it is not that there is a distinction between "defiled acts" and "undefiled acts"; rather, an act is defiled if the heart of the one who performs it is defiled.

The teachings divide the defiled and undefiled minds into four different categories. The first is the wholly defiled mind—the mind of ordinary deluded people and nonbelievers. The second is the wholly undefiled mind—the mind of the śrāvaka and pratyekabuddha.[95] The third is the mind that is both defiled and undefiled—the mind of the bodhisattva. The fourth is the mind that is neither defiled nor undefiled—the mind of a buddha.

These four categories, however, are simply provisional groupings intended to show the differences in spiritual attainment between ordinary people, śrāvakas, and the others. Generally speaking, when categorizing "defiled" and "undefiled" we can say that it is not just ordinary people and nonbelievers whose minds are defiled but also śrāvakas, pratyekabuddhas, and bodhisattvas. In the sense that śrāvakas and pratyekabuddhas no longer seek worldly rewards they are undefiled, but since they still shun samsara and strive for nirvana they have not yet realized the truly undefiled mind. Nor have the bodhisattvas, even those who have reached the level of the Ten Stages[96] or Equivalent Enlightenment,[97] since they have not yet completely severed delusion. The bodhisattvas' actions are undefiled, however, in the sense that they seek neither the rewards of the world nor the nirvana of the Hinayana, but strive only for Supreme Enlightenment.

According to the *Sutra of the Compassionate Flower*,[98] in ancient times there lived a cakravartin[99] by the name of King No-Thought-of-Conflict. He had an abundance of the seven treasures[100] and was surrounded by a thousand children. The regent at that time, named Treasure-Sea Brahmin, had a son who left the world, practiced the Way, and attained perfect enlightenment, becoming the Tathāgata Treasure-House. King No-Thought-of-Conflict, who venerated the Tathāgata, paved part of a park with gold and there erected a tower made of the seven treasures. This he appointed with lavish decorations and filled with all manner of offerings. That evening he lit thousands of votive lamps before the Tathāgata and his followers. He placed lamps on his own head, hands, and knees, and throughout the night paid homage to the Tathāgata. The king, accompanied by his princes and by the eighty-four thousand minor rulers under him, continued such offerings for three months.

The regent, Treasure-Sea Brahmin, had a dream in which he saw King No-Thought-of-Conflict, the princes, and all the others with the faces of wild boars, elephants, lions, foxes, or monkeys, and with their bodies defiled by blood. Among the group were a few figures in human form riding on small, broken-down carts. Upon awakening the regent went to the Tathāgata and described his dream.

The Tathāgata explained, "Neither the king nor the princes, nor anyone else who made offerings to me, had the heart that seeks the Mahayana.[101] Their wish was only to be reborn as gods, spirit kings, cakravartins, or men of wealth. Even those few who desired no reward in the heavenly or human realms but instead sought liberation were interested not in the Mahayana but only in the vehicle of the śrāvakas. The human figures and creatures with boar, monkey, and other animal faces that you saw in your dream represent the forms of the king and the others as they experience the eternal cycle of samsara in the human, preta, and animal realms. Those riding in the broken-down carts represent the followers of the Hinayana."

Upon hearing this, Treasure-Sea Brahmin went immediately to King No-Thought-of-Conflict. "The offerings Your Majesty made to the Tathāgata constitute causes for prosperity in the next life. Maintaining the precepts constitutes causes for a human or heavenly rebirth in the next life. Listening to the Dharma forms causes for wisdom in the next life. Why doesn't Your Majesty [transcend these things and] give rise to bodhicitta—the supreme mind that seeks enlightenment and the liberation of all sentient beings?"

The king answered, "Supreme bodhi is exceedingly profound and difficult to attain. For this reason I first seek rewards in the phenomenal world."

"The Way is plain and clear," replied Treasure-Sea Brahmin. "When the defilements are cut off, the Way is vast and boundless since there are no hindrances. You should strive for the place of true repose."

Thereupon the king returned to the palace, retired to a quiet place for single-minded reflection, and gave rise to bodhicitta. Treasure-Sea Brahmin went also to the princes and advised them in the same way that he had the king. Each and every one of them gave rise to bodhicitta. Afterward the king and the princes went together to pay homage to the Tathāgata, saying, "For three months we made offerings to the Tathāgata and the Sangha. The merit of this has now returned to us as supreme bodhi."

The Tathāgata praised the king, saying, "Well done, Great King! In the future, after immeasurable eons of time, you will attain true awakening in the Land of Repose, and will be called Tathāgata Amitābha."[102] All of the princes too received confirmation from the Tathāgata of their future realization of Buddhahood. The first was Avalokiteśvara,[103] the second was Mahāsthāmaprāpta,[104] and so forth.

King No-Thought-of-Conflict and the princes had performed vast numbers of meritorious deeds, yet these formed the cause of nothing better than rebirth in the realms of the gods, humans, pretas, or animals, or for attainment of enlightenment in the Hinayana vehicle of the śrāvakas. But because they transformed their way of thinking through the exhortations of Treasure-Sea Brahmin, they all gave rise to bodhicitta and received confirmation of their eventual attainment of Buddhahood.

Even in the present Latter Age of the Dharma, how can you fail to give rise to bodhicitta if, like King No-Thought-of-Conflict, you overturn the deluded mind and engage in meditation? Even if you cannot go this far, and are able to do no more than cultivate good roots in accordance with the sacred teachings, if you dedicate such efforts to the realization of supreme bodhi then surely you will acquire great merit. Such people are watched over by the Three Treasures and protected by the gods; although they have yet to attain enlightenment they will at least be born in a pure land, or, if born in the human or heavenly realms, they will be free of all adversity without ever striving to avoid it and be blessed by good fortune without ever seeking it out.

RENOUNCING AVARICE 4

Question: I fully understand that by abandoning the desire for prosperity, prosperity naturally comes one's way. But abandoning this desire is exceedingly difficult—how does one do it?

Answer: It is not difficult if one's desire to cast away avarice is as profound as one's desire for prosperity, though if one casts away avarice in the hope of obtaining good fortune this is no better than seeking happiness through moneymaking schemes.

Nor is it simply a matter of despising gain in the phenomenal world. In their desire for unconditioned nirvana, the Two Vehicles—the śrāvakas and pratyekabuddhas—still dwell in the Phantom City.[105] Even bodhisattvas of the Three Worthy States and the Ten Stages of Development,[106] because of their continuing desire for the Dharma, have yet to manifest the great wisdom of enlightenment. The moment we drop all desire for worldly success the inexhaustible storehouse of our Original Nature immediately opens, allowing us to use all of the treasures within—functioning that is infinite and profound, samādhi that is beyond all measure—for the limitless benefit of self and others. If you are going to give rise to desire at all, why not give rise to this Great Desire? Anyone who conceives this Great Desire can no longer be satisfied with arhatship or even the exalted status of a bodhisattva, let alone rewards in the human and heavenly realms.

PROSPERITY AND THE
SEARCH FOR THE WAY

Question: The ancient ascetics lived under trees and on top of crags, surviving on nuts and berries and wearing clothes made of grass. Is it wrong for a person, unable to follow their example, to seek long life and prosperity so that he may practice the Buddha Way?

Answer: Although seeking prosperity for the sake of the Way certainly differs from the desire for worldly gain, still such a seeker rejoices when his search is successful and grieves when it is not. He possesses one thing yet lacks another. He is satisfied for the moment, then yearns for what is next. Passing his days burdened by such petty cares will hinder the Way and will certainly never advance it. Finally the seeker approaches the hour of his death, only to find his practice immature owing to his pursuit of prosperity "for the sake of the Way." Will he then be able to ask that his life be extended so that he can die when his practice is complete?

The ancient masters taught that food is necessary only to maintain life, and that clothes are necessary only to ward off cold. Even the poorest person has food and clothing sufficient for that. Though what one eats and wears may not be of the finest quality, it is incomparably better than the wild foods and grass clothes of the ancient ascetics. Those who follow the Buddha Way without begrudging their very lives will, with the aid of the Three Treasures and the heavenly deities, always have sufficient food and clothing to maintain their practice. This is true even if they lack good karmic seeds.

When Dengyō Daishi[107] lay on his deathbed, his disciple Kōjō[108] approached him and said, "While you were with us we were able, thanks to your great virtue, to obtain sufficient food and clothing for the entire community and practice the Way without hindrance. But if the temple loses support after you're gone, then the monks may regress in their practice of the Way. Please tell us what to do if that happens." Dengyō Daishi responded, "In food and clothing there is no mind that seeks the Way, but in the mind that seeks the Way there are food and clothing." If you truly understand the wisdom of Dengyō's reply, then seeking prosperity for the sake of the Dharma seems foolish indeed.

THE MERITS OF THE BUDDHAS AND BODHISATTVAS

Question: The buddhas and bodhisattvas vow to fulfill the wishes of sentient beings. One would therefore expect them to comfort all beings and alleviate their sufferings, even if they were not specifically requested to do so. Why is it, then, that throughout the ages even people who pray wholeheartedly so rarely see their prayers answered?

Answer: I, too, entertained the same doubt some thirty years ago, when I was living as a hermit at Usuba in Jōshū.[109] It had not rained in quite a while, and one early summer day as I walked near my hermitage I noticed how dry and desolate all the fields and paddies appeared. I felt a deep sense of pity and wondered how the dragon kings[110] could be so lacking in compassion.

Then the thought came to me: "The dragon kings can make rain, but they feel no particular compassion for human beings. I feel compassion for human beings, but I lack the power to make rain. The buddhas and bodhisattvas, however, surpass the dragon kings in their power to make rain and surpass me in the depth of their compassion, so why do they not help in these times of misfortune? Some may say that our bad karma prevents the buddhas' aid from reaching us. This would mean, however, that karmic forces solely determine the suffering of sentient beings, and if poor karma can prevent salvation, then it is false to say [as the holy teachings do] that our prayers are answered by the buddhas and bodhisattvas. To those who protest that the sacred texts tell no lies, I say that, regardless of how things may have been in ancient times, nowadays I know of no one, aristocrat or commoner, who feels that his prayers have been truly answered.

"Buddha Bhaiṣajya-guru[111] vowed to heal our illnesses, yet few people are, in fact, free of illness. Bodhisattva Samantabhadra[112] promised to serve all sentient beings, yet the world is filled with impoverished people who have no one to aid them. Even if one does have many servants, who among them truly qualifies as a Samantabhadra, the 'Bodhisattva of All-encompassing Excellence'? In ancient times great teachers and holy monks appeared in the world and, through the efficacy of their spiritual powers, saved sentient beings from adversity. But the world was still young then and humanity's karmic load was light, so even if those teachers and monks had not employed their spiritual powers it is unlikely that things would have gone seriously wrong. The world is now defiled and corrupt, and humanity's virtue is shallow. Why is it that now, just when these holy figures with their spiritual powers are so urgently needed, they are all in nirvana or deep samādhi and do not appear in the world?"

Many doubts of this kind arose in me. Since they were not directly related to the One Great Matter,[113] however, I put the issue out of my mind and no longer concerned myself with it. However, after a month or two I remembered something.

In earlier times the poet-monk Saigyō[114] had tried to find lodging at the post station Eguchi. When a woman refused him a room at her inn, he composed a short poem: "Hard it would be to renounce the world, but will you begrudge me even just a temporary lodging?" Hearing this, the woman composed a poem in reply: "Knowing that you are someone who has renounced the world, I only thought to keep you from dwelling too much on this 'temporary lodging.'"[115] That which people generally regard as compassion becomes the cause of attachment to the causal world. Hence a lack of compassion and the failure of things to go as one wishes can actually help liberate one from the cycle of samsara.

I also remembered another story. There was once in Kyoto an outstanding scholar of the Chinese classics who, when at home, always sat his little son next to him to study the classic texts. Then, every day before going to work at his government post, the scholar would put the little boy in a crib just large enough for him to sit in, hang the crib from a beam with a rope, and leave the child with a book to read. Afterward, however, the boy's stepmother would feel sorry for him and let down the crib so that the child could play until it was time for the father to return, when she would put the boy back in the crib and hang it once again from the beam. The little boy resented his father's strictness and appreciated the kindness of his stepmother. When the boy grew up, his efforts enabled him to follow his father in the family occupation, and he was appointed secretary at the Grand Council of State. By then his childhood resentment toward his father's strict discipline had changed to gratitude, and he realized that his stepmother's kindness, so appreciated at the time, had actually been a hindrance. In the same way, I realized that I had completely misunderstood the benevolence of the buddhas and bodhisattvas, and I abandoned my mistaken view that in this Latter Age they show no compassion.

The buddhas and bodhisattvas made various vows, but at the heart of them all is the intention to liberate sentient beings from the beginningless delusion of samsara and lead them to the Awakened Shore of the original pure mind. The wishes of ordinary beings, however, all have their roots in the world of birth and death. Would it be truly compassionate of the holy sages to satisfy such desires?

Nevertheless, the buddhas and bodhisattvas do sometimes grant desires of a secular type in accordance with the nature and tastes of sentient beings, so that those beings may be gradually guided toward liberation. But they cannot be expected to fulfill the wishes of those for whom the satisfaction of worldly desire would encourage pride, attachment, and unrepentant self-indulgence. This is the nature of the holy sages' benevolence.

Thus the fact that throughout the ages the prayers of sentient beings have had no apparent effect can be seen as evidence that they *have* had an effect. In the same way, when doctors treat the sick they must sometimes give them bitter-tasting medicine and sometimes burn moxa on their skin. Foolish patients, misunderstanding their doctor's intentions, complain that they sought treatment in order to cure their pain, yet the treatment is making it worse. They suspect their doctor of lacking compassion, but it is not a matter of the doctor lacking compassion—the real problem is the patients' warped outlook.

In the transmission section at the conclusion of sutras,[116] the benevolent deities of the heavens take a vow in which they promise to protect all those who follow the teachings of the sutra, to keep them from misfortune, to provide them with wealth, to guard them from illness, etc. What they mean is that if people who are practicing the Buddhadharma meet with hardships owing to karmic seeds sown in previous lives and are thereby hindered in their practice, then the gods will remove those hardships so that those seekers will not become disheartened. Their vow was not taken for the sake of self-centered people with false views, who do not practice the Buddhadharma and wish to avoid misfortune while they chase after worldly fame and fortune. If you consider this carefully, you will see that it stands to reason that people's prayers throughout the ages have usually gone unanswered.

One day during the Heian period a nun came to worship at Kiyomizu-dera.[117] After bowing to the central image, she asked repeatedly, "Avalokiteśvara of Infinite Compassion, please remove those things I dislike." Someone near her, thinking this an odd request, asked her what she meant.

"Ever since I was a child I've loved loquats," she replied, "but the big pits are such a nuisance. So every year in May when the fruits are ripening I come here to pray that the pits might disappear. So far, however, my prayers haven't been answered."

The pits in loquats annoy everyone, but no one normally thinks of praying to Avalokiteśvara to solve the problem, which is of course what makes this story humorous. Looking around, though, we see many people offering sutras and mantras to the gods and buddhas in order to improve their life circumstances. Such people are not interested in the Supreme Way—they seek only to attain worldly happiness and avoid misfortune. That being so, was it really any sillier for the nun to pray that the loquat pits might disappear?

Suppose you went to the house of a rich man and asked for some little trifle. If that is all you wanted you could just as well have asked someone who wasn't wealthy, though you could of course respond that it makes sense to ask for something trifling since the rich are usually greedy and can't be expected to willingly part with anything of real value. The buddhas and bodhisattvas, however, are vast in their compassion, unlike the wealthy of the world. Prayers that seek no more than finite material happiness displease them; they desire only that people aspire to the Supreme Way. Thus those who go to them with requests for mundane things are even more foolish than those who would call upon a wealthy household and ask for something of no value.

People born in the land of Uttarakuru[118] always have enough food though they never cultivate fields, since the rice they eat grows wild. Though they never weave brocade, they dress in fine attire. They live for a thousand years and never die before their time. Among human kings the highest are the four types of cakravartin: the Iron-Wheel King, the Copper-Wheel King, the Silver-Wheel King, and the Gold-Wheel King.[119] Of these, the Gold-Wheel King possesses the most excellent karmic fruits of any human being; he rules over the four continents and has free use of the seven treasures.[120] His life span is said either to be infinite or to last eighty thousand years.

In the realm of desire[121] there are six heavens. The first and lowest is the Heaven of the Four-Quarter Kings, where the Four Heavenly Kings dwell.[122] In this heaven there is no lack of good fortune. Beings in this heaven live for five hundred years, with each day being the equivalent of fifty years in the human realm. The next level is the Heaven of the Thirty-three Gods,[123] located at the top of Mount Sumeru. The king of this heaven is Śakra,[124] among whose followers are Vaiśravaṇa and the other Heavenly Kings, as well as the sun, the moon, and the constellations. The fruits of Śakra's karma are by no means meager. His life span is one thousand years, with each day being the equivalent of one hundred human years. In the four heavens above the Heaven of the Thirty-three Gods the karmic fruits grow progressively better, with life spans doubling from stage to stage, until in Paranirmita-vaśa-vartin,[125] the sixth and highest heaven, life spans are sixteen thousand years, with each day being the equivalent of sixteen hundred human years.

However, although the beings dwelling in these heavens are deities, they are still born within the realm of desire, so that when their allotted time is nearly over they must all undergo the suffering of the five degenerations.[126]

Above the six heavens of the realm of desire are the realm of form and the realm of formlessness. Together, the realms of desire, form, and formlessness are known as the threefold world. Within the realm of form are the four meditation heavens. The deities in these heavens are perfect in their physical form and emit bright light from their bodies. In the first meditation heaven dwells the god Brahmā, king of the threefold world, who lives for one and a half kalpas. The fourth meditation heaven is not affected by the three calamities that occur during a kalpa of destruction.[127] In one of the subdivisions of the fourth meditation heaven, known as the Vast Fruit Heaven,[128] life spans are five hundred kalpas long.

In the realm of formlessness there are also four heavens, the deities of which are without physical form and therefore have no need for things like food, clothing, or wealth. Life spans are twenty thousand kalpas in the Heaven of Boundless Empty Space (the first of the four heavens) and eighty thousand kalpas in the Heaven of Neither Thought nor No-Thought (the fourth and highest of the formless heavens).[129]

Although such karmic fruits are wonderful indeed, they are all the result of conditioned good causes arising from samādhi in the defiled world. They are thus limited, and the deities will eventually have to be reborn in the evil realms. As the *Lotus Sutra* says, "There is no safety in the three worlds; they are like a burning house."[130] Thus the wise do not seek such rewards.

People born in the evil world of the five impurities,[131] regardless of how good their karmic circumstances may seem, cannot match the people of the northern continent of Uttarakuru, to say nothing of the gods in the heavens. Even the most long-lived of human beings rarely reaches one hundred years of age, yet one hundred years is but a single day in the Heaven of the Thirty-three Gods, and not even an instant compared to the eighty-thousand-kalpa life spans in the Heaven of Neither Thought nor No-Thought. What difference is there, then, between praying to the gods and buddhas for shallow and fleeting benefits and praying, like the nun, for the pits to be removed from loquats? Pathetic indeed it is to ask for insignificant things—even should your requests be granted—if it means living your life in vain and suffering rebirth in the evil realms. If instead you pray to attain the Supreme Way, you will experience, if not true awakening, then a strengthening of your good karmic roots augmented by the salvific spiritual power of the gods and buddhas, so that you will naturally avoid misfortune and pass your years in peace, not only in the present life but in many lives to come.

Although the buddhas have perfect freedom of function in all things, there are three things they cannot do. First, they cannot guide those with whom they have no karmic connection. Second, they cannot teach each and every sentient being. Third, they cannot alter fixed karma.[132] Fixed karma is either positive or negative karmic fruit that is brought about by positive or negative karmic causes from past lives. Even the buddhas and bodhisattvas with all their powers cannot affect it. The appearance of one's face, the degree of one's good fortune, the length of one's life, and the social standing of the family one is born into are all determined by fixed karma. Taoists like Zhuangzi,[133] not knowing that such things are the result of karmic causes, regarded them as part of the spontaneous workings of nature. Buddhism is different, teaching that those who suffer negative karmic results owing to negative karmic causes from the past will, if they understand the principle of causality, enjoy positive karmic results in future lives if they do not produce further negative causes in the present one.

When people give no thought to the fixed karmic circumstances of their present life, they fail to cultivate good causes for the next. Are not such people foolish? They are like the farmer who in the springtime fails to plow, fertilize, and water his paddies and is careless in tending his seedlings. When autumn comes, whatever rice plants he might have will barely yield straw, much less grain. Even if the farmer, disappointed with these results, proceeds to water and fertilize his paddies it will do no good—by then it is foolish to meddle with the crop in the hope that something might come of it. But if the farmer realizes that this year's failure was the result of his careless preparations in the spring and therefore prepares well for the following year's crop, he will certainly avoid the same unfortunate result.

One sutra says that through the power of a buddha and the power of the Dharma even fixed karma can be changed.[134] Although this is not the usual view in Buddhism, if a person forsakes his previous life of attachment and abides in true awareness, practices sincerely, and prays that the karmic circumstances of his life be altered so that he might complete the Way or be of benefit to other beings, then the power of a buddha and the power of the Dharma are able to influence even fixed karma. Hence the sutra's words, "Even fixed karma can be changed." However, if a person prays for long life and prosperity out of attachment to selfish desires, this avaricious mind is out of accord with Buddha-mind and thus the buddhas can neither hear nor respond to the request.[135] Therefore it is said that even the power of a buddha cannot prevail over the power of karma. Great Compassion forms the very essence of the buddhas, and thus they say that they feel compassion for all sentient beings as if those beings were their own beloved children. If the power of a buddha could easily cancel the power of karma, then no one would be allowed to fall into hell or to undergo birth in the defiled world and experience all of its sufferings.

When Śākyamuni was still alive, Prince Virūdhaka of Kośala was mocked by the Śākya clan and thus, following his enthronement, invaded Kapilavastu and slaughtered 99,900,000 Śākyas.[136] Seeing what was happening, the Buddha's disciple Maudgalyāyana[137] said to him, "Since in your great compassion you save all beings regardless of their relation to you, surely you would save even strangers from a tragedy like that which is befalling Kapilavastu. But those who are being slaughtered are all of your own clan. Why then do you not save them?" The Buddha replied, "Their slaughter is the result of karmic seeds sown in previous lives, and thus they cannot be saved."

Maudgalyāyana, though hearing these words directly from the Buddha, was still unconvinced. Using his supernatural powers, he gathered five hundred Śākyas who had not yet been killed and took them to the vicinity of the Heaven of the Four-Quarter Kings, where he hid them under a huge bowl that he conjured up. In this way, he thought, they can escape from Virūdhaka's attack. He then went to the Buddha and told him what he had done.

The Buddha said, "The influence of karma extends everywhere, and cannot be circumvented through supernatural powers. You were very clever, but the five hundred people under the bowl are now all dead." Maudgalyāyana flew to the place where the people were hidden, only to see that the Buddha's words were correct. The sutras relate many such stories, stressing that the workings of karma cannot readily be changed.

DIVINE PROTECTION

7

Question: If the power of a buddha and the power of the Dharma cannot easily change fixed karma, then what is the benefit of the Buddhadharma?

Answer: There are various levels of fixed karma. The shallowest level is the fixed karma whose effects appear in the present life. Next is the fixed karma whose effects appear in the next life. The deepest level is the fixed karma whose effects appear in lifetimes subsequent to the next. Karma that is shallower than fixed karma may manifest at any time, and thus is known as unfixed karma.

Depending upon the gravity of the karma, its effects appear either earlier or later, but karma, once produced, never disappears without giving rise to some type of effect. It cannot be erased except through the power of a buddha or the power of the Dharma, and even such powers are not effective unless one repents sincerely and seeks mercy. Even the great doctor Qipo Bianque[138] could not force cures upon his patients, but if the patients followed his instructions the diseases would soon disappear. It is the same with the buddhas. They cannot forcibly change the karmic circumstances of sentient beings, but, using their perfect knowledge of past, present, and future, they are able to see into the causes of those circumstances. They teach that poverty is the result of stinginess and greed; that short life is the result of killing; that ugliness is the result of impatience; and that humble birth is the result of contempt for others. If, following the buddhas' teachings, one repents of one's past errors and thereafter refrains from creating new karmic causes, there is no reason why the buddhas shouldn't be able to alter even fixed karma. But all day long people harbor wicked thoughts inside and perform evil deeds outside, even as they pray to the gods and the buddhas for happiness and long life. This being the case, how could the gods and buddhas possibly effect any change?

At the Grand Shrine of Ise offerings of *heihaku*[139] are forbidden, as is the reading of sutras and dhāraṇīs. I asked an Ise priest the reason for this several years ago when I was staying near the Outer Shrine during a visit to Ise.[140] He replied that when a person worshipped at the shrine it is necessary to undergo outer and inner purifications. The outer purifications involve eating vegetarian foods, keeping physically clean, and avoiding contact with sources of defilement. The inner purifications involve ridding one's heart of any desire for fame and riches. Since the desire for fame and riches is precisely what motivates virtually all *heihaku* offerings, this nullifies the inner purification. Hence the priests ban *heihaku* offerings, in the same way that a judge's assistant would refuse bribes from plaintiffs filing lawsuits at the court.

When a person lacks both status and wealth, it is because status and wealth led that person to produce evil karma in a previous existence. If people would simply renounce the desire for these things and remain pure of heart, then their allotted share of status and wealth would naturally suffice. Otherwise they can worship at shrines day and night, making offerings of *heihaku* and sacred horses, reciting sutras and dhāraṇīs, flattering the deities with song and dance, and still never get their wishes. Such is the will of the gods, expressed, it is said, in divine revelations.

While conversing with the Ise priest I asked him why Buddhist monks are not allowed in the vicinity of the main shrine buildings.

The priest replied, "One hears much talk about this, but it's all just supposition. Buddhism did not arrive from the continent until the reign of the thirtieth emperor, Emperor Kinmei,[141] so in ancient times, when the Ise divinity was enshrined at its present location, neither Buddhism nor Buddhists were present in Japan.[142] Thus, of course, no prohibition existed on Buddhist clerics worshipping at the shrine. In olden times visits to the imperial palace were never made in priestly robes. However, with the spread of Buddhism and the acceptance of that religion by the emperor, priests of great wisdom and virtue were invited to enter, and ever since that time they have been permitted access to the palace.

"At Ise Shrine we have never altered our ancient customs and traditions. Moreover, since we demand inner purification of worshippers, we were told in a divine oracle not to permit ceremonial performances. As a result, Buddhist priests simply stopped coming. Nevertheless, the Shinto gods are manifestations of the buddhas and bodhisattvas.[143] How then could they possibly disdain a true master of the Dharma? In the past, eminent priests have come here."

Having been told that it was permitted to visit, I went the next morning to the Inner Shrine. Looking around at my surroundings, I was deeply moved by the ancient rocks thickly encrusted with moss and by the giant trees with their huge intertwining branches. I wondered how many springs and autumns they had seen. It was as though I were looking into the distant past. The surrounding scenery was vast in scale, with clear rivers brimming with water and ranges of high mountains in the distance. The view seemed to stretch off to faraway lands not in Japan.

The shrine itself stood in the midst of all this. The ground upon which it was built had not been leveled, but retained the natural slope of the mountain. The roof of the shrine was thatched with reeds, and the rafter beams were straight. The timbers of the torii had no curve. The offerings of rice had been struck only three times with the mallet.[144] The Shinto priests, the shrine maidens, and the ordinary worshippers both highborn and lowborn all maintained silence as they walked in a respectful manner. This was the result of the deities manifesting their simple, unadorned divine presence to all people and dedicating the merit of their inner and outer purity to each and every age. How foolish it is to lose the blessings of this precious divine grace by chasing after fame and taking pride in one's prosperity, thereby turning one's back on the divine presence and forfeiting everything its purity can offer.

Long ago the Great Bodhisattva Hachiman manifested in the form of a Shinto god at Usa in the province of Buzen.[145] When the deity was being moved to Otokoyama in the province of Yamashiro 110 years later,[146] there appeared on the sleeve of the presiding priest Gyōkyō's[147] robe an image of Amitābha Buddha and his two attending bodhisattvas. This robe is presently kept in the so-called "image box" at the Otokoyama Shrine. Hachiman is said to have appeared before Kōbō Daishi[148] dressed in Buddhist robes. At that time Kōbō Daishi drew a picture of the bodhisattva, and the bodhisattva drew Kōbō Daishi's picture; the two images are preserved at the temple Jingo-ji in Takao, near Kyoto. These are all auspicious signs of the Bodhisattva Hachiman's desire to lead sentient beings to take refuge in the Buddhadharma and renounce the world of samsara.

Every year from the first to the fifteenth day of the eighth month the Otokoyama Shrine celebrates the Hōjō-e,[149] in which people go here and there to purchase a million fish to be released in the stream at the foot of the mountain upon which the shrine is located. In honor of this meritorious offering, Otokoyama's *omikoshi* (portable shrine) is carried in the early morning of the fifteenth day to the bottom of the mountain. There the officiants conduct a Buddhist service and musicians play court music. During this time the Shinto priests all wear dignified formal robes. However, when the service is finished the celebrants exchange their stately ceremonial attire for clean white robes. Then, wearing straw sandals and bearing white staffs, they make the return trip up the mountain. The procession resembles that of a funeral, in order to remind people that "in the morning, one is ruddy faced and prospering in the pathways of life; in the evening, one is white bones bleaching in the fields."

Hachiman Bodhisattva has promised to protect the righteous. Righteousness has many levels, however. The most genuinely righteous are those who have forsaken deluded thinking and awakened to the Way of truth. Even those who have not reached this level are truly righteous if they keep in mind the principle of impermanence, do not seek after fame or covet wealth, practice the path of benevolence, and faithfully refuse to take life. Guiding living beings to this path is the true significance of the Hōjō-e ceremony.

There is no one, high or low, lay or ordained, who does not revere Hachiman. However, even Hachiman is unable to fulfill his vow to protect all beings if people—though they be aristocrats or high priests—do not accept the path of righteousness. How much more so, then, for other people? What is true of the Ise and Hachiman gods is true also of all other gods, who, although they may differ in their methods, are the same in their compassionate intentions. How perverse it is to turn one's back all day on the divine will, then resent the gods because one's prayers go unanswered.

PRAYER AS AN UPĀYA[150]

Question: If that is true, should all prayers for worldly fame and gain be forbidden?

Answer: When I say that it's foolish to pray for worldly fame and gain, it is in the same sense that I say it is useless to pray for loquats with no pits. Even if your prayers are answered and you obtain pitless loquats, how many years of life do you have to enjoy them? Praying for fame and gain is no different. Difficult it is to alter fixed karma through prayer, and even if you succeed how long do the results last? You simply increase your worldly attachments and eventually fall into the evil realms. If you must pray for something, I recommend praying to attain the Unsurpassable Way.

However, people foolish enough to pray for something like pitless loquats, even if dissuaded from such requests by arguments such as these, would be unlikely to turn to the gods and buddhas and aspire to enlightenment. Instead they would drift through life, neither fostering devotion nor deepening their connections with the Way. It is preferable, therefore, to encourage such people to go to places like Kiyomizu-dera and pray for such things as pitless loquats; there is no reason to stop them from doing so. This is why esoteric Buddhism employs practices, such as *jōbuku* and *sokusai*,[151] that are associated with the manifest attainments.[152] Thus in the *Mahāvairocana Sutra* it is written that the formless and profound Dharma cannot be understood by the foolish, and so it is expressed in more concrete ways.[153]

SHINGON ESOTERIC RITUALS

9

Question: Some Shingon priests claim that the manifest attainments—the attainments with form—express the true spirit of esoteric Buddhism and that veneration of the formless is the standpoint of the exoteric traditions. What do you think of this?

Answer: From the standpoint of the true Buddhadharma, there can be no distinction between "with form" and "without form." But because the human mind functions in deluded as well as enlightened ways, "form" is distinguished from "no-form." The teachings of non-Buddhist traditions also discuss form and no-form, as do the Hinayana teachings, the expedient Mahayana teachings, and the true Mahayana teachings.[154] However, although all these traditions speak of "form" and "no-form," they differ in what they intend by these terms. The Profound and Formless Dharma spoken of in the esoteric *Mahāvairocana Sutra* is not the formless Dharma spoken of in exoteric Buddhism; much less does it correspond to non-Buddhist understandings.

A commentary on the *Mahāvairocana Sutra* says that both emptiness and nonemptiness are, ultimately, formless, and that that in which all form is immanent is the Samādhi of Great Emptiness.[155] "Emptiness" is that without form, while "nonemptiness" is that with form. In what sense, then, can one say that both form and no-form are formless? That which is beyond formlessness and which moreover contains all form is not what ordinary people conceive of as form. Therefore formlessness as taught in the esoteric tradition is said to be "the Dharma gate most subtle and profound."[156] It cannot be comprehended by the ordinary deluded mind and is thus beyond the reach of ordinary wisdom. Can it not be argued, however, that placing such emphasis on the formless is out of keeping with the true spirit of Shingon? This is so only if one interprets the formless of which we are speaking as corresponding to formlessness as understood in the exoteric traditions. Then one would have reason to reject it.

If a person who has reached formless attainment[157] performs *jōbuku* rituals in order to help guide deluded beings, he should not be criticized for using powers with form. His actions may have form, but the mind that inspires them is formless. On the other hand, if a person attached to worldly things and motivated by selfish desires for fame and wealth performs *kaji* rituals and esoteric ceremonies, whether for himself or for someone else, he will realize no benefits with form, much less ones without form. It is like a small child trying to use a sharp sword. He can easily injure or kill himself, and even if he escapes physical harm he might ruin the blade and render the sword useless by hacking at stones or dirt.

The ancient masters explained the principles of esotericism in a similar fashion. For example, the power of the *jōbuku* ritual could be used to subdue the wicked impulses and false views of unenlightened beings and guide them to the truth of the Buddhadharma. Similarly, evil people who obstructed the Buddhadharma and showed no inclination to change their erroneous ways could be ritually deprived of life so that, after the firm establishment of the true Dharma, they could be introduced to the Buddhadharma through the use of various expedients. Or a person who persecuted others and made it impossible for them to accept the Buddhist teachings could be subdued, so that those who wished to accept the Buddhadharma would be free to do so. In each of these cases bodhisattvas used such "negative upāya" only in order to advance the Dharma and benefit living beings, and never for the sake of secular fame and profit.

The *Nirvana Sutra* tells of how the Buddha, in an earlier rebirth as a king, noticed that a group of evil monks in his country were persecuting another monk whom they resented for his conscientious practice of the Dharma. The king subjugated the evil monks, thus helping the virtuous monk. Since the king acted solely for the sake of promoting the Buddhadharma, he incurred not even the slightest retribution.[158] It was the same in Japan when Prince Shōtoku prayed for the defeat of the Mononobe clan, led by Mononobe-no-Moriya.[159] If the prince had done so not for the sake of the Dharma but only in order to destroy an enemy and advance his own chances for worldly success, he would have suffered karmic retribution both in the present life (preventing him from making his contributions to the country's development) and in future lives (causing him rebirths in unfortunate circumstances). As the *Nirvana Sutra* says, to repay malice with malice is like attempting to extinguish fire with oil.[160]

The buddhas and bodhisattvas show the same concern toward each and every sentient being as they would toward their only child. Nor is any partiality seen in the compassion of the Japanese gods, being as they are buddhas and bodhisattvas who have taken on the form of deities in order to further their work of salvation. Thus if someone, for selfish reasons unrelated to the Dharma, were to ask the buddhas and deities to destroy his enemies and assist his allies, do you think they would do as he requested?

Those with true faith in the Buddhadharma do not consider themselves fortunate even if heaven rewards them with a long and peaceful life, because often it is precisely such minor good fortune that lulls people into complacency and weakens their motivation to follow the Way, causing them in the end to fall into the evil realms. Nor do Buddhists wish to live in an age with no Buddhadharma, though it be in a land as wisely governed as China during the reigns of the Three Sovereigns and Five Emperors.[161] Even if one lives in troubled times, there is no cause to lament as long as the Buddhadharma flourishes. Thus disciples of the Buddha, whether they follow the path of meditation, doctrine, or the vinaya, should pray for the vigor of the Dharma as they do for world peace, since their prayers are certain to be heeded by all beings who in former lives have deepened the vow and acquired the spiritual power necessary to advance in the Way.

There are some who say that killing with arrows, swords, or other weapons creates sinful karma, while killing with spells or rituals results in merit. This is a terrible misunderstanding. Using weapons to kill may be meritorious if one's intentions are like Śākyamuni's when in a previous life as a king he destroyed evil monks for the sake of the Dharma, or like Prince Shōtoku's when he prayed for the defeat of Mononobe-no-Moriya. But esoteric ceremonies and rituals performed for the sake of worldly fame and gain bring nothing but evil karma. This is why the *Brahmā Net Sutra*, as part of its injunction against the taking of life, forbids killing through the use of incantation or deviant mantras.[162]

Then there are those who say that no evil karma results from *jōbuku* that kill one's enemies with the aim of leading them to Buddhahood in their next rebirth. If such rituals were truly able to bring someone to Buddhahood in this way, then that would be wonderful indeed. But wouldn't this lead to the rash conclusion that such rituals are best directed not toward hated enemies but rather toward loved ones, so that they might become buddhas as quickly as possible?

PRAYING FOR INFLUENTIAL SUPPORTERS 10

Question: The Buddha said that the Dharma should be transmitted to monarchs, officials, and powerful patrons, both for the well-being of the supporters and the prosperity of Buddhism. Would it not stand to reason, then, that monks should pray for these supporters?

Answer: In teaching the Dharma to people like monarchs and officials, the Buddha did not intend that they use it to seek worldly fame and riches. His aim was that they might protect Buddhism, spread its teachings, and eventually leave the world of illusion. He taught them to pray for a peaceful world, for the safety of Buddhism's supporters, for the dissemination of the teachings, and for the well-being of all living creatures. If monks, too, pray in this spirit, then they do not contravene the Buddha's aim. Although we are now in the Latter Age of the Dharma, the situation of Buddhism remains fortunate, with monks, whether of the meditative, doctrinal, or vinaya traditions, free from obligations to serve in the military or in government office. Monks are occasionally asked to officiate at public prayer rituals, but there is no need to refuse such requests when the prayers are offered for worthy goals.

However, owing to the social disturbances of recent years, much of what goes on during prayer rituals in both the Kantō and Kyoto regions is quite strange and leaves one wondering how exactly it constitutes prayer. One of the fundamental principles of the Buddha's teaching is that everything is brought to completion through the harmony of causes and conditions and the dynamic of the Buddha's power and human receptivity.[163] The great teachers and prelates of ancient times used prayers for the nation and invocations against misfortune as upāya to guide beings to a deeper knowledge of the Way. Never did they perform such rituals for their own personal fame and gain. Because they themselves were embodiments of Great Compassion, they were venerated by everyone, from monarchs and court officials to the lowest classes. These forces—the faith of the populace, the virtue of the priests themselves, the power of the Buddha, and the power of the Dharma—all worked harmoniously together to bring about the causes and conditions that rendered the ceremonies effective.

Nowadays, however, the inner virtue of the priests cannot compare with that of the prelates of old. The faith of the believers, too, is weak. For example, believers ask priests to lead Buddhist prayer rituals as a type of public service, thus turning the priests into little more than government functionaries. Offerings for important ceremonies and esoteric rituals do not accord with established custom. When special prayer rituals are held the believers occasionally pledge to distribute the donations, but rarely is this done. This is true not only of prayer rituals but also of all Buddhist services. The reason that such things occur is that faith in the Buddhadharma is shallow. How then can one expect prayers to be answered and the roots of goodness to grow?

In Kamakura recently a Chinese doctor named Zhiguang has made a name for himself in the practice of medicine. Once when he was compounding a prescription known as *sokōen*[164] there was a man nearby who, desiring to try the medicine, pinched a bit between his fingers and tasted it. Noticing this, Zhiguang told him to take some more. Puzzled, the man asked why. "Each medicine has a proper dosage," replied Zhiguang. "If you take less, the medicine has no effect. If you're going to take it at all, you should take enough for it to fulfill its function." The point Zhiguang was making applies to prayer rituals and other Buddhist services as well. If one is going to hold such sacred events at all, one should approach them in a way that will make them effective. The success of a prayer ritual and the degree of resulting merit are determined solely by the depth of one's faith—they have nothing to do with the amount of the offering. Services and prayer rituals are well conducted if performed in such a way that everyone is inspired and the Three Treasures are moved.

The Buddha taught that rulers and influential people should be instructed in the Dharma because the poorer classes, although they may attain liberation through faith in whatever tradition their spiritual efforts in former lives have led them to, lack the capacity to protect and support the Dharma and spread the Buddhist teachings. Because of their duty to support the Dharma, those of the ruling classes who receive it should not limit themselves to faith in a single school and reject all others. Nor, if their faith does extend to all traditions, should they utilize those traditions to offer prayers directed toward secular goals. In this degenerate age, is it not a privilege to receive the teaching of the Tathāgata? Vowing deeply never to betray this trust, support Buddhism externally by building temples large and small and support it internally by fostering the true spirit of the Way, supporting all schools and forming whatever connections might help in guiding all living beings to the realization of enlightenment. This is the truest of prayer rituals and the most boundless of meritorious acts. Monarchs, high officials, and powerful patrons may have attained their positions as a karmic reward for their practice of the five precepts[165] and the ten good actions[166] in former lives, yet it is thanks to the providence of the Three Treasures that they were able to do so. If they now turn their backs on the teaching of the Dharma they are no different from those of low birth who do not receive the Buddha's teaching.

PRAYING FOR GOOD FORTUNE IN FUTURE LIVES

Question: Although it is foolish to pray for fame and fortune in the present life, would you agree that it is prudent to pray for good fortune in future lives?

Answer: That which we regard as our present life is, of course, the life that in our previous existence we regarded as our future life. Similarly, what in the present life we regard as our future life is simply our present life in the next existence. This being the case, prayers offered in one's past life for the sake of benefits in one's next life manifest as fame and wealth in the present life, and prayers offered in the present life for the sake of benefits in the next life will also manifest in that life as fame and wealth. The reason that such prayers are proscribed in the present life is in order to discourage interest in the dreamlike gains of the world and to encourage aspiration for the future attainment of the Supreme Way.

A person who renounces fame and wealth in his present existence and prays to obtain them in the next may appear to be more sensible than someone who prays in the hope of altering fixed karma, but he is equally foolish in his attachment to the phantom-like body and to future rewards. And even if a person prays to attain the Supreme Way, if that attainment is for himself alone then he, too, is foolish. The

Treatise on the Great Perfection of Wisdom states that it is not just for himself or herself or for a single sentient being that the bodhisattva cultivates the roots of goodness.[167] A bodhisattva is one who seeks the Supreme Way and cultivates myriad roots of goodness for the sake of all sentient beings.

Samantabhadra Bodhisattva made ten great vows. In the first of these vows, the vow to worship and respect all buddhas, he asked that "his body may divide infinitely and appear before the innumerable tathāgatas and venerate every one of them, and continue to do so from one instant to the next without tiring until the end of the universe." In his vow to make abundant offerings to all the buddhas he stated, "May I produce an infinite amount of wonderful offerings, appear before the innumerable buddhas, and donate those offerings to them, and continue to do so forever without tiring." The other vows are similar to these. In his ninth vow Samantabhadra took it upon himself to look after sentient beings, asking that his body might become infinitely divisible so that he might serve all sentient beings in accordance with their needs and with the same reverence that he would show a buddha, and that he might continue to do so forever without tiring. In the tenth vow, the vow to transfer all of his merit[168] to others, he asks that all of the merit he acquires through his vows to worship and respect the buddhas, to make abundant offerings to the buddhas, and so forth, be transferred to sentient beings everywhere so that they might realize enlightenment. A person with such an aspiration as this is one who truly prays for the Supreme Way.

Foolish people, even when they worship a buddha, direct their devotion only to the particular buddha in whom they believe. When they make an offering, they do so in the same spirit. Whether they hold memorial services for their deceased parents or perform prayer rituals for their benefactors, their intentions are selfishly directed solely toward those to whom they are personally obliged, never toward the entire universe and all its sentient beings. As a result the merit produced is never great. However, depending upon the time and circumstances, if the spirit behind the merit-transfer is generous then the resulting merit, too, is great, even if only a single buddha is venerated and only a single person is the object of the ritual.

Non-Buddhist teachings are concerned only with the present life and not with past and future existences, and thus speak only of fulfilling one's obligations toward one's parents and benefactors in this world. The Buddhist sutras, however, teach us that in our endless wanderings through the cycle of life and death all beings have been at one time or another related to one another as fathers and mothers, sons and daughters.[169] Thus one who has the bodhisattva mind does not limit his concern even to his ancestors of seven generations, much less to his two parents in the present life.

ADVANCED IN WISDOM, ADVANCED IN COMPASSION

Question: Unless one has liberated oneself, one cannot liberate others. What sense does it make, then, to defer one's own liberation and first cultivate virtue for the sake of other beings?

Answer: Sentient beings are lost in the round of samsara because their attachment to self causes them to seek fame and profit, creating various types of bad karma. However, if you forget yourself and arouse the desire to benefit all beings, then Great Compassion stirs within you and silently unites with Buddha-mind. Then even if you do not cultivate the virtues for your own sake, perfect virtue naturally accrues to you, and even if you do not seek the Buddha Way for your own sake, the Buddha Way is quickly realized.

Those who seek liberation for themselves only are Hinayana in spirit; even if they cultivate infinite virtues they are unable to realize Buddhahood even for themselves, much less lead others to liberation.

Among those beings who arouse the bodhisattva mind, there is a difference between bodhisattvas advanced in compassion and bodhisattvas advanced in wisdom. Bodhisattvas advanced in compassion are those who vow to liberate all sentient beings before themselves attaining the Buddha Way. Bodhisattvas advanced in wisdom are those who seek to attain the Buddha Way themselves before liberating all sentient beings. Although bodhisattvas of the latter type resemble the followers of the Two Vehicles[170] in that they seek their own liberation, they do so for the purpose of saving all other sentient beings and thus they possess the bodhisattva mind.

Although we distinguish between bodhisattvas advanced in compassion and bodhisattvas advanced in wisdom, there is no difference between the two in their aspiration to liberate all sentient beings. They are the same in that every merit they cultivate and every practice they engage in is directed toward this goal.

THE THREE TYPES OF COMPASSION

Question: The writings of the Zen masters recommend that we first seek to awaken our own minds and then, after having dealt with remaining relations and habits,[171] that we extend our concern to others. If this is so, would it not contradict the teaching that the bodhisattvas' vow is to liberate others before attaining liberation for themselves?

Answer: There are three types of compassion. The first is compassion directed toward sentient beings; the second is compassion based on the Dharma; and the third is compassion without an object.

Compassion directed toward sentient beings is the type of compassion that regards sentient beings suffering in the cycle of birth and death as actually existing and that strives to liberate these beings from the world of delusion. This is the compassion of the Hinayana bodhisattva. Although it is superior to the aspirations of the śrāvaka and pratyekabuddha, who are concerned only with liberation for themselves, it is nevertheless a substantialist view that adheres to the concept of benefit, and thus it is not true compassion. It is what the *Vimalakīrti Sutra* criticizes as "sentimental compassion"— compassion marked by affection and false views.[172]

Dharma-based compassion, which clearly perceives the illusory nature of all sentient and nonsentient existence that arises through dependent origination, is an illusory compassion that teaches illusory Dharma gates to liberate illusory sentient beings. This is the compassion of the Mahayana bodhisattva. Although it no longer entertains substantialist views and is therefore unlike sentimental compassion, this type of compassion is still not true compassion since it adheres to the concept of nonsubstantiality.

Objectless compassion occurs when, following the realization of enlightenment, the compassion that is an inherent virtue of Buddha-nature manifests itself and functions naturally to liberate all sentient beings, even when there is no conscious striving to do so. It is like the moon, which equally casts its reflection on water everywhere. Thus in spreading the Dharma there is no distinction between "teaching" and "not teaching," and in liberating people there are no notions of "benefit" and "no benefit."

This is true compassion. Those who practice compassion directed toward sentient beings or compassion based on the Dharma are obstructed by such compassion and cannot realize objectless compassion. This is what is meant by the maxim "Minor compassion hinders great compassion."[173] The Chinese Zen master Baizhang Huaihai had the same thing in mind when he warned, "Do not be greedy for petty gains and merits."[174] This is what the Zen masters mean in their teachings on compassion.

MAHAYANA COMPASSION

Question: Why do you disparage "sentimental compassion," when it is by recognizing the actual suffering of beings in the cycle of birth and death that the spirit of compassion arises? If one regards all sentient beings as illusory, how can one feel compassion?

Answer: There are different kinds of beggar in the world. Some beggars are born into outcaste households and are low in status from the start. Others are born into aristocratic households but fall into poverty owing to unexpected circumstances. Of these two types of beggar, aristocrats who fall into poverty usually arouse deeper feelings of sympathy than those who are poor from the start.

The compassion of the bodhisattva is similar to this. Sentient beings are originally one with the buddhas, with no characteristics of birth and death. But should a single deluded thought arise, then out of that no-birth-and-no-death appears—like a dream or a phantom—the form of birth-and-death. Mahayana bodhisattvas view all sentient beings as one would aristocrats who have unexpectedly fallen into poverty. In this they differ from Hinayana bodhisattvas, who believe there to be actual sentient beings sinking in the sea of samsara and who thus give rise to compassion marked by sentimental affection and false views.

The True Meaning of Kaji
and Kitō Rituals[175]

Question: The Shingon school practices *kaji* rituals to relieve the sufferings and misfortunes of sentient beings. Some people criticize the Zen school because it lacks such rituals. Is there any reason for this?

Answer: The esoteric schools teach that all of the ten realms of the sacred and mundane[176] are, without any change in their mode of being, manifestations of Mahāvairocana Buddha.[177] Thus there is no difference between the wise and the foolish and between aristocrats and commoners, nor is there any distinction between blessings and misfortune or between ease and suffering. What then is there to pray for; what then is there to seek? However, in order to guide those who have not yet realized this profound truth, the Shingon school utilizes the manifest attainments.[178]

Zen leaves such expedients to the doctrinal schools and points directly to Original Nature. If one realizes Original Nature, one knows that fundamentally birth and death are without form; this is true longevity. One sees nothing to call "misfortune"; this is true security. One leaves behind the notions of "poverty" and "wealth"; this is true gain. One sees that there is no one to despise as an enemy; this is true conquest. One understands that there is no disparity between "love" and "hate"; this is true love and respect. Once one realizes these principles, one sees that there is no reason to criticize Zen as ineffective when it comes to alleviating suffering and misfortune.

The *kaji* ceremony in Shingon—that is, the usual type of *kaji* ceremony performed for such purposes as removing misfortune and increasing wealth—is simply an expedient means for guiding ordinary people. Every living being consists of the six great elements[179] and the four universal mandalas,[180] and is one with and no different from Mahāvairocana Buddha. Ordinary beings, however, are not aware of this, so the Tathāgata taught the *kaji* of the three mysteries[181] as expedients. These are the genuine *kaji*.

There are any number of people nowadays who follow the esoteric practices but few indeed who seek to master the deepest secret teachings, advance to the practice of the true *kaji*, and experience the attainment of Buddhahood in this very body. Instead they concern themselves solely with worldly prayers, so that even those eminent prelates who strive to uphold the genuine esoteric teachings end up obliged to perform *kaji* rituals and secret practices, despite seeing this as contrary to the true spirit of their tradition.

Then there are Shingon priests who specialize in ritual and know nothing of the inner meaning of their tradition. Such priests, believing ritual practice to be the essence of esotericism, enhance their own fame and wealth by reciting prayers for their donors, with the idea that they're being of service. This is why the esoteric school has gradually declined to the point where it is now akin to yin-yang divination—a situation that conscientious Shingon priests deplore. Nevertheless, because of the expedient practices it has developed, there is some merit to Shingon even in its present condition.

When those who believe in the Zen school ask Zen temples to offer prayers for matters of no grave concern, they are sowing seeds for the destruction of the Zen teachings. Thus their prayers come to nothing, and any karma they create for themselves is negative. However, if people encourage Zen monks to devote themselves to *zazen* and promote the principles of their school, and if they ask the monks for instruction in the correct practice of the Way and strive to realize the teachings of the school's founders, then the Three Treasures and the deities will surely show compassion and aid them in their efforts. Even if they do not succeed in awakening to the Way and realizing the Dharma, they will certainly receive benefits equal to those of any worldly prayer.

The Kamakura regent Saimyōji,[182] a lay practicer who held the Zen teachings in high regard, established the great Zen monastery Kenchō-ji and installed as founding priest the Chinese Zen master Lanxi Daolong.[183] Lanxi censured as "monks without the spirit of the Way" those in his assembly who, even while striving seriously in their Zen meditation practice, devoted time to studying the sutras, commentaries, and Zen records. Far more blameworthy, then, are those who pursue worldly fame and profit! This is true not only of monks—everyone who believes in Zen, including supporters and their families, must do their utmost to awaken to their Original Nature.

Following Lanxi other great Zen masters came to Japan from Song-dynasty China, including Wuan Puning,[184] Daxiu Zhengnian,[185] and Wuxue Zuyuan.[186] All of them admonished monks and laypeople alike that nothing is more important than realizing Original Nature. The faith of the people was as deep as that of the monks. During the Kōan era,[187] when Japan was in utter confusion owing to the Mongol invasions, the regent Hōjō Tokimune,[188] a lay Zen practicer, remained calm and collected. Every day he invited Wuxue, who was then abbot of Kenchō-ji, and other prelates to discuss the Dharma. His attitude was so impressive that Wuxue made mention of it in his sermons. Later Tokimune established Engaku-ji to promote the welfare of the patriarchal school. This may have been why the Mongols failed to conquer Japan. Tokiyori and his son Tokimune were able to keep Japan safe for two generations, and both men are said to have died in a very inspiring manner.

Although Buddhism was venerated in this way during the lives of Tokiyori and Tokimune, the unfortunate fact is that "love of the world is heavy, faith in the Dharma is light." Thus even Zen temples came to be inundated with ceaseless requests for prayers on trifling matters, so that everywhere now the displaying of prayer tablets, the chanting of sutras, and the reciting of dhāraṇīs take precedence over the practice of Zen meditation. Moreover, the temples have numerous minor supporters, each of whom requests prayers. Monks concerned with fame and money treat these as great matters, thus forgetting the One Great Matter of enlightenment. How can this not but lead to the destruction of the Zen Dharma?

In the Zen monasteries of China, where the practice of Zen meditation is still given the highest priority, the only chanting done after the morning gruel meal is that of a single *Dhāraṇī of Great Compassion*.[189] The recitation of the *Śūraṅgama Dhāraṇī*[190] is something that started only recently, and even this practice is restricted to the summer training period. The custom of chanting the *Śūraṅgama Dhāraṇī* in the evenings began in Japan, where it is known as *hōsan*, a term that in China refers to a different ritual.[191] In the early years at Kenchō-ji no sutra chanting was performed during the day. However, at the time of the Mongol invasions they started reciting the *Avalokiteśvara Sutra*[192] as an incantation to protect the nation. This became a custom, and now sutras are chanted three times a day—before dawn, prior to noon, and in the evening. Although such services are not in the original spirit of Zen, now that they have become established practice no senior monks are willing to end them.

Moreover, this being the Latter Age of the Dharma, there are many monks who, despite belonging to the Zen school, find sutra recitation less burdensome than Zen meditation. For such monks it is unlikely that eliminating the extra chanting would be of any benefit. In addition, so doing would no doubt contravene the wishes of those temple benefactors who value worldly things. Therefore Zen temples everywhere conscientiously perform the thrice-daily sutra rituals, directing the merit thus gained toward the happiness of their believers and peace throughout the world. On the mornings of the first and fifteenth days of each month the monks assemble at the Dharma Hall to perform the *shukushin* ritual[193] not only for the emperor but also for peace in the world and harmony among all people.

Thus one shouldn't accuse Zen monks of not offering prayers. Recitation of the *Dhāraṇī of Great Compassion* and the *Śūraṅgama Dhāraṇī* brings benefits, described in the sutras, that are in no way inferior to those of the esoteric rituals. Nor should one underestimate the benefits of reciting the *Diamond Sutra* and the *Avalokiteśvara Sutra*. Nevertheless, if there is anything that the thrice-daily recitation of these sutras and dhāraṇīs is unable to accomplish, then simply reciting even more sutras and dhāraṇīs will be of no use and will only detract from the practice of meditation.

Offerings to Worldly Monks 16

Question: In this Latter Age of the Dharma all monks, whether of the meditation, doctrinal, or precept traditions, chase after fame and profit and neglect their practice. Some people say there is no reason to make offerings to such monks and that it is useless to sacrifice oneself donating land to the Sangha or constructing and maintaining temple buildings. What is your opinion?

Answer: Because only those with meager stores of good karma are born into the Latter Age of the Dharma, even people with all of the advantages, abilities, and education befitting their social station are rarely the equals of their predecessors. If everyone inferior to his or her predecessors was disqualified from succeeding to their predecessors' positions, the ranks of the courtiers and warriors would soon be much depleted. Yet, although they may not match their illustrious ancestors, today's courtiers and warriors do their best to maintain the family traditions, and for that reason the secular government still functions and the military retains its strength. It is the same with the Sangha. Although today's priests may not equal the great teachers and prelates of old, they continue the latter's practices and thus the meditative and doctrinal traditions continue to this day.

When Śākyamuni Buddha still walked the earth the Three

Treasures were different from what they are today. The Buddha Treasure was the flesh-and-blood Tathāgata himself; the Dharma Treasure was his living teaching; and the Sangha Treasure was the community of disciples who aided the Tathāgata in his work. Now, however, in this degenerate age long after the Buddha's passing, wooden images, paintings, and the like are worshipped as the Buddha Treasure; sutras, treatises, and other written texts serve as the Dharma Treasure; and shaven-headed individuals wearing robes are honored as the Sangha Treasure.

According to the sacred teachings, however, these are the very Three Treasures we are supposed to hold and maintain during the Latter Age of the Dharma. Although the genuine Three Treasures permeate our universe, they are not perceivable to us in the Latter Age with our poor karmic roots, and thus we cannot venerate the true Buddha and Sangha and hear the true Dharma. Nevertheless, does it not foster good karmic relations to honor even a buddha image painted on paper or carved from wood, to receive even the teachings expressed in written words, and to make offerings even to shaven-headed individuals attired in robes?

Beings born in the period between the extinction of Śākyamuni's Dharma and the coming of Maitreya, the future buddha, will be unable even to *hear* of the Three Treasures, much less cultivate the type of good karmic relations just described. If people make offerings to the Three Treasures of the Latter Age with the same degree of faith that people made offerings to the Three Treasures while the Buddha was alive, the merit they receive is just as great. Thus, instead of condemning the decadence of the Sangha one should lament the fact that one's faith does not equal that of the ancients, causing one to neglect the Buddha and Dharma and demean the Sangha, thereby inviting evil karma and generating no merit.

If one despises today's monks, saying that they are not like arhats or bodhisattvas or the great teachers and prelates of old, why would one stop with just the Sangha? The most finely carved or painted buddha image cannot compare even in the smallest degree with a living tathāgata, and the writings of the sutra scrolls cannot convey the ineffable Dharma that lies beyond all words and explanations. Yet we continue to venerate buddha images and sutra scrolls, even knowing that they do not represent the true Buddha and Dharma. Is it reasonable to do so and then scorn the members of the Sangha because they are not true monks? Would this not mean that the Three Treasures of the Latter Age are in fact just Two Treasures, with the Sangha Treasure missing? If one then says that all of the Three Treasures of the Latter Age are no more than idle talk, then these are the words of Māra and the heretics and do not even merit discussion. In the "Moon Store" section of the *Great Collection Sutra* the Buddha says:

> In the Latter Age to come, there will be in my Dharma those who, although they shave their heads and wear the robe, will break the precepts and live in a dissolute fashion. Even monks such as these, however, are the children of the Buddha. To slander them is to slander the Buddha; to injure them is to injure the Buddha. Anyone who supports and protects them will receive unlimited merit. It is similar to the way in which people in the world view gold as the most priceless of treasures, but, when gold is not available, regard silver as priceless. If silver is not available then copper is their treasure. If copper is not available then iron becomes precious. If iron is not available then pewter is coveted. In Buddhism, buddhas are the greatest of treasures. When there are no buddhas, bodhisattvas are the highest treasure. When there are no bodhisattvas, arhats are the highest treasure. When there are no arhats, ordinary beings who have attained samādhi are the highest treasure. When there is no one who has attained samādhi, those who perfectly maintain the precepts are the highest treasure. When there is no one who perfectly maintains the precepts, those who maintain them imperfectly are the highest treasure. When there is no one who maintains

them even imperfectly, then those who shave their heads and wear robes are the highest treasure. In comparison with those who are not of the Buddhadharma, they are most venerable. You devas, dragons, and yakṣa, protect my disciples and do not let the buddha-seeds perish.[194]

Such is the compassion of the Buddha. Do not disregard the request of the Buddha because of the disreputable behavior of the monks.

A man who drinks saké ends up with bleary eyes, a tottering walk, slurred speech, and a confused mind. Yet, foreseeable though these unbecoming effects are, they don't particularly bother those who enjoy drinking. Those who detest saké because of its befuddling effects are usually teetotalers who have no taste for alcohol anyway. Similarly, those who reject the Buddhadharma because of the failings of the monks are those who never had much use for Buddhism from the start.

Something that generates merit for sentient beings is known as a "field of merit,"[195] of which there are two types: fields of reverence and fields of compassion. Fields of reverence result when one venerates and makes offerings to a wise and holy person; fields of compassion result when one feels compassion for and makes offerings to animals or to people in humble circumstances. If one makes offerings to a selfish and ignorant monk, one will receive at least the field-of-compassion merit.

A piece of wood left as it is will act for neither good nor evil. But one can carve this piece of wood into the image of a buddha and venerate it in the same spirit that one would a true buddha, in which case the accruing merit would be the same as if it really were a buddha. Treat it with contempt, however, and evil karma is certain to result. If this is true even of a lifeless piece of wood, how much more so is it true of human beings, all of whom possess Buddha-nature? Even an ignorant, shameless monk becomes a field of merit if one regards him with faith and respect. If one slanders him, however, evil karma will follow without fail. In the *Brahmā Net Sutra* it is written, "To offer a discriminatory special invitation to [such a worthy group as] five hundred arhats or bodhisattva-monks will not generate as much merit as inviting one ordinary monk, if it is his turn."[196] However, it is also said that if one wishes to hear about the path to liberation from a "good friend,"[197] then it is permissible to offer a special invitation to someone of virtue.

People often criticize shameless, precept-breaking monks, yet feel free to engage in similar behavior themselves because they are laypeople. This way of thinking is mistaken. When their allotted days are finished and they face King Enma,[198] do they think the fact that they were laypeople will win them forgiveness for the daily evils they committed and free them from punishment in hell?

The fact that the sacred texts forbid criticism of the Sangha's failings does not, however, imply a type of favoritism toward the ordained. It is intended solely to help the laity avoid the serious transgression of harming the Buddhadharma, not to suggest that it is permissible for the Sangha to break the precepts and act in a shameless manner.

Although laypeople tend to forget the evil karma that accrues when they criticize the monks' improper behavior, the monks, for their part, do not reflect sufficiently upon the fact that the laypeople's criticism is the result of the monks' own inappropriate conduct. Instead, they insist on admonishing the laity not to censure the Sangha and demean the Buddhadharma. Would that I could turn things around so that the laity would know the clergy's point of view and the clergy would know the laity's point of view. Then this corrupt world would instantly become the realm of the True Law.

BUDDHISM AND GOVERNMENT

Question: There have been leaders who became so involved in culti-vating the roots of goodness that it hindered them in government and impeded their ability to rule. Why was this?

Answer: In a sacred text it is written, "Good fortune without wisdom is the enemy of three lifetimes."[199] Owing to good fortune, one ends up spending one's life performing only secular good and thus misses the opportunity to illuminate the mind-ground. This is good fortune without wisdom as the enemy of a single lifetime. Because of the secu-lar good one has performed, one achieves a fortunate rebirth in the human or heavenly realms. One's attachments to the world thereby deepen and one's evil habits increase. Even if one avoids creating much evil karma, one's mind is distracted by political affairs and one's free time is occupied with entertainments, preventing practice of the true Dharma. This is good fortune without wisdom as the enemy of two lifetimes. By the next rebirth the roots of one's worldly good-ness, generated during one's earlier life, are exhausted, and there is an increase in the influence of the fundamental ignorance rooted in the beginningless past. As a result one falls into the evil realms. This is good fortune without wisdom as the enemy of three lifetimes.

In texts like the *Sutra on Trapuśa and Bhallika*[200] the Buddha does indeed expound that one should practice conditioned virtues such as the five precepts and the ten good actions. This is known as the human and deva teaching.

The Buddha, when guiding those whose poor karmic habits from previous lives make them unable to practice the true Dharma, would utilize their desire for rebirth in the human and celestial realms by advising them to practice the secular virtues, and in this way would gradually lead them toward the highest teachings.

Thus, in view of the fact that we live in the Latter Age of the Dharma, it is fine to practice good works in the belief that devotion in the present life will bring good fortune in the next, and there is no need to discourage this. Nevertheless, it is the true intention of the Buddha that such practice be done in such a way that it does not become "the enemy of three lifetimes."

Whatever good acts one may do, if one has not yet awakened to the mind-ground, those acts never go beyond the level of secular virtue. This is why the masters of the contemplative and doctrinal schools recommend that one first illuminate the mind-ground before engaging in good works. Tiantai Zhiyi,[201] for example, in his system of six stages of practice[202] that clarifies the process of awakening, forbids those at the second stage[203] from preaching the Dharma for the benefit of others and from chanting sutras and dhāraṇīs for their own benefit, on the grounds that at this stage such activities constitute a hindrance to the Way. Only at the third stage of practice is sutra and dhāraṇī chanting permitted; at the fourth stage some preaching of the Dharma is allowed; at the fifth stage one practices the six pāramitās[204] along with the Tendai meditations; and at the sixth stage one is able to correctly practice the six pāramitās and benefit others.

In the *Essential Teachings of Meditation Master Foguo Yuanwu Zhenjue* there is an essay entitled "Awakening Nature and Encouraging Good,"[205] in which it is stated that one should first awaken to one's true nature and only after that cultivate the roots of goodness. Virtuous deeds performed by one who has not realized the mind-ground give rise only to conditioned results and thus cannot lead to freedom from illusion. One may preach the Dharma and guide people, but since this is based on sentimental compassion it is not truly transformative guidance. This is why secular virtue is discouraged and practice of the true Dharma encouraged.

If those who warn against overinvolvement in the cultivation of good roots are doing so for the sort of reasons mentioned above, then this is commendable advice. However, if their true purpose is only to stress worldly affairs and demean the Buddhadharma, then their intention is demonic indeed. Those who receive birth in the human realm, whether their station in life is high or low, all do so because of their practice of the five precepts and the ten good actions in former lives. People of exceptional good fortune who show unusual vitality and strength of character are those who were especially dedicated to these practices, and who also performed numerous additional meritorious acts.

The fact that you are respected throughout the land as a military leader is solely because of your stores of good karma from former lives.[206] Nevertheless, there are in the world those who oppose you, and even among those who serve you as retainers there are few who are truly selfless in following your commands. In view of this, I would suggest that your performance of meritorious acts in your earlier lives might not have fully sufficed. Could you then be said in your present life to be excessive in your practice of the virtues?

Comparing the amount of evil committed since the first year of the Genkō era[207] with the amount of good that was done, which of the two is greater? During this period, how many men have been slaughtered as foes, leaving their wives, children, and other dependents to wander about with nowhere to go? The deaths of those who have fallen in battle, enemy and ally alike, all constitute sinful karma for you. Fathers have lost their sons, and sons have lost their fathers. The number of those who have suffered in this way is beyond all reckoning. If they could at least receive compensation for their loyalty they would have some consolation, but those who are not daimyos or who lack influential connections have no way of gaining your ear, and thus their appeals go unanswered. Their resentment will not soon disappear.

Even now I hear talk of victories, but such victories are simply the slaying of more enemies and the amassing of more evil karma. How many shrines, temples, inns, and homes in the cities and countryside have been burnt or destroyed, how many properties have been confiscated to provide supplies for the military or rewards for loyal vassals? As a result of this, shrine rituals are seldom performed and temple services have been neglected. People who possess estates but are not themselves warriors can no longer control their lands. Lodgings have been requisitioned, leaving many people with no place to dwell. Good government is not being practiced, and the sorrow of people both highborn and lowborn grows ever deeper. It is entirely because of this that the land is not at peace. Why then are you so concerned about the overcultivation of virtue? If only everyone would devote themselves to the good works that you mention then this world would truly become a Pure Land. In what way could this hinder governance?

Since ancient times many kings and ministers both in Japan and abroad have been devout believers in Buddhism. Among them have been some who espoused Buddhism for the sake of secular rule, while others have taken the reins of government in order to promote Buddhism. Although leaders who put their trust in Buddhism in order to improve the quality of their secular rule are superior to evil kings and ministers who lack all faith in the Dharma, their true concern is with prosperity and benevolent governance. Although the populace is thereby spared for a time the suffering of hunger and cold, neither the highborn nor the lowborn are spared the suffering of birth and death. In this sense even the rule of the Three Sovereigns and Five Emperors is not truly worthy of praise, since Buddhism was not yet known in their lands.

In contrast, leaders who rule for the sake of Buddhism are truly lay bodhisattvas, skillful in guiding the populace to the Buddhadharma. In Japan, Prince Shōtoku constructed temples and pagodas, enshrined Buddhist images, lectured on the sutras and treatises, and commented on the holy texts, even as he handled all of the various affairs of state. This is what it means to govern wisely for the sake of Buddhism.

When, at the beginning of the Seventeen Article Constitution,[208] Prince Shōtoku wrote that relations between the highborn and lowborn should be harmonious and amicable and that the Three Treasures should be revered, it was in order to emphasize that government should be conducted for the sake of the Buddhadharma. For this reason no one in the land opposed the prince's rule while he was alive, and in the seven centuries since his death all have honored his achievements. The only one to oppose him was Mononobe-no-Moriya,[209] who was in the end defeated by the prince. Moriya was an important minister in the government and was an outstanding figure in politics, yet he was severely punished because of his obstruction of the prince's virtuous works. This is all stated in the records preserved at Tennō-ji, written in the prince's own hand.

Elsewhere, Emperor Wu[210] of the Liang dynasty is sometimes criticized for having lost his kingdom to the general Hou Jing[211] because of his involvement in good works and his consequent neglect of his political duties. What, then, of the Tathāgata Śākyamuni, who as crown prince under King Śuddhodana was expected to succeed to the throne, but who instead left the world and secluded himself in the Himalayas where he suffered hunger and cold? Would one censure him for renouncing the glory of the throne, saying he was unduly concerned with the Way? On several occasions Emperor Wu of the Liang also attempted to leave his position and retire from the world, but each time the imperial court would not allow it. Finally the emperor tried to ensure his retirement by selling himself to the temple as a slave. Even then his ministers refused to permit it, returning the temple's money and restoring the emperor to the throne. It is hard to imagine that the emperor felt any great regret about his position having been usurped by Hou Jing.

Viewing your present circumstances, it is evident that you cannot leave the world like the Tathāgata Śākyamuni or Emperor Wu of the

Liang. If, like Prince Shōtoku, you advance the secular law for the sake of Buddhism, then that would be most commendable. I have heard that the army of loyal soldiers you are presently raising is solely for the purpose of advancing the Buddhadharma. Thus I am confident that this nobly motivated undertaking will not meet defeat, even if everyone in the land were to join together in opposing you. I have offered you these straightforward words in the hope that, if they cause those who criticize you to turn from their deluded views, then they will have been of some benefit.

18

DEMON-WORK

Question: It is said that those who practice the Buddhadharma run the risk of falling into the realm of the demons. Why is this?

Answer: Everything that hinders the Buddha Way is called "demon-work." If one persists in demon-work, then one inevitably falls into the realm of the demons. This is explained in detail in the *Śūraṅgama Sutra*,[212] the *Great Calming and Contemplation*,[213] and the "About Demons" chapter of the *Great Perfection of Wisdom Sutra*.[214] Because of the length of the relevant passages I cannot directly cite them here. To summarize, there are two types of demon, "outer demons" and "inner demons."

The Demon King and his minions who come from the outside to torment practicers of the Way are all outer demons. The Demon King dwells in the sixth and highest heaven in the realm of desire and is known as Tenma, the Celestial Demon. Beings like *tengu*[215] are among the minions of the Demon King. The Demon King regards all beings in the three realms as his subjects and is thus intent on obstructing those who enter the Buddha Way. He is not concerned about those who care only for worldly things and ignore the practice of the Buddhadharma, since such people can never escape the round of birth and death.

Demons can all fly, emit light from their bodies, and read the past and the future. They can appear in the form of buddhas and bodhisattvas, and they are eloquent in preaching the Dharma.

In the *Nirvana Sutra* it says that one day when Ānanda[216] was returning from an outing he saw on the way nine million celestial demons, all of whom had taken the form of buddhas and looked exactly like the Tathāgata. All were preaching the Dharma and criticizing each another. Ānanda stared at them, unable to tell whether his actual teacher, Śākyamuni, was among them. Seeing this, Śākyamuni had Mañjuśrī chant a dhāraṇī, upon which all of the celestial demons fled.[217] If even Ānanda was liable to such deception, how much more so are foolish people? If the celestial demons can manifest as buddhas and preach the Dharma, how much more readily may they take on other forms and speak of other things? People in the world who are impressed by abilities like raining flowers from the sky and emitting light from one's body are certainly in the realm of the demons.

Even if practicers are not tormented by such outer demons, they may still harbor delusion within their own minds. This may take various forms: adhering to evil views, indulging in conceit, clinging to meditative states, taking pride in their wisdom, falling into the Two-Vehicle mind and seeking liberation for themselves only, or attempting to benefit others out of sentimental compassion. All such things hinder the attainment of Supreme Enlightenment and are thus referred to as inner demons. Other things that prevent completion of the Way, such as illnesses that lead one to abandon training or death resulting from one's own actions, also relate to the realm of the demons.

Another variety of inner demonic obstruction is seen in people who practice too compulsively, sitting *zazen* at every free moment and tearfully lamenting how long it takes to attain enlightenment. Habitually slothful students encounter a different type of obstruction when they decide to engage in a bit of meditation and end up like people with chronic indigestion who suddenly overindulge in food.

It is an inner demonic obstruction to excessively venerate one's teacher, to the point of engaging in repugnant behavior like eating his excrement and drinking his urine. Overly critical students, however, face their own type of inner demon when they notice faults in their masters' behavior and therefore reject the Buddhadharma.

When strong passions like greed, aversion, and ignorance arise they, too, form a type of demonic obstruction. On the other hand, when one is overly fearful of the rise of deluded passions and is overcome with remorse when they do, this is also a type of demonic obstruction.

Such obstructions sometimes arise as the result of bad attitudes on the part of the practicer. At other times it is precisely because the practicer's attitude is sincere that hindrances appear as part of a demonic attempt to destroy that sincerity, in the same way that a candle flares up just before it burns out. If one remains calm and undisturbed regardless of what happens, one cannot go wrong.

19 CONCEIT

Question: I can understand why a person would fall into the realm of demons by entertaining evil views, but why would a person enter this realm because of wisdom, virtue, and miraculous powers?

Answer: It is similar to when a person serves loyally on the battlefield and is rewarded for outstanding service. If that person, proud of his reward, starts acting presumptuously then he is certain to incur punishment. The fault is not with the reward but entirely with the attitude of conceit that arose because of the reward.

It is the same with the Buddhadharma. As followers of the Way gain experience in practice, the fruits of their training mature day by day, and their spiritual powers may come to excel those of other people. If these people then begin to take pride in their limited wisdom and virtue they will undoubtedly fall into the realm of the demons. From ancient times there have been practicers in both the doctrinal and contemplative schools who have entered this realm. Even among those who devote themselves to practices for rebirth in the Pure Land there is something known as "rebirth in the demonic realm." None of these consequences is the fault of the Buddhadharma itself, but they are solely the result of arrogance regarding one's wisdom, virtue, and supernatural powers. If, in addition, a person holds false views, denies the principle of cause and effect, and praises himself while vilifying others, he falls straight into hell without even entering the realm of the demons.

The *Sutra on Purifying Karmic Hindrances* explains how even the practice of the six pāramitās can constitute a hindrance to the Way, saying that one who practices giving (*dāna*) may come to hate the avarice he sees in others, while one who practices maintaining the moral code (*śīla*) may criticize those who break the precepts. Similarly, one who trains in contemplation (*dhyāna*) may shun those with scattered minds, while one who has attained wisdom (*prajñā*) may look down upon the foolish.[218] The point is not that the practice of the six pāramitās constitutes demon-work, but that progress on the Way can be hindered by a possessive, dualistic attitude that sees oneself as right and others as wrong.

As long as one has such an attitude, everything one does is demon-work, even if one arouses the mind that seeks the Way and practices the six pāramitās. How much more so for those who practice to gain wisdom, eloquence, and supernatural powers for the sake of worldly fame and profit. Such ambitions are all the work of one's inner demons. Outer demons, perceiving this, give such people the wisdom, eloquence, and supernatural powers that they desire.

Confused, these people fail to see that their abilities are the work of demons, regarding them instead as the result of their own virtues. Thus they grow conceited and fall into the demonic realm.

Question: Although the clergy may have greater detachment than the laity, no ordinary mortal can be without dualistic attachments. If all of one's practice done in an attitude of dualistic attachment is demonwork, doesn't this mean that the training done by ordinary people can never result in realization of the Buddha Way?

Answer: Every act can bring either benefit or loss; the difference depends upon how it is handled. Handled poorly, a situation will bring loss; handled well, it is certain to result in benefit. Thus when someone who was rewarded for loyalty is later punished for boasting of his reward, you do not therefore conclude that acts of loyalty are meaningless, since the fault lay not with the loyalty but with excessive pride. Even if a feeling of pride does arise at having been rewarded more than others, if a person refrains from arrogant behavior in the knowledge that such behavior can bring ruin to himself and his household, then with the accumulation of further services and acts of fealty he can not only improve his personal standing and that of his family but also perform immeasurable services for his lord and for society.

In Buddhism, too, you may hear of someone with great achievements in the practice and great merit in the Way who nevertheless ends up in the realm of the demons as a result of dualistic attachments. If you therefore abandon your own practice, to which path will you turn to attain liberation from the realm of birth and death? Despite the differences in the various schools of Buddhism, in any of them a person who maintains an attitude of dualistic attachment and pride in his attainments will find it hard to escape the realm of the demons. But one who rejects the Buddhadharma and refuses to practice will fare even worse, falling straight into the three evil paths. Entering the demonic realm is not the result of Buddhist practice but of conceit over one's attainments in the Way.

No one is free of dualistic attachment who has not yet reached the level of sagehood. Even if thoughts of dualistic attachment arise, realize that they are all the work of demons and do not cling to them. If you experience minor insights and benefits, even if they seem out of the ordinary, do not be satisfied with them. Though you understand nothing, do not become discouraged. When your practice finally matures, the marvelous light of your Original Nature will suddenly manifest, and you will naturally realize the infinite functioning of virtue. Then you will not only dispel your own delusion but also provide the immeasurable benefit of guidance to all sentient beings. If you can do this, then all of the celestial demons and heretics will become good companions, and no obstacles to the Buddha's work will remain. This is what the layman Vimalakīrti meant when he said, "The whole host of demons and the non-Buddhist believers are all my attendants."

ZAZEN-INDUCED BREAKDOWNS

Question: Some people hesitate to do *zazen*, seeing how Zen meditators occasionally suffer mental breakdowns. Are such breakdowns really the result of *zazen*?

Answer: If the fact that Zen practicers occasionally suffer breakdowns causes a person to reject *zazen*, it is because that person has insufficient karmic resources for the practice. After all, there are individuals who have never done *zazen* and are solely concerned with secular matters who have experienced similar breakdowns. Does this cause people to reject worldly affairs?

Breakdowns that occur during meditation are sometimes caused by demonic spirits who enter the practicer when he takes pride in a minor insight, or by delusive apparitions that torment the practicer as the result of past karma. Occasionally a meditator who is attached to the notion of a quick enlightenment will overstrain himself physically and mentally, disrupting his circulation and precipitating a collapse.

Breakdowns occur for these and various other reasons. They are not the fault of *zazen*. Moreover, breakdowns are temporary affairs, and people almost always recover. When they are over one should simply return to the mind that seeks the Way. Those who do not meditate for fear of breakdowns are destined for long stays in hell, with little chance of release. This is true madness indeed. Therefore do not fear that *zazen* causes madness. What one should truly fear is rejecting the practice of *zazen* because of a few cases of madness.

DEALING WITH DEMONIC OBSTRUCTIONS 22

Question: What should we do when demonic obstructions arise?

Answer: The doctrinal schools have various methods for this, but I will not consider them here. In the Zen school, if one believes that the mysterious principle of the separate transmission outside of the teachings is perfectly realized in each individual, with no distinction between the wise and the foolish, and if one believes that this principle has been changeless throughout the ages, then one should know that possessing even extraordinary wisdom and virtue is nothing more than fantasy and illusion and is nothing to be attached to. An ancient once said, "Even if there is something that is superior to nirvana, cut it to pieces."[219] Those who believe in the Ultimate Tathāgata of Self-Nature[220] do not place any special value on things like the three bodies and the four wisdoms,[221] nor do they look down upon even the lowliest sentient beings. Were their bodies to manifest the special marks of a buddha and were their heads to radiate halos, they wouldn't regard it as anything special. If one is like this, how can inner or outer demons possibly find a place to enter?

Zen Master Daoshu[222] of the Tang dynasty lived on Mount Sanfeng. One day a stranger dressed in unusual clothing began to appear at his place and walk in the vicinity of his hermitage. Sometimes he would appear in the form of a bodhisattva and sometimes in the form of a celestial being or a Taoist sage. Occasionally he would emit an eerie light or speak in mysterious tongues. This went on for ten years, and then the stranger came no more. The master said to one of his disciples, "For some time a celestial demon was coming and trying to disturb me with displays of various transformations. I faced the matter by neither looking nor listening. Finally he ran out of transformations, while my no-look-no-listen response could never be exhausted. As a result he withdrew and disappeared."

This is one method of dealing with demons, and one that works not only with the demonic realm. In all situations both favorable and adverse, if you remain like Master Daoshu your practice of the Way will quite naturally come to fruition. This is what Bodhidharma intended when he said, "Outside, cut off relations with all things; inside, have no concerns. Make your mind like a wall, and you will certainly attain the Way."[223] If you can be this way not only during the ordinary situations and interactions of everyday life but also when facing death, you will not be troubled by karmic conditions.

The Zen master Huangbo[224] writes in his *Essentials of the Transmission of Mind*:

> When an ordinary person is about to die, he should merely contemplate the five skandhas to be all-empty and the four elements to be without self.[225] The true mind is without characteristics and neither goes nor comes: when one is born the [mind-]nature does not come [into one], and when one dies neither does the nature go [anywhere]. Peaceful, perfect, and serene, the mind and its realms are identical. If one can only now suddenly achieve comprehension in this fashion, you will...be a person who has transcended the world.... If you see buddhas...coming to greet [and escort you to the Pure Land], with all the various phenomena [involved in such visions], then have no thought of following them. If you see various phenomena

with evil characteristics, neither should you have any thoughts of fear. Simply forget your mind and identify yourself with the dharmadhātu. These are the essentials [of meeting death].[226]

SUBDUING DEMONS WITH NO-MIND

Question: Just as someone who is drunk is often unaware of the fact, so those in the demon realm don't realize they are there. Thus learning the secrets of demon quelling may be of little use when those secrets are really needed. Is there any way a beginner can avoid the realm of the demons?

Answer: Fearing the demon realm and seeking to avoid it is already to be in the demon realm. Nāgārjuna said, "Entertain thought and you fall into the demons' snares. Entertain no-thought and you will escape them."[227] An ancient worthy said, "Apart from mind there are no demonic obstructions. Attain no-mind and the demons are subdued."[228] This is why Daoshu's approach of not looking and not listening was effective against the demon that sought him. If one clings to the form of the buddha realm, it becomes the demon realm; if one forgets the form of the demon realm, it becomes the buddha realm. The true practicer is neither attached to the buddha realm nor afraid of the demon realm. If one has this attitude, then one will neither cling to notions that one is enlightened nor grow discouraged with the practice, and all obstacles will of themselves disappear.

It is also important to make a vow in front of the Buddha. In the *Sutra of Complete Enlightenment* it is written:

Sentient beings in the Latter Age should make the pure Great Vow. "May I now abide in the Buddha's perfect enlightenment; may I meet good teachers without encountering non-Buddhists or the Two Vehicles; may I steadily cut off obstructions and ascend to the pure jewel-palace of liberation."[229]

One who has this spirit, even if just a beginner, will by the power of this great vow go from one lifetime to the next without ever falling in with demons or nonbelievers. Such a person will be guarded by the host of buddhas and protected by all the deities, and thus without fail will escape all hindrances and attain to the stage of nonretrogression.[230]

PART II

THE PROFOUND WISDOM
OF ORIGINAL NATURE

Question: It is fully reasonable that the search for prosperity, which causes hindrances to the Way, should be restrained. But one would expect wisdom to be helpful to the Way. Why then does the Zen school disparage scholarly understanding and intellectual aptitude?

Answer: The reason that the Buddha has the title "Most Honored of Two-legged Beings" is that he is fully endowed with both merit and wisdom. Thus these things in themselves are not to be despised. The reason that followers of the Way are discouraged from intellectual pursuits is to encourage them to relinquish their attachment to material good fortune and the defiled wisdom of the secular world, as well as to seek the Great Wisdom of their own inherent truth. Such wisdom is the undefiled, supermundane treasure of the Dharma. Knowledge gained through studying the texts of the sutras and commentaries, through memorizing the teachings of a master, and through thought based on deluded views is nothing more than a type of property acquired through various worldly stratagems. Those who are wise in this sense may appear superior to the unlearned, but their wisdom is actually an obstacle in that it can hinder them from attaining enlightenment. The ancient masters warn us that the foolish are hindered by foolishness, and the wise are hindered by wisdom.

Thus if those who understand that the profound wisdom of Original Nature is immanent in everyone but is obstructed by ignorance and knowledge can let go of both the true and the false that arise in their minds, then they will without fail come into accord with this profound wisdom. It is like a drunken man becoming sober and returning to his senses.

WISDOM AS AN IMPEDIMENT

Question: The wisdom of the non-Buddhists and Two Vehicles is not that of the true path, and thus it must constitute a hindrance to the Way. Must the wisdom of the Three Worthy States and the Ten Holy Stages[231] also be rejected as a hindrance?

Answer: In the teachings it is said that wisdom can lead to confusion. It is like moxibustion, which is important in alleviating pain during an illness but which, once the illness is cured, becomes a source of pain.

The teachings also tell us that the realization of one's former faults advances one to the next level on the bodhisattva path. For example, when one realizes the shortcomings of the wisdom of the first stage of bodhisattvahood, one has become a bodhisattva of the second stage. When one realizes that the wisdom of the second-stage bodhisattva is still imperfect one has become a third-stage bodhisattva. It continues in this way until one realizes that even if one fully illuminates the profound principle of the Dharma-nature with the wisdom of a bodhisattva of Equivalent Enlightenment,[232] this is still within the realm of fundamental ignorance. Fundamental ignorance is severed when even the wisdom of Equivalent Enlightenment is forgotten and one subtly unites with the profound wisdom inherent in us.

When we realize this, we see how superficial are discussions of the wisdom and function of Equivalent Enlightenment and Marvelous Enlightenment.[233] Thus in the Zen school we do not regard Equivalent Enlightenment and Marvelous Enlightenment as anything special, to say nothing of the other levels of bodhisattva wisdom. Huangbo writes, "Even Marvelous Enlightenment is the Phantom City."[234] Hearing these words, Zen followers may grow conceited and scholars indignant, but this is because both base their understanding on words and therefore fail to grasp the mysterious principle of the Zen school. No one who conformed with the profound wisdom of Original Nature would become conceited or indignant, nor would such a person value wisdom and despise ignorance.

Scholarly Understanding and Profound Wisdom

Question: The profound wisdom of Original Nature is inherently ours, but from the beginningless past it has never manifested because ignorance obstructs it. If we now cast aside wisdom and return to ignorance, would not profound wisdom fail to manifest, just as it has until now?

Answer: People unable to divine their own fortunes call upon fortune-tellers and trust what they are told. Even if they are unable at the moment to see any indications of the truth of the fortune-tellers' readings, they believe that when the time comes the signs will appear. When one hears the profound teachings of the Dharma but is unable to attain awakening oneself, one puts one's trust for the time being in the Buddha's words. This is known as "faith" or "accepting the evidence of the sacred teachings."

Scholarly understanding can become a hindrance to the Way, however, and the Zen school is not the first to point this out; there are many clear statements to this effect in the sutras. For example, in the *Lotus Sutra* the Buddha says:

> When Ānanda and I were at the place of Void King Buddha, we both at the same time conceived the determination

to attain anuttara-samyaksaṃbodhi. Ānanda constantly delighted in wide knowledge [of the Law], and so has not yet attained anuttara-samyaksaṃbodhi, while I constantly put forth diligent effort and therefore have succeeded in attaining anuttara-samyaksaṃbodhi.[235]

According to the *Śūraṅgama Sutra*, "Ānanda was solely concerned with listening to the Buddha's teachings on the Dharma, and thus did not attain the power of the Way."[236] The *Sutra of Complete Enlightenment* says, "Sentient beings in the Latter Age wish to attain the Way but do not seek enlightenment, preferring instead to study the teachings and foster their sense of self."[237]

Some people say that the reason they look down upon the learned is because the latter only record and memorize words and letters and do not understand the underlying meaning. Those who say such things do not yet understand the distinction between words and meaning. The *Laṅkāvatāra Sutra* says:

Those who wish to attain enlightenment should seek out the company of the learned. To be learned is not to be knowledgeable about words, but to be knowledgeable about meaning. "Meaning" is separate from mental cognition and verbal expression.[238]

What most people refer to as "meaning" is simply words and phrases.

Question: The six pāramitās[239] are the foundation of bodhisattva practice. Among the six, prajñā pāramitā, the perfection of wisdom, is supreme, because without it the remaining five cannot reach completion. Why, then, do you criticize wisdom?

Answer: The word *prajñā* is Sanskrit; the Sino-Japanese translation is *chie* 智慧. The word *wisdom* applies to many different types of wisdom: true wisdom, deluded wisdom, provisional wisdom, wisdom that knows reality as it is, and so forth. What most people think of as wisdom is the correction of ignorance through understanding the various Dharma teachings. According to the *Sutra of Complete Enlightenment*, however, both wisdom and ignorance are equally prajñā.[240] What the sutra means is not that ignorance when corrected becomes true wisdom but that when activity-consciousness[241] arises through the agency of ignorance, then within the profound wisdom of perfect enlightenment the forms of "wisdom" and "ignorance" are perceived. Such perception is deluded thought. If on this basis one attempts to rectify ignorance into wisdom, one does no more than multiply deluded thought.

The word *prajñā* can also be translated as "awakening," and as "the Way." The Zen master Nanquan Puyuan said, "The Way has nothing to do with knowing or not-knowing. 'Knowing' is delusion, 'not-knowing' is vacuity."[242] Some students of Zen think that to understand the principle of the Original Nature is to awaken to the Way. If this is so, why does Nanquan say, "The Way has nothing to do with knowing"? Others think that obliterating all intellectual understanding and abiding in empty silence constitutes awakening to the Way. If this is so, why does Nanquan say, "The Way has nothing to do with not-knowing"?

If you simply let go of all such understandings and ardently investigate day and night the place of this "letting go," when the time is ripe you will encounter the profound wisdom of Original Nature. Then you realize for the first time that the essence of the Way has nothing to do with either ignorance or wisdom. If you come this far, you see that ordinary wisdom and ignorance are not external to you but are created within yourself.

Although one who knows the principle of impermanence, recognizes the law of cause and effect, and discards secular fame and gain is wiser than the ordinary deluded person, this level of attainment will not result in the realization of Buddhahood. Nor does the fact that the bodhisattvas of the Three Worthy States and the Ten Holy Stages have gained insight into illusion[243] or attained nirvana wisdom[244] mean that they have realized Buddhahood. When one attains the stage of a bodhisattva of Equivalent Enlightenment one transcends the wisdom of the Three Worthy States and Ten Holy Stages and enters Diamond Samādhi.[245] At this time the profound wisdom of Marvelous Enlightenment manifests for the first time.

This profound wisdom is inherent and fully realized in everyone. Thus those of the highest capabilities can awaken to this innate wisdom immediately, without first passing through the Three Worthy States and the Ten Holy Stages. This is what an ancient master meant when he said, "For the great ones, one breakthrough accomplishes all,"[246] and what the *Avataṃsaka Sutra* intends when it says, "At the time one first awakens the aspiration for enlightenment one has already attained full realization."[247]

Followers of the expedient teachings who feel that even a bodhisattva at the highest of the Ten Stages has not yet realized Marvelous
Enlightenment, much less an ordinary person shallow in understanding, have no belief in this innate wisdom, perceiving wisdom to be
nothing more than the correction of one's ignorance.

Preaching the six pāramitās and myriad practices and establishing the fifty-two stages of bodhisattvahood are both directed toward
those of medium and inferior capabilities. The special emphasis on
prajñā pāramitā is an upāya intended for those unable to immediately
awaken to Original Nature, to provide them with a raft of illusory
wisdom so that they might eventually reach the Other Shore of Original Nature. This is the reason that the doctrinal schools allow a certain degree of scholarly understanding, although such understanding
is not the true goal of these schools. The most important purpose of
the raft is to carry people across the river to the opposite shore. Foolish people, however, fail to understand the raft's true function and
therefore grow attached to it and refuse to leave it behind.

The Buddha and the ancestors appeared in the world and preached
the various Dharma gates in order to create a raft that could convey us
across the river of deluded, inverted thinking to the Other Shore of
Original Nature. Even if you board it, the raft cannot land you on the
Ground of Original Nature if you refuse to get off. A person who is
able to fly can, of course, go directly to the other side without need of
a raft; similarly, a person of the highest capabilities can immediately
awaken to the Ground of Original Nature without needing to acquire
the wisdom of the Three Worthy States and the Ten Holy Stages. If
one exhorts such a person to scholarly learning, it is like giving a raft
to someone who is able to fly—it would only be a hindrance. This is
why the Zen school has a distaste for learning.

However, among Zen practicers there are those who construct
rafts out of the words of the Zen masters and grow proud in the belief
that their rafts are superior to the rafts of the doctrinal schools. Such
rafts may indeed be wonderful, and those who dwell contentedly
upon them indulging in pleasant pastimes as they drift aimlessly in

the current are perhaps superior to those who remain on this shore idling their lives away without ever trying to cross the river, but both types of people are the same in that they never reach the Other Shore. The bodhisattvas of the Three Worthy States and the Ten Holy Stages may be riding a superb raft, but as long as they continue to dwell on it they have yet to transcend transformational samsara.[248] How much more so those who are satisfied to dwell on the rafts of the provisional and Hinayana teachings?

Question: There are those who, believing something similar to what you just said, neither seek wisdom nor study the teachings of the sacred texts. Yet they do not attain enlightenment. Why is this?

Answer: Realizing the fallacy of the belief that accumulating scholarly knowledge constitutes enlightenment, some people abandon it in an attempt to bring themselves into accord with the Way. Hindered by such deluded thinking, however, they never achieve the accord they seek.

The *Avataṃsaka Sutra* says, "How strange that all sentient beings are fully endowed with the wisdom and the virtuous form of the Tathāgata, yet are unable to realize this because of attachments and deluded thought."[249] It is like a man of great strength and marvelous skills who suddenly becomes ill and is left as weak as a three-year-old and unable to use his abilities. One day he sees a healthy man doing amazing tricks and performing acts of unusual strength. Envying the man and forgetting that he himself possesses the same abilities when he is well, the sick man attempts—ill though he is—to learn the other man's skills and manifest the same strength. Before he can reach his goal he exhausts himself physically and mentally; his illness worsens, and in the end he suffers the agonies of death. If this man had kept in mind that the skills and strength that he sought were already his and that only his illness made him unable to use them, he would have focused on curing his illness first. His strength and skills would then have returned of themselves.

Training in the Way is similar. Although the wisdom and the virtuous form of the Tathāgata are innate in us, we cannot manifest and use them because the illnesses of deluded thinking and inverted notions block us from doing so. Not understanding this truth, many people, as they lie on their sickbed of deluded thought, hear of the sages' displays of wisdom and virtue. Envious, they take up the study of Buddhist and non-Buddhist texts, transcribe and memorize the words of the masters, seek out supernatural powers, or pray for special talents or eloquence. All such things simply worsen the underlying illness of deluded thinking. When, then, can our innate wisdom and virtue ever appear?

STOP DELUDED THINKING

Question: What is "deluded thinking"?

Answer: It is deluded thinking to regard the Pure Land and the defiled world as separate, and to conceive of a difference between ignorance and enlightenment, and between ordinary beings and sages. It is also deluded thinking to assume that the Pure Land and the defiled world are not separate, or that there is no difference between ignorance and enlightenment or ordinary beings and sages.

It is deluded thinking to see a distinction in Buddhism between Mahayana and Hinayana, between the provisional teachings and the true teachings, between the exoteric teachings and the esoteric teachings, and between the path of meditation and the path of doctrine. It is deluded thinking to see all of Buddhism as equal and of one flavor, with no superior and inferior among the schools. It is deluded thinking to regard the Buddhadharma as walking, standing, sitting, and reclining, or seeing, hearing, recognizing, and knowing. It is also deluded thinking to believe that Buddhism is to be found somewhere outside of all such activities.

It is the deluded thinking of ordinary beings to think that things truly exist. It is the deluded thinking of the Hinayana to regard all phenomena as impermanent. It is the deluded thinking of non-Buddhists to believe, based on various doctrines, that the self exists eternally or that the self is extinguished upon death. It is the deluded thinking of the bodhisattva to know that all phenomena are empty and illusory and to awaken to the true form of the Middle Way.[250] It is the deluded thinking of the scholastics to ignore the separate transmission outside of the teachings and to adhere to doctrine. It is the deluded thinking of Zen practicers to believe that there is a Dharma gate, known as "the separate transmission outside of the teachings," that is superior to doctrine.

If you believe all of these statements and therefore conclude that all points of view are deluded thinking, this too is deluded thinking. In olden times, whenever National Teacher Fenzhou Wuye was asked a question, he would simply say, "Stop deluded thinking!"[251] If you see through this single phrase, then your inherent wisdom and virtue will manifest of themselves.

WORDS AND DELUDED THINKING

Question: The Dharma gates that you criticize above are all teachings found in the sutras, commentaries, and sayings of the ancient worthies. Why, then, do you refer to them as deluded thinking?

Answer: No one who has reached the Ground of Original Nature is hindered in any way by utilizing various Dharma gates as upāya to guide learners, just as speaking of fire does not burn the mouth. The learner who has yet to realize Original Nature, however, interprets the meaning of his or her teacher's words with a mind still ruled by the passions, and therefore everything becomes deluded thinking. Why is it nowadays that in the doctrinal schools even those who have perfectly mastered the secret oral teachings never equal the founders and ancient worthies of their traditions? It is because none of these oral transmissions conveys the ancient worthies' true intention.

Zhiyi, the founder of the Tendai school, commented, "I received succession from Nanyue Huisi. I do not rely on others for confirmation."[252] A commentary on the *Mahāvairocana Sutra* says, "Mind confirms mind; mind awakens mind. This is what is known as the realization of enlightenment. It is neither attained nor awakened to through the mediation of others."[253] Who among the exoteric and esoteric teachers has ever claimed that scholarly mastery of the texts constitutes the true meaning of the Buddhadharma? Why is it that even among supposed Zen masters there are those who, although they seem proficient in examining students and critiquing the sayings of the ancients, are not nearly as free as the ancients when facing loss or standing on the brink of death? It is because their understanding does not reach the ancient ones' level of realization. Master Yunmen said, "If *this* were a matter of words and letters, would there be anything unexpressed in the Tripiṭaka? If that were so, then what need was there for Bodhidharma to come from the West?"[254]

Nonpractice
Is the Greatest Delusion

Question: May we then say that applying one's mind to practice is deluded thinking, that the doctrinal and meditative teachings are nothing but twigs and leaves, and that the person who acts in accordance with his deluded passions is the true person of the Way?

Answer: Such a view is the most deluded of all deluded thinking. The *Sutra of Complete Enlightenment*, in its discussion of the four faults, refers to it as "the fault of allowing things to be as they are."[255]

KOAN PRACTICE

Question: If seeking merit and wisdom are disparaged, is it then not problematic that learners would seek enlightenment by working with koans?

Answer: An ancient master said, "Do not consciously seek enlightenment."[256] If a learner consciously seeks enlightenment, he is not truly working on koans. Yuanwu Keqin commented, "It is not necessary for a person of superior abilities to contemplate the words of a koan."[257] This shows that koan work is not the Zen master's main concern. Even if, out of compassion, he has the student work on a koan, such work is not the same as reciting the *nenbutsu* to gain rebirth in a buddha land or chanting sutras and dhāraṇīs to accumulate merit. Koans are not assigned so that one may be born in the Pure Land or realize Buddhahood and the Way. Nor is a koan some kind of strange puzzle or an expression of Zen doctrine. It is simply that which cannot be grasped by the ordinary mind—that is the nature of a koan. It can be likened to a dumpling made of iron. Faced with that which the "tongue" of ordinary consciousness cannot taste, you chew away and chew away, and finally you chew right through. Then, for the first time, you realize that this iron dumpling has nothing to do with the five tastes and six flavors of the world.[258] Nor is it the flavor of the Dharma or the taste of the doctrine.[259]

Question: Those who misunderstand the doctrinal and Zen teachings and fall into biased views should rightly be admonished. But there is no need to condemn those who understand the doctrines correctly without getting caught up in the web of doctrinal thought, as well as those who grasp the essence of Zen without sinking into the Zen sickness. If, however, you say that the teachings of both the doctrinal schools and Zen are not truth, wouldn't someone who realizes Original Nature be the same as a deluded person?

Answer: In Original Nature the concepts of "wise man" and "fool" do not exist. People who carelessly persist in speaking of "the wise" and "the foolish" are the true fools; the truly wise are those who do not perceive either one or the other. To regard as wise a person who is quick-witted and articulate is the worldly way of looking at things. A person who has attained the wisdom of the Original Nature does not give rise to conceited thoughts like "I am wise," since with the realization of Original Nature the notions of "wise" and "foolish" are no longer conceived. And it is not the case that such people actually regard themselves as wise but just don't *show* this to others.

When the four great elements[260] are in harmony and one feels at ease in both body and mind, one needs the secrets of the medical texts no more than one does effective medicines or healing rituals. However, when the four elements are out of balance and the 404 ailments appear,[261] then medical treatment is important. Doctors make their examinations and compound their prescriptions in accordance with the illness. Just as there are many different types of sickness, so too are there many different types of treatment. Despite the variety of treatments, however, the purpose is always the same: to relieve the suffering of the patient and return him or her to the state of comfort and well-being that existed prior to the illness.

The reason that people go to a doctor and seek treatment is to rid themselves of their sickness and pain, not to study what is written in the medical texts. If the doctor's treatment cures their illness, then the patient is healthy and free of pain. The cure was the result of the treatment, but once the patient is well she has simply returned to the original state of health she was in before she became ill—her health is not something bestowed upon her for the first time by the doctor. Nor would one say that returning to well-being requires mastering medical knowledge and learning clinical technique.

The same is true of Buddhism. In Original Nature there are no concepts of "enlightened" or "deluded," "sacred" or "profane," and thus there is no need for the doctrinal or meditative teachings. However, the illness of fundamental ignorance soon arises and sentient beings are filled with suffering and inverted views. The Buddha took pity on them and, in his capacity as the Great Medicine King, taught various types of Dharma gates in accordance with people's different natures and inclinations. Despite the differences in these Dharma gates, however, when one examines their objectives, one finds that all are wholly intended to cure sentient beings of their disease of discriminating between enlightened and deluded, sacred and profane, and to guide them back to the peace of their Original Nature. The goal is not to teach the various Dharma gates themselves. If people rid themselves of the disease of fundamental ignorance and deluded thinking, they no longer wander in the realm of birth and death and no longer discriminate between enlightened and deluded, sacred and profane.

Such people have experienced the unconditioned great liberation and are rightly called people of great enlightenment.

Enlightenment is not a matter of mastering the various teachings of the doctrinal schools, or of illuminating the practices of the Five Houses of Zen. There are seekers in this Latter Age who believe that the true goal of the Buddhadharma consists of learning the doctrines and understanding Zen. This is what "turning the medicine into the disease" means.[262] The ancient masters referred to this as "the sickness of doctrine and the sickness of Zen."

Question: You seem to be saying that it is a mistake for beginning students to master the profound principles of the teachings and then practice in accordance with that understanding. However, other people claim that it is wrong to begin practice without first studying the doctrines. Is there a reason for what they say?

Answer: It is like a person who has a serious disease. If he wants to put off treatment until he studies under a doctor and masters the medical texts, his illness will have worsened and taken his life long before he is finished. If, instead, he goes to a doctor and explains his symptoms, then the doctor will determine the nature of the illness and prescribe a suitable medicine, or burn moxa on the appropriate points. The patient himself has no idea what ingredients were compounded to make the medicine, nor why the physician selected certain moxibustion points and not others. He simply puts his faith in the doctor in the belief that, if he dutifully takes his medicine or burns the moxa, his disease will eventually get better.

The practice of the Way is similar to this. You may believe that in order to realize Original Nature you must first master the various Buddhist teachings, and only then, with these as a basis, embark on the actual practice of the Way. However, we have at most a hundred years of life, and the Buddhist teachings are infinite. Long before you have studied them all, your allotted years will have passed and your learning will have been for nothing. Unaware, you will be dragged along by karmic forces, unable to escape the cycle of birth and death. It is for this reason that the masters of the Zen school show learners no more than a word or a phrase, and even that word or phrase is intended not as a spur to practice but as a means to directly indicate Original Nature. If the learner is too dull to realize Original Nature immediately, then he should use the word or phrase as a koan to help him focus on that which cannot be understood through ordinary thought. Then, when the time is ripe, an eternity of delusion will immediately vanish.

FUNDAMENTAL WISDOM AND ACQUIRED WISDOM

Question: If people, at a single word from a good teacher, realize enlightenment and attain the realm unrelated to either doctrine or meditation, would this not hinder them from benefiting others?

Answer: In the teachings it is explained that the wisdom of the Buddha is of two types. The first type, known as fundamental wisdom, is the inner realization of the Buddha. The second, known as acquired wisdom, is the understanding of how to teach others through the use of expedient means. The doctrinal and meditative teachings of the buddhas and masters are all expedients for teaching others. In other words, all teachings that students of meditation and doctrine understand with the thinking mind, whether they see them in the sutras or hear them from their teachers, are expressions of acquired wisdom. Those who have themselves experienced the inner realization of the Buddha should deepen their own acquired wisdom and dedicate themselves to benefiting others and saving all sentient beings by propagating the meditative and doctrinal teachings. The tathāgatas of the three periods of time and the masters throughout the ages have all followed this path.

Those who have not yet experienced this inner realization should make its attainment their first priority. If they wish to reach this realm they should transcend the domains of "doctrine" and "meditation"—only then will they be able to attain it. No one who clings in his or her heart to the teachings of doctrine or meditation will ever awaken to Original Nature. An ancient master said, "When the sight of the buddhas' and patriarchs' teachings is like the sight of bitter enemies, only then do you have the capacity to receive them."[263] It is also said, "Get to the root, and don't worry about the twigs."[264]

It is like planting a tree. If the roots take hold then the branches and leaves will naturally thrive, and the tree will produce flowers and fruit. Thus when you first plant the tree you concentrate on the roots rather than the upper parts, and while the tree is taking hold you limit your pruning to no more than a few branches. However, it would be mistaken to think that a tree is planted for the sake of the roots alone. The reason the roots are so carefully tended is so that the branches, flowers, and fruit will thrive.

A person may have realized Original Nature, but if he has failed to grasp the Living Patriarch's methods of salvation then he is still unclear about the Great Dharma. Such a person, although his self-realization may be genuine, cannot serve as a teacher since he lacks the means to help others. This is what is meant when it is said, "The intent is understood, but the words are not."[265] There are others who understand something of the ancient masters' use of expedients but whose own eyes are not yet clear. In this case it is said, "The words are understood, but the intent is not";[266] these people, too, cannot teach.

An ancient master said, "For one who has yet to attain realization, it is better to study the intent than to study the words; for one who has attained realization, it is better to study the words than to study the intent."[267] "Intent" refers to the intent of Bodhidharma, the First Patriarch. "Bodhidharma's intent" refers to the Original Nature innate in every human being. "Words" refers to the respective expedients used by the Five Houses of Zen. The intent is the root; the words are the branches and leaves. The beginning student should first of all thoroughly grasp the intent of the Patriarch and not dwell, lifeless, amid the words.

The ancient masters, after awakening to the Patriarch's intent, would spend thirty to fifty years in intensive refinement, eliminating their remaining karma and residual hindrances. This type of training is known as "nourishing the sacred embryo." When the process fully matures everything is united into one, and there naturally appears the lucid eloquence and appropriate functioning that enables complete freedom in helping other people. At this stage, "both the intent and the words are understood."[268]

There are also people, of course, who can neither see clearly nor understand the expedients of the Five Houses. About such people it is said, "Neither the intent nor the words are understood."[269]

If, some time after a tree has been planted, its branches and leaves, flowers, and fruit still fail to thrive, one can conclude that the tree has not successfully taken root. If one then changes the soil and keeps it properly watered and fertilized in the succeeding days and months, one can be confident that the roots will take and the rest of the tree will flourish. The foolish person, however, unaware that the reason for the tree's poor growth lies in its roots, attempts to make the branches grow and the flowers blossom, never realizing that by so doing he weakens the roots even more. Similarly, if a person who has understood Bodhidharma's intent still lacks the powers of eloquence, functioning, and transformation, he should not concern himself with trivial matters but instead abide in the awareness of Original Nature, eradicate the notions of a substantial self and substantial objects, and get to the source of both deluded desires and sacred understanding. The ancient masters tell us that it is easy to realize the Dharma but difficult to maintain it. "Maintaining the Dharma" refers to the practice of cultivating the sacred embryo.

Latter-day students with a spiritual bent who have experienced something like the shadow of enlightenment (not true enlightenment) seldom undertake the practice of cultivating the sacred embryo. Such students, convinced of their fundamental grasp of the truth but concerned that they still lack eloquence and the other powers, set out to study the doctrinal and meditative teachings in the hope that through the providence of the buddhas and patriarchs they will gain what they seek. As a result they further obscure their Original Nature and end up falling into the realm of the demons.

Still other students, glimpsing the shadow of enlightenment and thinking it to be Original Nature, hold fast to their experience in the belief that this constitutes cultivation of the sacred embryo. Continuing such "cultivation" for a thousand lifetimes or ten thousand kalpas would accomplish nothing more than increasing one's ignorance. Even if during this time one accumulates some merit, in the end it would only cause further wanderings in the realm of samsara. It is like planting and watering a tree with no roots. Such a tree, if given fertilizer and blessed with spring rains, might for a time send forth new leaves and sterile flowers, but before too long it is certain to die.

Question: What is the difference between studying the intent and studying the words?

Answer: Authorities on poetry originally drew the distinction between words and intent. When discussing a particular poem, for example, such authorities may note that it is refined and elegant in its wording but deficient in its underlying intent. The Zen school identifies a similar distinction between expression and meaning when it borrows the terms "words" and "intent" from the poetry critics, although it uses the terms in a rather different sense.

Zen has many specialized expressions relating to the category of "words," such as *kōjō* and *kōge*, *nahen* and *shahen*, *hajū* and *hōgyō*, *kinjū* and *sakkatsu*, *sangen* and *sanyō*, *goi* and *kunshin*, and so forth.[270] Certain latter-day students believe that a clear understanding of the differences in the way these various expedients are used constitutes "attaining the intent" and that freely employing them in *mondō* when teaching people constitutes "attaining the words." Even that which these students regard as intent is actually in the category of words. Nevertheless, some say that this approach is the basis of a combined study of the intent and the words. This explanation sounds plausible enough, but the reasoning behind it is off the mark.

Question: You say that beginners should first of all study the intent. By teaching through the use of koans, however, aren't you encouraging them to study the words?

Answer: Taking up the sayings of the ancient masters does not necessarily imply the study of words. Of course, if one attempts to analyze the sayings from the standpoints of *hajū* or *hōgyō*, or deliberate on them from the perspectives of *nahen* or *shahen*, this unquestionably constitutes "studying the words." Even if one sits silently facing a wall, as long as one continues to classify and compare random bits of knowledge and conjecture, one is still in the realm of words.

Letting go of all such reasoning and speculation and working directly on a koan is one method of studying the intent. If, when reading the records of the ancient masters or listening to the sermons of enlightened teachers, one can aim directly for the essence without giving rise to logical interpretations, then one is truly studying the intent. Once the student has clearly awakened to the intent of Bodhidharma, the student's teacher may explain the differences between the Five Houses of Zen and discuss such expedients as *hajū*, *hōgyō*, *yokuyō*, and *hōhen*.[271] This is the "word" aspect of training, and unless one learns it one cannot become a skillful guide to other people. When an ancient master called the failure of enlightened people to investigate words and phrases a "great disease," this is what he meant.[272] This applies not only to the expedients of the Zen school. One should be familiar with the systems of the doctrinal schools; the teachings of Confucius, Mencius, Laozi, and Zhuangzi; and the writings of the non-Buddhist teachers and secular thinkers.

Among those studying Buddhism today, those with a true desire to seek the Way are few. Their concerns being more with fame and vanity, they take up the study of the meditative and doctrinal teachings before awakening to the nature of the self. If in so doing they gain so much as a single insight they proclaim themselves teachers and start deceiving ordinary people. If among their students there is anyone whose ideas agree with their own they readily grant their seal of approval. This is a great error.

We must carefully consider the ancient masters' admonition that those who have yet to attain realization must first study the intent. This is a distinction that must be made. Fundamentally, however, there are no distinctions to be made, and the masters of our school had no desire to establish "word" versus "intention." As a man of old said, "Intent deeply influences words; words deeply influence intent. Intent and words move together. One must be very careful in this regard."[273]

THE IMPORTANCE OF PRACTICE

Question: Although we are now in the Latter Age of the Dharma, the traditional lineages of the Buddhist and non-Buddhist teachings survive. There are people who understand the principles taught by the ancient sages and tirelessly preach the teachings of their schools. Yet among the Confucians there are none who, like Confucius and Mencius, personify the five cardinal virtues.[274] Nor do followers of the various Buddhist traditions deport themselves according to their founders' standards. Masters of the Zen school are skilled in answering koans, preaching the Dharma, and teaching students, but when in the realm of birth-and-death, happiness-and-sorrow, they rarely show the same freedom from bondage seen in the masters of old. Why is it that, if the transmission of the Dharma has remained unchanged from the past, the behavior of its followers is so different?

Answer: The sutras warn that even those who have heard numerous sermons are no different from the unlearned if they don't engage in practice. Even in secular matters, it is easy to understand something intellectually but difficult to put that knowledge to practical use. We like to think we're as capable of carpentry or woodwork as any craftsman, but when we try to use an adze or plane we find we can barely shave a piece of wood. This is because people rarely make the effort to learn the requisite skills unless they intend to become carpenters, and thus they cannot equal even the most inept of professionals. Those born into carpenter households practice the skills from childhood, so that even the clumsiest of them is capable of following the family trade.

Nowadays those who study the Buddhist and non-Buddhist teachings concern themselves only with the scholarship of their respective traditions and never attempt to cultivate the underlying spirit. This is the reason they never approach the level of the sages of the past. In ancient times when Confucius taught the five cardinal virtues of benevolence, righteousness, propriety, wisdom, and sincerity, all of his disciples did their best to cultivate these virtues. Confucius certified one disciple's attainment of benevolence and another's attainment of righteousness because he recognized the virtues of benevolence and righteousness in those disciples' hearts. He would never have acknowledged their attainment if they had merely demonstrated knowledge of those virtues without manifesting them in their lives. People who study Confucianism nowadays simply memorize the teachings and then call themselves masters without ever practicing the virtues as a Way. Thus, though their knowledge of benevolence and righteousness equals that of Confucius and Mencius, they differ not a whit from ordinary people regarding the presence of these virtues in their hearts.

Even when the Buddha himself was alive, not everyone had the superior karmic roots necessary to attain complete emancipation. Nevertheless, those of medium and inferior roots who listened to his teachings and practiced according to their understanding would invariably benefit to the extent of their capacities. Later, in the early years after the Buddha's nirvana, everyone who followed a particular school and practiced its teachings profited as their abilities allowed. This was because, despite the differences in their talents, those people who had the good karmic roots to accept the Buddhadharma were all concerned, not with worldly fame and profit, but with liberation from birth and death and the emancipation of all sentient beings.

People born in the Latter Age have shallow stores of karmic merit. Thus householders who follow Buddhism are generally concerned with secular gain, and even those who become homeleavers are primarily interested in wealth and status. For this reason they have no desire to accumulate merit through spiritual practice, finding all the satisfaction they seek just studying the doctrines and principles of the various schools. As they advance in knowledge they grow ever more arrogant. While ordinary people adhere only to the notion of a personal self, those who study the Buddhadharma add to this the concept of a substantial Dharma.[275] As a result, while they may be in no way inferior to the sages of old when it comes to discussing the teachings, when it comes to practice they are no better than the most ignorant of ordinary people.

In trades that require manual skills, such as carpentry or blacksmithing, you will never be regarded as a competent workman if you can't actually plane a piece of wood or forge a piece of iron, regardless of how eloquently you may be able to explain how these things are done. Mere intellectual knowledge will never allow you to make a living in a trade. Present-day artisans, although born in the Latter Age, are in no way inferior to their ancient counterparts because from their earliest years they actually practice the essentials of their craft.

If students of the Buddhist and non-Buddhist traditions would only do as the craftsmen do, how could they not equal the masters of old? Surely such students would still surpass ordinary people in moderating their human passions and ego attachments, even if they were of inferior aptitude and unable to attain full liberation in the end. Nowadays, however, students pay no heed to the depravity of their minds or the shallowness of their practice, as long as their scholarly understanding exceeds that of other people. Thus it is only to be expected that the followers of the various Buddhist schools cannot equal the ancient sages.

The ancients said that it is better to gain a foot through effort than a fathom through persuasion. That is why the masters of the Zen school have always urged students to set aside their intellectual knowledge and thoroughly investigate their own minds. However, present-day Zen students read the recorded sayings and dabble in literature, becoming proud if their accomplishments are above average and feeling no shame at having never awakened to the truth. For this reason, although the Zen school and the doctrinal schools differ in their practices, they are alike in being unfaithful to the conduct of their founders. This is how Buddhism is degenerating in the Latter Age. Could anything be more deplorable than this?

Practice over Understanding

Question: Should someone who strives solely for an intellectual understanding of the meditative and doctrinal teachings and never engages in practice be disdained as no better than an ignorant person?

Answer: The monk Budai said, "If one has mastered both practice and doctrine, there is no need to keep the form of a monk."[276] Then there are those who take the tonsure yet neither practice nor study. Such as these cannot be called disciples of the Buddha—compared to them, monks who at least devote themselves to intellectual studies are admirable indeed. Still, if one becomes a disciple of the Buddha, Budai admonishes us, then become a *true* disciple of the Buddha.

Why is it that the doctrinal schools advocate scholarly understanding? It is to motivate people to practice in accordance with their understanding. What is the purpose of encouraging practice? It is to help people realize enlightenment. Is it a wise person who gains nothing from his encounter with the true Dharma (so rarely met with!), using his knowledge not as an aid to liberation but as a ticket to worldly fame and profit? If even those who enter the doctrinal schools are in error if they focus exclusively on scholarly learning, how much more so is this the case with followers of Zen.

BODHICITTA

Question: How does one arouse bodhicitta?[277]

Answer: Buddhism speaks of three levels of capacity: superior, medium, and inferior. Those of superior capacities are known as bodhisattvas. *Bodhisattva* is a Sanskrit word in which *bodhi* means "enlightenment" or "Way," and *sattva* means "sentient being." Although distinctions exist between householders and world-renouncers, basically everyone who seeks the Buddha Way for the sake of all beings is a bodhisattva.

The Buddhist teachings discuss various kinds of bodhicitta, but there are two fundamental types: ordinary bodhicitta and true bodhicitta. Ordinary bodhicitta is the mind which, realizing that everything alive must eventually die and that all that prospers must eventually decline, abandons fame and profit and retreats from the world. Nāgārjuna said, "To recognize the impermanence of the world is known, provisionally, as bodhicitta."[278] Since it is from the shallow that one enters the deep, one who has not aroused ordinary bodhicitta cannot arouse true bodhicitta. This is why masters of the Zen school, even as they point directly to Original Nature, always stress to their students the transient nature of existence.

However, if one merely spurns secular ambition out of fear of impermanence and never gives rise to the true mind of the Way, then one is still being foolish. In the days of old, Xu Yu, hearing that Emperor Tang Yao wished to hand over the throne to him, washed out his ears in the River Ying, and Chao Fu led his ox home so it would not drink of the water in which Xu had washed his ears.[279] This may seem an admirable example of detachment from secular power as well as from ordinary wealth and fame, but Xu and Chao are still only sages in the ordinary sense, lacking the true mind of the Way. Generally people think that the mind of the Way involves renouncing worldly ambitions, making a hut for oneself in the mountains, and purifying one's mind with the sound of waterfalls or wind in the pines. This way of thinking is similar to that of Xu and Chao and cannot be called the true mind of the Way. The *All Dharmas Are without Actions Sutra* says that if one dwelling in the quiet solitude of the forests and mountains thinks of himself as superior to ordinary people he will not attain even a heavenly rebirth, much less Buddhahood.[280]

The true mind of the Way is the awakening of the mind that has faith in Supreme Enlightenment. Supreme Enlightenment is what is called *anuttara-samyaksaṃbodhi* in the sutras. *Anuttara* means "supreme." *Samyaksaṃbodhi* means the true, perfect enlightenment of the buddhas. Since *bodhi* can also be translated as "Way," the term rendered as "Supreme Way" in the sutras refers to *anuttara-bodhi*. This Supreme Enlightenment, perfect and complete, is inherent in everyone; there is not less of it in ignorant people nor more of it in sages, and it has remained unchanged throughout the ages. Faith in this is called the true mind of the Way.

A sutra says, "From the moment bodhisattvas first awaken the aspiration for the Way, they seek Supreme Enlightenment steadfastly and without faltering."[281] The sutra's position is that bodhisattvas, from the time they first awaken to the aspiration for the Way, seek Supreme Enlightenment without becoming distracted by fame or wealth or the views of either the Hinayana or the expedient Mahayana teachings. Be that as it may, if one has no more than a *belief* in innate Supreme Enlightenment and does not actually partake in it, then one cannot be said to have the true mind of the Way. This is what the *Nirvana Sutra* speaks of when it states that bodhicitta is impermanent and subject to birth and death, and it is not the eternal, indestructible Buddha-nature.[282]

However, when the *Avataṃsaka Sutra* says, "In anuttara-bodhi there is no regression in the past, no regression in the present, and no regression in the future,"[283] it refers to the innate bodhicitta possessed by everyone. In the Shingon school this is known as "pure bodhicitta." The *Mahāvairocana Sutra* says, "What is enlightenment? It is to know your own mind as it truly is."[284] A commentary on this sutra has the following exchange:

> "If the mind itself is enlightenment, why don't all sentient beings attain Buddhahood?"
>
> "It is because they don't know the mind as it truly is. If they knew mind as it truly is they would attain perfect awakening the moment they first aroused the aspiration for enlightenment."[285]

When people whose aspiration does not partake of innate bodhicitta abandon the things of the world and devote their days to practice, they take pride in the strength of their resolve and their capacity for training, and thus they invariably fall into the realm of the demons. Conversely, if their resolve weakens and they become distracted by worldly concerns, they are overcome by feelings of depression and as their end approaches they grow terrified of remaining caught in the round of birth and death. Hindered by their feelings of arrogance and fear, they increasingly obscure their innate bodhicitta.

If beginning practicers experience such feelings, they should know that these erroneous notions arise because they are not yet in accord with the Supreme Way but that they will without fail come into accord with it if they let everything go and directly investigate what *is*.[286] Then they will know for themselves that true bodhicitta neither arises nor fades away. In the *All Dharmas Are without Actions Sutra* it is written, "If one seeks enlightenment, there is no enlightenment in one.... If one sees enlightenment as something with form, that distances one from enlightenment."[287]

REDUCING WORLDLY PASSIONS

Question: When people of superior capacities directly awaken to Original Nature, then nothing in their surroundings can distract them. Even if they have not realized enlightenment they are not disturbed by outside conditions owing to the firmness of their aspiration for the Way. However, those of inferior capacities are not as firm in their aspiration. Even if they have faith in Buddhism they remain caught in worldly ambitions and influenced by circumstances both favorable and adverse, making it difficult for them to engage in single-minded *zazen*. Is there anything such people can do to reduce their worldly passions?

Answer: Those circumstances that suit our desires we regard as favorable; those that go against our desires we regard as adverse. We love the former and hate the latter. Through desire we invite birth; through aversion we receive death. Thus favorable and adverse circumstances together create the conditions for transmigration in the realm of birth and death. Ignorant people, not understanding this, reject that which opposes their wants and wish only for that which fulfills them.

The word *sahā*[288] is a Sanskrit term that can be interpreted to mean "lack" or "insufficiency," because people born into this sahā world, having meager stores of karmic virtue, are unable to fully satisfy any of their desires. Yet even so they continue searching for fulfillment, which is like seeking coolness in the midst of fire. If you want everything to proceed according to your wishes, you should find a way to emancipate yourself from this sahā world. Here in this world of insufficiency, the more you seek to satisfy your desires the more you suffer in body and mind, and the more evil karma you accumulate for the future.

There is an old poem that says, "Does anyone truly realize that passing one's life in happiness is not what this world is about?" If one understands the meaning of this verse, then the inability to find fulfillment in this world becomes in itself an excellent teaching, encouraging people toward emancipation. If people are not attached to satisfying their desires, then nothing will go against their desires. What causes suffering is not the external world but the flaws in one's own mind.

Once, when I was living in a small temple in the countryside, there was a quarrelsome monk among our community. One day he came to me and said in a repentant way, "This belligerence of mine is such a bad habit. How can I overcome it?"

I replied, "If you know the best way to fight, then the desire to fight will leave you. Let me teach you the best way to fight. Those who are skillful at warfare seek out the enemy general and pay no attention to the common soldiers, knowing that if the general is slain then the other soldiers will succumb. You should discern who the general is among the enemies arrayed against your mind.

"Even if other people strike and abuse you, that will never cause you to fall into hell. What will land you in hell is the anger that you nurse as a result of such attacks, anger that burns away all the merit you have accumulated from eons of good deeds. Thus the general who is harming you is not another person but your own mind. When the urge to quarrel arises, first look to that impulse and slay it."

Hearing this, the monk left with tears in his eyes. From that time on he became a much more gentle person.

In those days the small temple still had no bath, so the monks would bathe at a nearby temple belonging to one of the doctrinal schools. The dipper used to scoop hot water from the tub was made of a section of bamboo about five inches long, with the bamboo joint located right in the middle so that water could be ladled out using either end. It was made in this way to prevent people from ladling out too much water at one time. One of the monks in our temple would get annoyed every time he saw this dipper and would complain about the miserly spirit of the temple's priest.

Finally I said, "Originally there is no form of 'big' or 'small' in anything. Bodhisattvas who have left behind all deluded notions of 'big' and 'small' and have realized inconceivable emancipation are able to put Mount Sumeru inside a poppy seed without the poppy seed getting any bigger or Mount Sumeru getting any smaller. Vimalakīrti's room was a mere ten feet square, yet it was able to hold thirty-two thousand lion's seats that were each eighty-four thousand yojanas high.[289] If there were no notions of 'big' and 'small' in your mind, then you could scoop up the entire ocean in that bamboo dipper. Thus it is not the priest's spirit that is miserly, but yours. I myself haven't realized inconceivable emancipation and so the forms of 'big' and 'small' still remain, but because I accept and clearly discern this principle I don't get annoyed like you." The monk told me that after hearing my words he no longer felt irritated when he saw the dipper.

This is an issue that relates not only to the size of dippers, of course, but also to such matters as status, length of life, wealth, rank, social conditions, and interpersonal relations. All of these mundane matters, despite their variety, are nothing more than passing dreams and images floating up from the deluded mind. The time we spend selecting this and rejecting that from among these illusions would be far better employed letting go of the calculating mind that makes such discriminations. If one can let go, one will cease discrimination regarding not only status and health but also Pure Land versus defiled world and sage versus ignorant being. What is there to rejoice about; what is there to lament?

If one cannot let go, one should, when one notices one's mind becoming confused by the illusions of the world, repeatedly think to oneself, "No matter how high one's birth, how long one's life, how vast one's wealth, how exalted one's rank, how few one's enemies, or how peaceful one's nation, the rewards of the human world cannot equal those of the celestial realms. And even if they could it still would not be enough, since we do not live forever. Conversely, a person humble in birth and rank and living in a lawless land should not lament, bearing in mind that the human state, regardless of its circumstances, is still preferable to that of the four evil paths.[290] This is all the more so when one has the great good fortune to encounter the Buddhadharma. Why would one bother with the trivial gains of the world?"

Teachings that make this point are presented in the form of various parables used not only by the doctrinal schools but also by the founding masters of the Zen school.

Bodhidharma identified two types of people who attain the Buddhadharma: those who enter by principle and those who enter by practice. People who enter by principle are those who go directly to Original Nature without relying on training. People who enter by practice are those who, hearing of Original Nature, believe in it and grasp its import, but, having no inner realization of it, practice various indeterminate upāya in order to bring about this realization. Bodhidharma explained four practices for this: the first is to accept injury, the second is to accord with conditions, the third is to seek nothing, and the fourth is to accord with the Dharma.

Among the many and varied people in the world are some who hinder and harm us. Animals and demons too sometimes cause us serious harm. Among the eight types of human suffering,[291] this is known as "the suffering of encountering beings one dislikes." Such suffering is all retribution for the suffering one has caused to these beings in previous existences. Similarly, being afflicted with the sufferings of poverty and illness is retribution for stinginess, avarice, and unethical conduct. If you think of suffering in this way, it will cause you neither anger nor sorrow. To reside peacefully in this outlook is the practice of accepting injury.

Or again, you may be happy, possessing a greater degree of rank, wealth, fame, and talent than other people. These, however, are simply your rewards for cultivating samsaric merit-roots in previous existences. One should recognize that one does not possess these things forever and not become proud of or attached to them. This is the practice of according with conditions.

As Dharma gates these two practices are not particularly profound, but their underlying principles can be understood by anyone. They are therefore helpful for those followers of the "teaching outside of the teachings" who, having shallow reserves of merit, become confused and forget the Buddhadharma when they encounter either excessively adverse or excessively fortunate circumstances. Although deep in their minds they retain their connection with the Dharma, they lack the capacity to deepen their practice under challenging conditions. But if they keep these two principles in mind and remain undisturbed while facing circumstances both fortunate and adverse, their practice will naturally mature. For this reason these two practices were the first ones to be mentioned by Bodhidharma.

"Accepting injury" and "according with conditions" are not the same as the Taoist sage Zhuangzi's practice of keeping the mind motionless during pleasure and pain, which Zhuangzi defines as the Way of Nondoing. Rather, they are teachings similar to those expounded by many masters of the Zen school. The recent Zen master Zhongfeng[292] of Mount Tianmu, for example, warns in his *Admonitions* primarily against the distortions of worldly attachment. And yet there are those of limited understanding who slight this as a non-Buddhist or Hinayana teaching, saying it is not a teaching of Bodhidharma's tradition.

Unlike the doctrinal schools, however, the Zen school does not differentiate between shallow and profound levels of teaching and preach according to the capabilities of the student. Sometimes it speaks of mundane principles, sometimes of supramundane truths. It adheres to no fixed paths—its methods are simply expedients to help people, releasing what is stuck and freeing what is bound.

An ancient said, "If it is understood, then you can employ it skillfully on the Way; if it is not understood, it becomes ordinary mundane truth."[293] That is, one can reveal the abstruse principles of transcendence, but if the student does not comprehend them they become no more than worldly teachings. Conversely, if people listening to worldly teachings thereby escape their attachments and fetters and directly realize Original Nature, then these worldly teachings become profound gates to the Dharma.

Even if a person encountering favorable or adverse circumstances remains undisturbed in spirit, should he abide in that state without clarifying the Original Nature then he will attain no more than rebirth in the northern continent of Uttarakuru.[294] Those who attain the fruit of arhatship have forever cut off the three poisons of greed, aversion, and ignorance and have transcended the three realms, but they have not attained the true principle of the Mahayana. Thus the *Sutra of Complete Enlightenment* states, "To stir up thinking is delusion; to stop thinking is also delusion."[295] Nevertheless, you shouldn't be averse to first understanding commonplace truths and moderating worldly feelings, and then practicing the Buddhadharma.

Even if you have calmed the worldly desires and are single-mindedly practicing the Buddhadharma, if you retain the desire to gain enlightenment, Buddhahood, supernatural powers, or eloquence you will never realize Original Nature. Therefore Bodhidharma established the third practice, that of nonseeking. The *Diamond Sutra* is making this point when it says, "Throw away the Dharma, to say nothing of that which is not Dharma."[296]

This does not mean, however, that Zen practicers should regard nonseeking as the ultimate. Seeking nothing, you encounter the source everywhere; you are troubled by neither circumstances nor surroundings, nor do celestial demons or nonbelievers hinder you. Arriving at this stage, there is no separation between awake and asleep, between remembering and forgetting. Seeing, hearing, and perceiving are all one and the same. Thus Bodhidharma established the fourth practice, that of practicing in accordance with the Dharma.[297] Even this, however, is still a stage of attainment and mustn't be regarded as the realm of Great Repose.

Question: As long as our worldly feelings of joy and anger or love and hatred are not yet extinguished, would we not be best off endeavoring to subjugate them and only when they are gone beginning our practice toward the realization of Original Nature?

Answer: Having had the good fortune to obtain birth in the human world and encounter the Buddhadharma, so rarely met with, if you do not awaken to the Original Nature in this life, in what life do you expect to do so? We cannot be certain of remaining alive from one breath to the next. Those uninterested in turning their minds to secular affairs for even a moment will have little difficulty maintaining their practice even if worldly feelings happen to draw them. Should mundane feelings arise upon encountering certain circumstances, such people's awareness of the place from which these feelings of attachment and aversion emerge is so powerful that those very thoughts contribute greatly to their practice. However, the moderation of worldly feelings using more ordinary methods is recommended for those whose aspiration is not yet strong enough to prevent them from becoming distracted when confronted by challenging circumstances, and who consequently forget to maintain their practice.

In any event, it is not necessary to eliminate worldly feelings before beginning practice toward the realization of Original Nature. Those who have realized the fruit of arhatship do not have thoughts of aversion or attachment regardless of what circumstances they find themselves in, but such people cannot be said to have truly realized the Dharma. Ordinary people pressed by the passions who enter enlightenment even though their feelings of joy and anger are not yet extinguished—such people have truly realized the Dharma. Thus it cannot be said that one must first eliminate worldly feelings and only then attain enlightenment. Even as one remembers to lessen deluded feelings when they arise, one must not neglect practice toward the realization of Original Nature.

It is said that those with a profound aspiration for enlightenment forget to eat and sleep. Although such people feel hunger and fatigue, they maintain their practice while eating and sleeping and are thus not hindered by these activities. However, people who lack this level of aspiration will become exhausted and ill if they go without food or sleep. Since this is a hindrance to their practice, they are encouraged to take something to ease their hunger and to lay out their bedding to rest. This is not to say, however, that they should set aside their practice while eating and sleeping.

The ancient masters taught that when walking, be fully aware of walking; when sitting, be fully aware of sitting; when lying down, be fully aware of lying down; when seeing or hearing, be fully aware of seeing or hearing; when perceiving, be fully aware of perceiving; when happy, be fully aware of the happiness; and when angry, be fully aware of the anger. This is the strict yet kind and careful advice of the ancients. Practice in this way, and you will attain enlightenment without fail.

TO SEE THINGS AS ILLUSION
IS NOT THE ULTIMATE

Question: Many of the Mahayana sutras preach the Dharma gate of regarding all phenomena as illusions or dreams. The Zen masters, too, speak of this approach. Should, therefore, meditation on the illusory nature of things be a fundamental practice of Mahayana students?

Answer: When the respective Buddhist schools teach that all phenomena are like dreams and illusions, their words are similar but they mean different things. Nevertheless, the general import is the same.

The popular expression "life is like a dream" points to the transient nature of all existence. Mahayana Buddhism, however, intends something else in its parables that refer to dreams and illusions. It says that the various phenomena that appear in dreams are all utterly without substance, yet they are clearly and distinctly *there*. They resemble the shapes a conjurer creates with his large handkerchief, which takes on various forms like people or horses and yet is not really any of these. This is what Mahayana Buddhism means when it likens phenomena to illusions (the sutras use the example of a conjurer and his cloth since such performers are common in India). In other words, though the ten thousand things have no substance, their forms are clearly manifest. The similes of the moon in the water and reflections in a mirror point to the same thing. The doctrinal schools have teachings that speak of "mysterious illusion,"[298] which is different in meaning from the doctrine that "all things arising through causality are illusory."

Practicers of the Buddhadharma are apt to fall into the views of the non-Buddhists and the Two Vehicles. Although the doctrines espoused by non-Buddhists are diverse, they basically comprise the two categories of annihilationism and eternalism. Annihilationism posits nonbeing; eternalism posits being.[299] This implies a total of four possible views: the view of being (eternalism), the view of nonbeing (annihilationism), the view of both being and nonbeing, and the view of neither being nor nonbeing.

The teachings spoken of by Mayahana practicers today may resemble those of true Mahayana Buddhism, but when their positions are examined some are found to fall within these four non-Buddhist views. Although the sermons of the Buddha may also be seen to fall within these four views, the Buddha's true wisdom transcends them. That is, in order to eradicate the view of being the Buddha preaches the emptiness of all things; in order to eradicate the view of nonbeing he preaches the immutability of all things; and so forth. Those who do not know the true intention of the Buddha, however, regard these expedient teachings as the truth.

Although the Two Vehicles—the śrāvakas and the pratyeka-buddhas—practice somewhat dissimilar teachings, both aspire to escape transmigration in the three realms by extinguishing body and mind and returning to unconditioned nirvana. Such a view is directly opposed to the Dharma principles of Mahayana, and if one truly understands the teaching that all phenomena are illusory then one will naturally avoid falling into such non-Buddhist and non-Mahayana views. A person with such understanding knows that one can speak of the immutability of things without holding to substantialism and that one can speak of the emptiness of things without holding to nihilism.

Thus viewing all phenomena as illusory is an aid to realizing the ultimate reality of the Middle Way.[300] For that reason it is called the first gate to the Mahayana; it is not considered a teaching of the absolute truth, but it is provisionally recommended in the doctrinal schools as a means of eradicating the substantialist and nihilist views of ordinary people and non-Buddhists, and of eliminating the Two Vehicles' attachment to emptiness. The "Types of Mind" chapter of the *Mahāvairocana Sutra* focuses its teachings on the phantasmal nature of all things that arise through causality,[301] while the *Sutra of Complete Enlightenment* and the *Laṅkāvatāra Sutra* urge one to drop even this understanding.[302]

That which is called *samāpatti* in the "three methods of contemplation" is a form of contemplation on illusion. That is, one provisionally arouses the image of "wisdom" and extinguishes the image of "ignorance" in order to ascend to the crystal palace of fundamental purity.[303]

Zen leaves such expedients to the doctrinal schools, and practicers of Zen should not use contemplations of this type. The reason that masters of the Zen school speak of the illusory nature of phenomena is not so that practicers will hold this concept in mind and use it as an object of meditation. Rather, they hope that by knowing the spectral nature of both Buddhadharma and worldly affairs learners will be encouraged to drop everything and focus on the direct realization of Original Nature. As the Third Patriarch Sengcan wrote in the poem *On Believing in Mind*, "A dream, an illusion, a flower in the sky—how could they be worth grasping? Gain and loss, right and wrong—discard them all at once."[304]

Question: Is it mistaken to regard phenomena as illusory when facing the various circumstances of life, even while knowing such thoughts to be useless?

Answer: The Zen practice of "dropping everything" is not the same as the non-Buddhist and Two-Vehicle practice of suppressing all evil thoughts and not allowing them to arise. The latter practice is like trying to use blood to wash off blood. Someone who suffers from an eye disease may look up and see various flowery forms appearing and disappearing in the sky. If the person doesn't recognize this as an effect of the disease he will regard these forms as real. He may therefore become annoyed by them or, conversely, find their presence pleasing. When his eye problem disappears so too will these floating forms. What, then, was there to get annoyed by or attached to?

The practice of the Way is similar to this. The disease of ignorance obstructs our mind's eye, causing us to perceive spiritual matters and worldly matters, good thoughts and bad thoughts, and all sorts of other flowery forms overlying the true emptiness of Original Nature. If we clearly understand this fact, we can remain the master, calm and unmoved, even when thoughts of good and evil well up owing to the still unhealed defects in our way of perceiving things. Like mirrors reflecting forms, our minds need exert no effort. Applying our minds in this way is what is known as Mahayana practice. An ancient master said, "Entertain no thoughts of good or evil." Also, "Advance directly toward Supreme Enlightenment, and don't concern yourself with right and wrong." Also, "There is nothing to practice. Simply let go—that is enough."[305]

DETACHMENT
IS NOT ENLIGHTENMENT

Question: If you let go of everything and hold no thoughts in your mind of either the Buddhadharma or the affairs of the world, would this be called the Ground of Original Nature?

Answer: Bodhidharma said, "Outside, cut off relations with all things; inside, have no concerns. Make your mind like a wall, and you will certainly attain the Way."[306] Dahui Zonggao commented, "This suggests that dropping all relations and remaining motionless on the inside are the means of entering the Way. If you regard this as the way of truth, then you go against Bodhidharma's true intention."[307]

JUDGING RIGHT AND WRONG

Question: The old masters say that a true practicer of the Way does not speak of the rights and wrongs of others. Although I agree with this, such judgments nevertheless arise during my dealings with both lay and ordained people. How should I deal with this?

Answer: Saying that true practicers of the Way do not speak of the rights and wrongs of others does not mean that they simply don't speak of such things even though they are in fact thinking about them. Rather, a true practicer of the Way sees no difference between self and other, and thus perceives no rights and wrongs about which to speak. Sengcan, the Third Patriarch, said, "In the Dharma-realm of Thusness there is no self and other."[308] A sutra says, "Dharma-nature is like the vast ocean and cannot be said to have right and wrong."[309] If we have not realized this truth, then notions of self and other remain. If the notions of self and other remain, how can we avoid perceiving right and wrong? As long as we perceive right and wrong we are not true practicers of the Way, even if we do not give voice to our judgments. Rather than attempting to avoid speaking of the faults of others, students of the Mahayana should thoroughly examine themselves and ask *who* it is that speaks of other people.

The *Sutra of Complete Enlightenment* says, "They take the four great elements to be the attributes of their bodies and the impressions of the six sense objects as the attributes of their minds."[310] The meaning of this passage is that what the ordinary person regards as self is not the true self. If one's concept of self is incorrect, then so too is one's concept of other. If one's views of both self and other are not true, how can one speak of right and wrong?

There are those regarded as Way practicers who say nothing about the faults of other people, but who in their hearts see them as good or evil, rate them as intelligent or foolish, judge how much or how little understanding they have, or evaluate the direction of their training. The direct attainment of Supreme Enlightenment is impossible for such individuals. That is why I urge you to never concern yourself with views of right and wrong. But even if you drop all views of right and wrong and do not distinguish between self and other, if you still haven't seen your Original Face before your parents were born you cannot be called a true follower of the Way. You must turn your light inward and illuminate your own mind: Who is it that distinguishes between self and other and gives rise to thoughts of right and wrong, gain and loss?

Centuries ago, when Nanyue[311] first called upon the Sixth Patriarch, the Patriarch asked him, "*Who* is it that has come here?" Nanyue withdrew, unable to answer. Eight years later he had a deep understanding. He called upon the Sixth Patriarch again and answered his question, saying, "If you explain it, you miss the mark."[312] For the first time he received the Sixth Patriarch's confirmation. Nanyue's failure to understand when he was questioned at the time of their first meeting might be attributed to a certain dullness, but actually it was because of his unusual aptitude that he was bewildered by the Sixth Patriarch's question and had to withdraw. Had it not been this way, he would not have attained enlightenment even in a thousand lifetimes.

Nowadays when people of inferior capabilities come to inquire about the Buddhadharma, I ask them who it is that is inquiring. Some are dumbfounded and reply out of their usual deluded thinking that they are so-and-so, giving their names. Others think they should inquire into who it is that asked the question, while still others, recalling the saying that one's own mind is buddha, produce all sorts of responses like raising their eyebrows, blinking their eyes, raising an arm, or thrusting out a fist. There are also those who hold to the concept that the mind is without substance and separate from all form; modeling their response on Nanyue's "Explain it, and you miss the mark," they answer, "Above, nothing to seek; below, nothing to let go of!"[313] Some, figuring that anything involving questions and answers is bound to be superficial, give out a great shout. Others shake their sleeves and walk out, believing it is the teaching of Zen not to get involved in such discussions. The likes of these will never attain enlightenment even when Maitreya appears in the world.[314]

Zen Master Baizhang, after each of his formal sermons, would call out to the monks of the assembly. When the monks looked toward him, he would ask, "What is *that*?" This question, known at the time as "Baizhang's sermon-closing words,"[315] was intended neither to teach the essentials of practice nor to test the monks' understanding. What *did* Baizhang intend, then? If you understand this straightaway, ignorance that has persisted from the eternal past will vanish in an instant.

Long ago there was a monk named Eminent Scholar Liang.[316] He was thoroughly versed in the sutras and commentaries and was deeply conversant with the doctrines, and he had gathered around himself students to whom he had taught the Dharma for many years. One day he called upon Zen Master Mazu Daoyi,[317] and the two engaged in various questions and answers. Finally Liang, unable to agree with Mazu, got up to leave. As he was going Mazu called out, "Eminent Scholar!" When Liang looked at him, Mazu asked, "What is *that*?" Liang suddenly experienced a great awakening.[318]

Although he had long since mastered the teachings of the sutras and commentaries, Liang had yet to experience enlightenment. Why did he suddenly attain a great awakening at Mazu's single phrase, "What is *that*?" You must realize that that which Liang awakened to is not found in the teachings of the sutras and commentaries. Those who devote their entire lives to intellectual understanding would more profitably have spent their time directly observing the arising and passing of thoughts, whether walking, standing, sitting, or reclining. Practicing in this way, how could anyone fail to experience enlightenment, like Nanyue or Scholar Liang? How unfortunate to spend all of one's time in intellectual pursuits. How much worse, though, are those who squander their lives speaking of right and wrong and chasing after worldly fame and profit? Are they worthy of having received a precious human birth?

THE EFFECTS OF PRACTICE

Question: There are people who lose heart because they have had faith in Zen and practiced its teachings for many years yet have seen no results. Others would not begrudge the practice if they were certain it would lead to enlightenment before they died, but they fear that the end result may be nothing more than a lifetime of exerting themselves in body and mind, with no liberation in the next life either. Is there any basis for such thinking?

Answer: When such people say they have experienced no results even after long years of practicing Zen, what sort of results do they mean? Some people rush about the world seeking fame or coveting wealth. Some pray to the gods and buddhas in order to escape disaster and invite good fortune. Some study the Buddhist scriptures and Chinese classics in the hope of acquiring wisdom. Some engage in esoteric practices in order to acquire supernatural powers. Some practice the arts and other skills in order to become more accomplished than others. Some try various therapies in order to cure disease. In activities such as these one can speak of results or no results.

Zen practice, however, is qualitatively different. Where would one look for results? An ancient master said, "It is present in all people and complete in everyone. There is not less of it in ignorant people nor more in sages."[319] Another ancient master said, "The Way is complete like the great void, without deficiency, without excess."[320] To think we have obtained results from practicing the Buddhadharma is like thinking there is excess in the void; to think we have obtained no results is like thinking there is deficiency in the void. If there were truly some excess or lack, the words of the buddhas and patriarchs that "there is not less of it in ignorant people nor more in sages" would be untrue.

Then there are those who give up on the practice before they even start, on the assumption that any practice they might do is wasted if it doesn't lead to enlightenment. Such people are the most foolish of all. If you entertain such worries what can you ever hope to accomplish, either in Buddhism or in worldly endeavors? After all, are there not people who, no matter how difficult the task, think through every possibility and exert every effort in an attempt to achieve success? People who quit before even giving Buddhist practice a try are those whose karmic burden has weakened their aspiration for the Buddhadharma.

If worry about whether practice will ever lead to awakening causes you to avoid it for your entire life, what will you do in your next existence? Do you think that if you fail to awaken through your own efforts you can hire someone to have enlightenment for you? If another person's practice could bring about awakening, do you think that the buddhas and bodhisattvas of the myriad universes would have allowed sentient beings to continue wandering in the realms of delusion?

The True Meaning of Zazen

Question: The ancient masters teach us that *zazen* is of no benefit if one is unclear in applying the mind. Thus some people claim that it is useless for ignorant people to sit in meditation. Is there anything to what they say?

Answer: The reason the masters spoke in this way is to correct the efforts of those who aspire to awaken to the One Great Matter[321] but never seek out an able teacher, sitting instead in an absent-minded manner and believing that this is *zazen*. They were not saying that ignorant people gain nothing from *zazen*. What would it profit a person to avoid meditation and spend his life in ignorance on the grounds that "*zazen* is of no benefit if one is unclear in applying the mind"? Entering the Buddhadharma is not a matter of a single lifetime's practice.[322] Those born with the superior capacities that allow them to realize sudden enlightenment are those who in previous lives have persevered in the practice of *zazen* even though they were unclear about it. Those who in this life continue in their meditation despite a lack of clarity will in subsequent lives be people who "gain a thousand insights at a single word."

Other people say that *zazen* is a difficult practice beyond the reach of ordinary people, and that it is therefore more appropriate for such people to engage in easier, more relative practices such as reading sutras, reciting dhāraṇīs, and chanting *nenbutsu*. The sutras tell us, however, that if one's aspiration is wrong then all practices are in vain.[323] Relative and absolute practices may differ, but any practice, if done for the wrong reasons, will produce nothing more than karmic causes for rebirth in the three realms of existence. Conversely, a person with the right aspiration in following the Mahayana can engage in any practice without error. Nevertheless, it would be a mistake to assume that the practice of *zazen* is something unusual, and that therefore it would be better to start with more relative practices. To say that *zazen* is an unusual practice reveals a misunderstanding of its inner meaning.

Zazen is not peculiar to the Zen school. It is taught in all of the exoteric and esoteric schools as well as in the Hinayana and non-Buddhist traditions, although the way that *zazen* is understood in these various paths varies in some ways. *Zazen* in the non-Buddhist and Hinayana paths may differ with regard to whether it is defiled or undefiled in nature,[324] but it is the same in that the essence of the practice is to keep the body still and not give rise to thought. In the Pure Land school *zazen* consists of the sixteen contemplations;[325] this was the central practice of the Dharma master Huiyuan and others.[326] *Zazen* in the exoteric and esoteric schools takes various forms, but generally it involves contemplating the doctrinal principles of the respective schools. In any event, it is an error to assume that *zazen* is a practice limited to the Zen school, simply because it has disappeared in most other schools with the coming of the Age of the Latter Dharma.

Zazen in the Zen school is not about stilling the body and suppressing the mind, so one need not dismiss sitting toward the wall and letting go of thoughts as a difficult practice. *Zazen* does not involve contemplation of doctrinal principles, so one cannot claim to lack the intelligence for it. *Zazen* requires no wealth, so poverty is no hindrance to its practice. *Zazen* requires no physical strength, so even the weak can do it. The Buddhadharma does not conflict with the human passions, so one cannot say one is too worldly to practice it.

Devotions like offering incense and making prostrations are bodily practices, so they cannot be done when one is engaged in something else. Reading sutras, reciting dhāraṇīs, and chanting the *nenbutsu* are oral practices, so they cease when one is speaking of other things. The contemplation of doctrinal principles is an intellectual practice, so it cannot occur when one is occupied with other thoughts. However, Zen cultivation does not depend on the body, the mouth, or the intellect. How, then, can it be called difficult?

TRUE PRACTICE

Question: I can understand why you say that Zen cultivation depends on neither the body nor the mouth. But if it does not depend on the mind, why then do you speak of "applying the mind in practice"?

Answer: Saying that Zen cultivation does not depend on the body, the mouth, or the intellect does not mean that, like the non-Buddhist samādhi of no-thought or the Hinayana samādhi of extinction, it involves annihilation of the body and mind. What ordinary people regard as body and mind are illusory, like flowers in the sky. One should avoid believing that these illusions truly exist and, based on that belief, practicing devotions and austerities with the body, chanting sutras and dhāraṇīs with the mouth, and contemplating doctrines with the mind. This is what the prajñāpāramitā sutras attempt to convey when they teach that there is no eye, no ear, no nose, no tongue, no touch, and no mind.[327] Similarly, the *Great Collection Sutra* says, "Enlightenment cannot be attained by the body, nor can it be attained by the mind, because both body and mind are illusions."[328] The *Sutra on the Meditation to Behold the Buddhas* says, "Buddha cannot be attained through mind, nor can buddha be attained through matter." It also says that "it is not attained through the body, it is not attained through knowledge."[329]

Ordinarily people think that it is by means of the eye that they can see form; by virtue of the ear that they can hear sound; and by way of the mind that they can know the supramundane Dharma. Thus, they believe, if the eyes go blind they cannot see forms; if the ears go deaf they cannot hear sounds; and if the mind becomes senile they cannot conceive of the Dharma. It is because of a single thought of delusory attachment that there arise such distinctions between "see" and "not see," "hear" and "not hear," and "understand" and "not understand."

The *Śūraṅgama Sutra*, as evidence that perception can take place even without the six sense organs,[330] says:

> Aniruddha, after losing his eyesight, was able to see the three thousand worlds as though they were held in the palm of his hand. Upānanda, though deaf, could hear sounds. The Goddess of the Ganges, though lacking a nose, could smell scents. Gavāṃpati could taste flavors though his tongue was abnormal. Sunyatā, the God of the Void, could feel though he had no body. Mahākāśyapa had rooted out the six sense consciousnesses and yet had perfect understanding."[331]

People unfamiliar with these teachings are surprised to hear that true practice does not depend upon the activities of body, mouth, or mind.

THE STRIVING OF NONSTRIVING

Question: In the Mahayana teachings it is said that in a single moment of awareness one practices the contemplation of the three truths[332] and that in one's very body one performs the three mystic practices.[333] Since these practices all involve the body and the mind, are they therefore of no value?

Answer: Buddhism does not reject even Hinayana cultivation or covetous merit-accumulation through observance of the precepts, much less the profound practices of the Mahayana exoteric and esoteric schools. This does not mean, however, that there is no distinction between the various upāya used in Buddhism to guide sentient beings. Thus the methods employed by the Zen school differ from those of the doctrinal schools.

The Dharma gates of the doctrinal schools, based on the view that sentient beings and buddhas are separate, attempt to guide the former into the realm of the latter. The Dharma gates of the Zen school, however, seek to bring sentient beings directly to the Ground of Original Nature, prior to the separation of sentient beings and buddhas. Thus Zen does not involve itself with practices dependent on body, mouth, and intellect, nor does it recognize the contemplation of the three mysteries.

Sengcan, the Third Patriarch of Zen, said, "Using the mind to seek the mind—is this not a great error?"[334] An ancient worthy said, "Where there is no striving—there is where all buddhas strive!"[335]

THE ABSTRUSE TEACHING
OF THE ZEN SCHOOL

Question: If not striving is true striving, would you say that Zen practicers lack the mind that seeks the Way and idle their time away?

Answer: Would you call "practicers of the Way" those who dislike applying their minds to the Buddhadharma, or those who, indulging their worldly passions, pass their lives in vain? An ancient master said, "If you strive, you enter the path of the Two Vehicles; if you neglect to strive, you fall into the realm of ignorant beings."[336] This is the abstruse teaching of the Zen school.

Question: If the Zen school does not involve itself with contemplation of the three mysteries owing to its emphasis on "the Ground of Original Nature prior to the separation of sentient beings and buddhas," why is it that from ages past students of the Zen school have engaged in practicing *zazen*, and good teachers have been careful to explain the correct and incorrect ways of applying the mind in practice?

Answer: When one is writing a poem or composing a song, it is important first to understand the theme.[337] If the theme of the poem is the moon, for example, it doesn't help to think about flowers. One must take the same approach with Buddhism. The Original Nature of which Zen speaks is inherent in everyone and is perfect and complete in each individual; there is no less of it in ignorant people and no more of it in sages. If you take up Original Nature as your theme but then start thinking of yourself as a deluded person who must engage in practice for the purpose of attaining enlightenment, you are turning away from your theme. Just as a person seeking inspiration for a poem about the moon should not contemplate flowers, so those with their hearts set on Original Nature should not cling to the concept of themselves as deluded beings and seek enlightenment outside.

Therefore, as long as one has not clearly experienced that which is inherently complete in every individual, one should drop all misguided notions that maintain the usual distinction between delusion and enlightenment and between secular and sacred. Instead, one should investigate directly for oneself or under the guidance of a teacher. This is not the same as engaging in such practices as reciting the *nenbutsu* to achieve rebirth in the Pure Land, chanting dhāraṇīs to gain supernatural powers, or concentrating on the contemplations taught in the doctrinal schools in order to grasp the foundational principles. People who follow such practices have lost sight of the central theme, which is the realization of Original Nature.

Examining the ancient masters' paths to enlightenment, we see that in those early times even people unable to attain immediate awakening had such strong faith that they never asked how they might apply their minds so as to bring them into accord with Original Nature. They simply asked direct questions, such as, "What is Buddha?" "What is Zen?" "What is the true meaning of the Buddhadharma?" "Why did Bodhidharma come from the West?" "What is the place from which all buddhas arise?" The students' questions were direct, so the teachers' answers were also direct: "This very mind is buddha!" "The juniper tree in the garden!" "East Mountain walks on the water!" These answers were all direct pointers to Original Nature and were not intended as devices to be employed in training.

Nevertheless, students unable to understand these pointers would take up the "word-heads"[338] indicated by the masters and delve into these direct indications of Original Nature for one or two days, one or two months, or even five or ten years. Although this period of investigation can be referred to as training, it is not the same as the cultivation carried out by the doctrinal schools, in which stages of understanding, practice, and realization are established and various types of contemplation are performed.

This difference is why the Zen school calls itself "a separate transmission outside of the teachings." Forgetting this, people nowadays ask teachers how to apply their minds in training. Some teachers comply, in the belief that by guiding students in koan work they can bring them to a realization of Original Nature, much as *nenbutsu* might be chanted for the sake of rebirth in the Pure Land or dhāraṇīs recited in order to acquire supernatural powers. As a result students start discussing which attitudes toward training are best and passing judgments on the various utterances of teachers. This is nothing but superficial, worldly chatter.

DIRECT GUIDANCE

Question: There are two approaches to working on the koans: to do so with a deep sense of questioning, and to do so with no sense of questioning. Which of these approaches is correct?

Answer: The Zen masters' methods have no fixed paths—they are like sparks from a flint or flashes of lightning. Sometimes masters say to work on a koan with a deep sense of questioning, and sometimes they say to have *no* sense of questioning. All such advice springs forth spontaneously in the course of the master's direct dealings with the student; it is not something the master prepares in advance and remembers for future use. For that reason this sort of instruction is known as "face-to-face guidance."[339]

It is useless to chase after the masters' spontaneous teachings in an attempt to formulate them into fixed teachings. The guidance of a clear-eyed master, whether it be to doubt or not to doubt, will never hinder the student, whereas the guidance of a master who lacks the clear eye will invariably blind the student.

The Use of Koans

Question: Some masters say that beginning students must always start by working on koans. Others say that koan work is merely peripheral. Which of these two explanations is correct?

Answer: This is in essence the same as the discussion about "questioning" versus "not questioning." At one point a koan is given to a student to work on, at another point it is taken away and the student has to let go. Both approaches are simply techniques used by the teacher as appropriate, and not according to some established system. The ancient masters used to ask their students if they were one with their koan. If you are one with your koan, then there is nobody working on the koan and no koan being worked on. If you have reached that stage, how can there be any difference between using and not using koans?

In any event, Zen masters both assign koans and take them away as expedients to guide people who have yet to reach the stage of oneness. Such functioning is not to be judged on the basis of ordinary feelings. If a person lacking the clear eye comes up with interpretations of the ancient masters' words and transmits these to students in the form of set teachings, he commits a great error. This is what the ancients were criticizing when they spoke of "taking the true Dharma and binding people with it."[340]

MASTER ZHAOZHOU SAID "WU!"

Question: Many eminent Zen masters, including Dahui Zonggao, recommended the koan "Zhaozhou's *Wu*," and assigned it to students in its original form.[341] Recently, however, the Ming-dynasty master Zhongfeng Mingben has added words to the original koan, saying, "What was the reason that Zhaozhou said '*Wu*'?"[342] Why did he do this?

Answer: Students in former times were not shallow in their desire for the Way. Unconcerned with physical discomfort and prepared to travel any distance, they sought far and wide for good teachers. Zen masters, in their compassion, would utter a word or two to help them. These words were intended only as direct pointers to Original Nature—the meaning was not in the words themselves. Superior students were able to perceive this meaning apart from the actual statements. What need, then, was there to engage in further discussions regarding other words and phrases?

Even those slower students who got caught up in the master's utterances soon saw that the words were like iron spikes, impenetrable to ordinary thought. However, their aspiration for the Way being strong, their hearts were filled with deep questioning. Forgetting to eat and sleep, they pursued this questioning until, after one or two days, or after one or two months, or, in some cases, after ten or twenty years, they finally broke through. Although the time required depended upon their karmic propensities from previous lives, none of them failed to break through within the span of their lifetimes. This is what an ancient master meant when he said, "Where there is great doubt, there is great enlightenment."[343]

In this way, no one was ever told by the ancient masters to take their words and use them as koans to contemplate upon. Nor did the ancient masters ever advise anyone either to doubt or not to doubt what they said. However, people nowadays lack strong karmic propensities for practice and their aspiration for the Way is shallow. Hearing a master's words, they contrive intellectual interpretations and then quit Zen, convinced that they have already attained enlightenment. Others, too dull-witted to devise such explanations, simply lose interest. It is out of compassion for such people that Zen masters from the time of Yuanwu Keqin and Dahui Zonggao developed koan practice as an expedient means.

Nowadays the aspiration of students is so weak that their questioning shows no real energy. Some treat the ancient koans like set patterns or models, as though cultivation were a matter of passing one's days convincing oneself that one owns other people's possessions. Zhongfeng Mingben therefore attempted to spur such students into arousing the great doubt.

In the original "Zhaozhou's *Wu*" koan, a monk asked Zhaozhou Congshen, "Does a dog have Buddha-nature?" Zhaozhou answered, "*Wu!*" [No]. If the questioning monk grasped the unspoken meaning behind Zhaozhou's answer, then of course no question would have arisen in his mind. However, if he didn't understand he would naturally have wondered what the master meant. By inquiring deeply into Zhaozhou's response from the heart of his own inner questioning, the monk would certainly have experienced a great realization.

People nowadays, however, with their shallow aspiration, not only fail to grasp the master's meaning but also lack the inclination to question what it is. Thus they end up passing their lives in idleness.

Such people, although they have a causal connection with the Way insofar as they have entered the practice, cannot hope to directly experience enlightenment. For that reason Zhongfeng, in his grand-motherly kindness, encouraged the student to inquire into the reason *why* Zhaozhou replied *"Wu!"*

Some people might say that Zhongfeng spoke as he did because koans should be understood by giving rise to a spirit of questioning, and that, if so, this would contradict Dahui's teaching, "Do not apply thoughts and concepts to the mind-root."[344] Other people say it is inappropriate to add words to the koans of the ancient masters. Such critics do not understand Zhongfeng's intention.

CULTIVATION AND
WORLDLY ACTIVITIES

Question: It is said that some people practice in the midst of worldly activities and other people perform worldly activities in the midst of practice. What is the difference between the two?

Answer: The Japanese term signifying "practice" or "cultivation," *kufū*,[345] was originally an everyday word in China that meant something to the effect of "leisure." The concept of *kufū* as practice is one that applies to all activities. For farmers the growing of crops is *kufū*; for carpenters and plasterers the construction of buildings is *kufū*. Drawing on this secular meaning, the word came to indicate cultivation of the Buddhadharma for seekers of the Way.

People who cultivate Original Nature itself experience no separation between practicing in the midst of worldly activities and performing worldly activities in the midst of practice. For beginners, however, it is appropriate at first to recognize such a separation. Those who are still unsteady in their capacity to focus on the Way should follow a schedule in which they perform their worldly activities to the best of their ability and then practice *zazen* at set times during the day. This is why the present monastic custom of sitting four times a day was instituted about two hundred years ago. Prior to that Zen monks would meditate under trees, on top of rocks, or together in monasteries, practicing day and night for the sake of the One Great Matter with no thought given to food or sleep.

In this Latter Age of the Dharma, however, not everyone who enters the clergy does so for the sake of the Dharma. Some reluctantly don Buddhist robes on the command of their parents; others enter the temple in order to escape the hardships of worldly life. Even people like these, who enter the clergy unwillingly, do so because of beneficial karmic influences from former lives, and thus they're not completely averse to practicing *zazen*. Nevertheless, they lack a genuine aspiration for the Way, and therefore when eating meals or drinking tea their appetites distract them from the Buddhadharma, and when reading sutras or chanting dhāraṇīs their focus on these relative practices causes them to lose sight of Original Nature. Occupying themselves with such trifling matters, they can easily neglect their cultivation of the fundamental and pass their lives in vain.

The four daily sittings of *zazen* are an expedient established for people such as these. This does not mean, of course, that they should cease their cultivation outside of these four periods. People with a true aspiration for the Way need never waste their time; there are people who ceaselessly cultivate the fundamental regardless of what they are doing, whether eating, dressing, reading sutras, chanting dhāraṇīs, going to the toilet, washing up, greeting other monks, or speaking to guests. Those who can do this are said to "practice in the midst of worldly activities."

Although such people are superior to the aforementioned practicers who perform their worldly activities to the best of their ability and then practice *zazen* at set times during the day, they still differentiate between practice and worldly activities and are therefore anxious that they might be distracted by those activities and forget their cultivation. This is because they regard things as existing outside of the mind.

The ancient masters tell us, "The mountains, rivers, the great earth, and everything that exists are all oneself."[346] If you have made this truth your own, then no activities are outside of cultivation. You put on your clothes and eat your meals in cultivation; you walk, stand, sit, and lie down in cultivation; you see, hear, perceive, and know in cultivation; you experience joy, anger, affection, and pleasure in cultivation. Those who can do this are said to "perform worldly activities in the midst of practice." This is the practice of nonpractice, the striving of nonstriving. For those who can apply the mind in this way, remembering and forgetting are both cultivation and it makes no difference whether they are asleep or awake. An ancient master said, "The Way is found in pleasure and pain and adverse circumstances."[347] Another ancient master said, "The Way exists in all things."[348] Both statements are making this same point.

But even realization to this degree is still no more than a stage of realization, and doesn't yet attain to the true teaching of the patriarchs.

Question: If there is no difference between worldly activities and practice, why is it that masters of both the doctrinal and the Zen schools urge their students to set aside all activities and cut off relations with all things?

Answer: An ancient master said, "In the Buddhadharma there are no fixed forms. What is important is responding to circumstances."[349] None of the Dharma gates used by the masters to guide students have fixed forms. Since it is a universal principle of Mahayana Buddhism that no separation exists between the Buddhadharma and secular affairs, how could any master that supports the Mahayana—regardless of the differences between Zen and the doctrinal schools—say that Buddhist practice is to be found outside of worldly activities? However, those who have not yet understood this principle view the activities of the world in an illusory and inverted way. In their compassion, Zen masters encourage such people to set aside all worldly concerns as a temporary expedient to help them relinquish their attachments. Good masters teach in accordance with their listeners' capacities, so they do not bind themselves to predetermined patterns.

During the time of the Buddha there was a man named Devasarva. For five hundred lifetimes he had resided in the celestial realms, and in this lifetime he had been born into the luxury of the royal household of Śākyamuni's father, King Śuddhodana. When King Śuddhodana encouraged five hundred members of the Śākya clan to enter the Sangha,[350] Devasarva was one of those requested to do so. Owing to the lingering karmic influences of his many lifetimes in the celestial realms, Devasarva had a love of fine clothing and lavish residences.

When he heard Śākyamuni admonish the members of the Sangha not to adorn their clothing or habitations, Devasarva thought to himself, "I was born into a wealthy household and lived in a mansion decorated with gold and silver inlays. My clothes were embroidered with beautiful threads. Yet I wasn't satisfied even with that. How then can I wear coarse clothing and live in a rude dwelling? I should return home for a while, satisfy my desires, and then come back." He called upon the Buddha and informed him of his decision to leave.

The Buddha called his attendant Ānanda and told him to go to the royal palace, borrow a number of beautiful ornaments, decorate a room with them in a way that would please Devasarva, and have him spend the night there. Ānanda did as he was told, and Devasarva slept in the beautifully appointed room. That night, his ordinary desires having been fulfilled, Devasarva's unruly thoughts ceased of themselves and the clarity of wisdom immediately filled his mind. Toward the end of the night he realized arhatship and flew through the air.

Ānanda was puzzled, and asked the Buddha about this. The Buddha responded, "There are people whose aspiration for the Way grows through adorning their clothes and houses. For such people adornment is an aid to practice. There are other people whose aspiration for the Way diminishes when they adorn their clothes and houses. Such practicers must be cautious about ornamentation. Realization of the Way and its fruits is entirely a matter of the practicer's mind and has nothing to do with clothes or dwellings."[351] Thus people today, if they are like Devasarva, will not be hindered in their practice of the Way even if they have a taste for beauty in their homes and clothes. However, when people without the slightest desire to apply their minds to the Buddhadharma use examples like that of Devasarva to claim that their love of finery and riches does not constitute a hindrance to the Way, this is the work of the celestial demons.

From ancient times many people have enjoyed designing landscape gardens, piling up earthen mounds, arranging rocks, planting trees, and directing flows of water. Although the resulting gardens resemble each other in appearance, the spirit behind them is often quite different. Some people have little personal interest in gardens but have them made as decorations so that visitors will admire the beauty of their residences. Other people, whose love of landscape gardens is part of the same craving for material things that drives them to collect the rare treasures of the world, seek out strangely shaped rocks and unusual trees to place in their gardens. Such people have no appreciation for the gentle refinement of the garden; what they love are worldly things.

Bai Letian[352] dug a small pond and planted bamboo around the edge to create a garden he was very fond of. In a poem he wrote:

> Bamboo is my friend
> because its heart is open.
> Water is my teacher
> because its nature is pure.

Those in the world who love landscape gardens and share the feelings of Bai Letian are truly free of worldly things.

There are also people who by nature are modest and unaffected, and have little interest in the secular. Such people find nourishment for their souls in the recitation of poetry and the appreciation of beautiful scenery. This is the sort of person that the expression "the chronic disease of beautiful scenery, the incurable illness of lovely views"[353] is referring to. One might call them secular people of refined taste. But if such people are lacking in the spirit of the Way, even such refined qualities become the basis for future rebirths in the samsaric realm.

Still others use landscape gardens to ward off sleepiness and boredom as an aid in their practice of the Way. This is something truly noble and is not at all the same as the delight ordinary people take in gardens. However, since such people still make a distinction between gardens and the practice of the Way, they cannot be called true Way-followers.

Then there are those who regard mountains, rivers, grass, trees, tiles, and stones to be their own Original Nature. Their love for gardens may resemble worldly affection, but they employ that affection in their aspiration for the Way, using as part of their practice the changing scenery of the grasses and trees throughout the four seasons. One who can do this is truly an exemplar of how a follower of the Way should consider a garden.

Therefore it cannot be said that a love of gardens is necessarily a bad thing, or necessarily a good thing. In gardens themselves there is no gain or loss—such judgments occur only in the human mind.

The Chinese have always loved tea for its healthful effects in promoting the digestion and clearing the mind, although the medical texts warn against drinking too much—just as medicines are harmful if the prescribed dosage is exceeded, so tea can have ill effects if taken in excess.

Long ago in China, people like Lu Tong[354] and Lu Yu[355] esteemed tea as a way to dispel sleepiness and melancholy and thereby facilitate study. In Japan the same effects of tea were valued by people like the Saint of Toga no O[356] and the founder of Kennin-ji[357] as aids in the practice of the Way. However, the often excessive indulgence in tea that one sees nowadays cannot be good for the health, much less for study and practice. It simply increases worldly expenses and sows seeds for the decline of Buddhism. In this way, whether a love of tea does harm or good is entirely dependent upon the attitude of the individual.

This is not simply a matter of *sansui* gardens or tea drinking; it applies equally to such arts as poetry and music. The various forms of poetry and music all have their distinctive qualities, but they share the purpose of bringing harmony and refinement to the coarse human mind. However, the present fashion of performing the arts as public entertainment fosters ego attachments, and consequently it has the opposite effect of diminishing refinement and increasing coarseness. It is for reasons like this that teachers of the doctrinal and Zen schools sometimes tell their students that worldly activities are not separate from practice and sometimes tell them that they should set aside all such activities when they practice. There is nothing to be surprised about in this.

58

Question: An ancient master said, "There is nothing to practice. Simply let go—that is enough."[358] Another said, "Do not think of good or evil."[359] Yet another said, "Gain and loss, right and wrong—discard them all at once."[360] If it is as they say, then Zen practice would consist of ridding oneself of all understanding. This would be the same as the "sudden teachings" of the Kegon school, which rejects all names and forms and stresses the purity of intrinsic nature. It also resembles the Sanron school's teachings on "fundamental emptiness" and "the single reality of śūnyatā beyond all phenomena."[361] And what would be the difference between the Zen teaching and the esoteric teaching to purge the deluded passions?

Answer: Although the words of the other traditions are similar to those of Zen, the meaning is not the same. First, it is a great error to suppose that what Zen understands as training consists of eliminating all views and conceptions. An ancient master said, "It cannot be sought through thought, it cannot be gained through no-thought. It cannot be reached through words, it cannot be penetrated through silence." He also said, "Thought and no-thought, words and silence—all are Buddhadharma."[362]

The master's two statements are poles apart; which of them is true?

Both statements are simply expedients and should not be taken literally. Thus the Zen teaching to "let everything go" does not mean what the doctrinal schools do by "purging defilements" and "cutting off deluded passions." Although Zen distinguishes true from false, this differs from the teachings established by the Hossō school. The esoteric tradition teaches that "all things, just as they are, are the Way" and "ordinary phenomena are identical to absolute reality," but these concepts do not represent the realization of ultimate truth. This cannot be grasped through reason but is only truly known after enlightenment. If one claims that the teachings of the Zen and doctrinal schools are the same on the basis of the similarity of their words, why limit the comparison to Zen and the doctrinal schools alone? Confucianism, Taoism, and even ordinary secular literature contain statements that are much the same.

There are followers of Zen who regard it as the standpoint of their school to base all understanding upon the words of the ancients, to make no use of reason, to disregard all distinctions in rank, and to retain no traces in their minds of either the Buddhadharma or secular reality. The ancient masters ridiculed this way of thinking, dismissing it as "spade Zen." Since the spade is a tool used to dig things up and throw them away, it was used to symbolize the position that Zen involves discarding all understanding.

59

ORIGINAL NATURE AND SUPERNATURAL POWERS

Question: Do those who have attained to the Dharma always manifest supernatural powers and marvelous activities?

Answer: Attainment of the Dharma is not necessarily related to the possession of supernatural abilities, since even celestial demons and nonbelievers who know nothing of Buddhism can display such abilities. Even among Buddhists, those who have realized arhatship and thus possess the three knowledges and six powers[363] cannot be said to have fully attained to the Dharma since they have yet to awaken to the doctrinal principles of the Mahayana. Bodhisattvas advance in the mysterious function of the supernatural powers as they progress through the Three Worthy States and the Ten Holy Stages, but they too have not fully attained to the Dharma.

What are generally referred to as the six supernatural powers are: (1) the "divine eye" power to clearly see anything, even beyond distant mountains and rivers, (2) the "divine ear" power to hear any sound, even beyond distant mountains and rivers, (3) the "other mind" power to know the thoughts of other people, (4) the "past life" power to know one's own and other people's previous existences, (5) the "divine realm" power to freely go or fly anywhere, and (6) the "defilement-ending" power to eradicate the deluding passions.

These powers vary somewhat according to who possesses them. Demon kings and nonbelievers, for example, only attain the first five powers and never the sixth, the "defilement-ending" power. As a result they are unable to escape the world of samsara and eventually lose their supernatural abilities. The arhats, although they do possess the sixth power since they have extinguished the defiling passions of the three realms, have not truly liberated themselves from delusion since they have yet to completely sever the root of ignorance. The same can be said of bodhisattvas of the Three Worthy States and the Ten Holy Stages.

An ancient master said, "Even if you have attained the six supernatural powers, know that there is one further power."[364] This "one further power" is inherent to both ordinary people and sages and is not weaker in one and stronger in the other nor inferior in one and superior in the other. All supernatural powers and marvelous activities, as well as all perception, all knowledge, and all physical action, are dependent upon this "one further power." Ordinary people, however, not realizing that they employ this power all day long, search for mundane abilities outside. Layman Pang's statement "Supernatural power and marvelous activity—these are drawing water and carrying wood"[365] reflects the function of this "one further power" in every bodily activity.[366]

The ancient masters told us that each and every one of us possesses a spiritual light. The *Sutra of Complete Enlightenment* is referring to this inherent spiritual light when it speaks of the "Samādhi of the Treasury of Great Light."[367] The three types of light that emanate from a buddha—bodily light, wisdom light, and supernatural light[368]—all originate in this Treasury of Great Light. And it is the functioning of this Great Light that gives ordinary people the ability to distinguish east from west and black from white.

Not recognizing their inherent light, however, deluded people search outside for illumination in the secular world. If one has not awakened to this inherent spiritual light, then even infinite bodily light is no more than a firefly's glow. Celestial beings, luminous though they are, eventually fall into the dark paths, while arhats of the highest attainment and bodhisattvas of the later stages, though they too emit light, have not yet left the realm of ignorance. This is because, distracted by lesser power and light, they lose sight of the great power and light of Original Nature. Thus students of the Mahayana must first of all have faith in this great power and light. If one can truly awaken to these, the ignorance of countless kalpas will be eradicated and the karmic ties of myriad lives will be loosed. Then for the first time one can send forth infinite light, destroy the delusion and ignorance of sentient beings, employ vast supernatural powers, and refute the false teachings of celestial demons and nonbelievers.

SIGNS AT THE TIME OF DEATH

Question: It is often the case that people who earnestly cultivate the Way of the Buddha experience inauspicious deaths, while those whose practice was not especially serious die in a praiseworthy fashion. Moreover, people whose lives were hardly laudable sometimes leave behind śarira[369] after their cremations, whereas people of wisdom and virtue often do not. Why is this?

Answer: Phenomenal things have no fixed form. Sometimes what appears to be good is actually bad; sometimes what appears to be bad is actually good. It is the same with appearances at the time of death. Fortuitous signs or circumstances may accompany the deaths of practicers whose lives were quite disreputable; this is occasionally the result of celestial demons attempting to deceive the dying individual or confuse other people. In other cases the positive signs that appear are those said to accompany the death of a person whose good behavior, though still in the realm of delusion, destines him or her for rebirth in the human or celestial realms.

The signs associated with the deaths of those to be reborn in these higher realms are explained in the sutras as: bearing no ill will during their final illness toward other people, retaining few attachments to secular life, experiencing only mild physical suffering, and undergoing no mental torment. They meet their end calling the names of the buddhas and bodhisattvas or the gods and saints. Among them, those destined for rebirth in such heavens as Trāyastrimśa[370] are greeted as they die by celestial beings whose fragrance scents the room and heavenly maidens who fill the air with music. Even with such auspicious deaths, however, these people must eventually return to the evil realms when their stores of good karma are spent.

In this way, sometimes people whose deaths seem admirable turn out to be unworthy of respect. Others whose deaths seem inauspicious are actually quite virtuous, their ominous death signs being conjured up by celestial demons in order to shake the virtue of the people around them (in such cases, however, those who are dying do not themselves see the inauspicious signs). In other cases people practice the true Dharma but do not attain complete liberation because the fruits of their efforts have not yet matured and karmic hindrances persist from former lives. For this reason they may even fall into the evil realms for a time.

However, though their deaths may be inauspicious, such people will eventually realize liberation because of the enduring power[371] of their true Dharma practice. For example, the daughter of Sāgara the Dragon King was born into the realm of the animals owing to her past karma, but the manifestation of the enduring power of the Mahayana enabled her to attain correct enlightenment at the age of eight.[372] When you think about it, as she faced the end of her previous life just prior to being reborn into the realm of the animals, surely the signs that accompanied her death could not have been auspicious!

One time when the Buddha was out walking he noticed an abandoned child in the grass by the roadside. A large number of people were looking at the child, who was extraordinarily fair of complexion. The Buddha went to the little boy and asked him a number of questions about the Dharma, all of which the child answered. The Buddha, taking him by the hand, encouraged him to remember the virtuous deeds of his past lives and to manifest his supernatural powers. Hearing these words, the little boy immediately rose into the air, assumed a seated posture, and from his body emitted a great light that illuminated the three thousand worlds. Seeing this light, Brahmā, Indra, and the eight types of guardian deities all gathered around the child and received marvelous benefits. The Buddha therefore declared that the child was to be called Marvelous Light Bodhisattva and certified his attainment of enlightenment.

The Buddha related the story of Marvelous Light Bodhisattva, saying that ninety-one kalpas in the past, when Vipaśyin Buddha[373] appeared in the world, there were two bodhisattvas. One, named Bodhisattva Sagacious Deva, realized the nonbirth and nonextinction of all existence. He had few desires and enjoyed living alone. The other bodhisattva, named Bodhisattva Abundant Wealth, enjoyed ascetic practice. He became friendly with Sagacious Deva and looked after him, but he also enjoyed visiting the homes of laypeople and participating in worldly affairs. When Sagacious Deva admonished him for this, Abundant Wealth felt resentful and angrily insulted him, saying that Sagacious Deva had been a deserted child whose parents no one knew. Because of these spiteful words, Abundant Wealth was conceived in the womb of a prostitute and abandoned at birth in each successive lifetime for the next ninety-one kalpas. Only with his rebirth at the time of the Buddha was his evil karma finally exhausted, allowing his former meritorious roots to appear.

Thus, owing to the various causes and conditions involved, those whose deaths are accompanied by inauspicious signs are sometimes people of superior merits and sometimes people destined for the evil realms. The latter are those who did not practice the Buddhadharma during their lifetimes and generated only evil karma.

Then there are people who pass away in the sitting or standing postures at the time of their death and attain liberation. This occurs with people who have realized the unity of inside and outside and penetrated the barrier of life and death. An ancient master said, "Dying in the sitting or standing posture occurs through the power of samādhi."[374] Even among those who have attained to the Dharma, those whose samādhi power is not fully mature have yet to realize complete liberation. Nevertheless, such people would not suffer deaths accompanied by inauspicious signs. Even if a person has not yet attained complete liberation, anyone whose mind is free of samsaric influences can be called a true practicer of the Mahayana. Conversely, confirmed arhats, though fully liberated and displaying the eighteen mysterious manifestations[375] at the time of their death, are not called attainers of the Dharma.

There were masters of the Zen and doctrinal schools who died in inauspicious ways, such as in accidents or disasters,[376] but this was simply the result of residual karma manifesting in the form of an inauspicious death. Moreover, these incidents are utilized as expedients for liberating other people, so these masters do not deserve censure for the way they died.

It is said that śarira remain when pratyekabuddhas are cremated, even though pratyekabuddhas, as followers of the Hinayana, have not attained the Dharma. Even ordinary laypeople, if they have achieved samādhi, are reported to have produced these relics. The tathāgatas of the three periods of time who appear in the world as buddhas always leave behind śarira after their deaths as a way of encouraging gods and humans to accomplish meritorious deeds.

Since the time of Śākyamuni, certain Buddhist masters have manifested śarira as part of their vocation of disseminating the Buddhadharma. Other masters leave no such relics behind, though auspicious signs accompany their deaths. One cannot really know the reasons for this. The *Sutra of the Great Treasure Collection* says, "The śarira of the tathāgatas flow from formless prajñā; prajñā is the essence of the śarira; śarira are the function of prajñā. Foolish people believe in śarira with form, but have no faith in formless prajñā."[377]

Zen Master Wuxue Zuyuan[378] wrote the following verse:

> Buddhas and ordinary people are equally illusions;
> If you seek substantial forms, that is just dust in your eyes.
> This old monk's śarira envelop the universe;
> Don't scatter cold ashes in the empty mountains.

In short, it is an auspicious sign if śarira appear after a person's death, but this does not necessarily mean the person had attained to the Dharma.

PART III

THE GROUND OF ORIGINAL NATURE

Question: What is the Ground of Original Nature?

Answer: Ordinary words and images cannot represent that which is prior to the separation of sacred and mundane, enlightened and deluded. Even the transcendental teachings cannot approach it. However, in order to guide ignorant people it is referred to by such names as the Ground of Original Nature, the One Great Matter, the Original Face, and the Master. All point to the same thing. "Sacred," "mundane," "enlightened," and "deluded" are all notions provisionally established with each passing moment of thought. With the flow of successive thought-moments these illusory notions take on a false reality and deceive the human mind. It is because of this deception that the Ground of Original Nature is obscured.

BUDDHA-NATURE AND THE
GROUND OF ORIGINAL NATURE

Question: Is what is called in the teachings "mind-ground" or "Buddha-nature" any different from "the Ground of Original Nature"?

Answer: The doctrinal schools are referring to the same thing, speaking as they do from the standpoint of the fully revealed Mahayana teachings. However, the doctrinal schools teach that with the arising of a single instant of delusion there occurs a provisional separation of ordinary beings and buddhas, and it is from this standpoint that they discuss mind-ground and Buddha-nature. In this way their position is different from that of the Zen school, which holds that the Ground of Original Nature precedes any separation between ordinary beings and buddhas. When a person awakens to the Ground of Original Nature, then everything—from the Buddha-nature, mind-ground, tathāgata-garbha,[379] suchness, and Dharma-nature of which the doctrinal schools speak, all the way to the earth, mountains, rivers, grass, tiles, and stones that ordinary beings perceive—partakes of the Ground of Original Nature. It is not necessary to accord a special significance to the label "Ground of Original Nature."

THE TRUE FORM OF THE GROUND
OF ORIGINAL NATURE

Question: Although it is said that everyone inherently possesses the Ground of Original Nature and that it is fully realized in each of us, no one has ever seen its form. Where is it located? Is it in the body or is it in the mind? Or is the entire body-mind the Ground of Original Nature? Or is it somewhere else, separate from the body-mind?

Answer: An ancient master said, "Without leaving where it is, it is eternally clear and serene. When seeking, know that it cannot be found."[380] The Ground of Original Nature is not in the body-mind, nor is it outside of the body-mind. It is not correct to say that the entire body-mind constitutes the place of Original Nature. It is not sentient being nor is it insentient being, nor is it the wisdom of the buddhas and the sages. Yet from out of it are born the wisdom of the buddhas and the sages, the body-minds of all beings, and everything including all the lands of the world. For this reason it is provisionally referred to as the Ground of Original Nature.

The *Diamond Sutra* states, "All buddhas and the Dharma of the highest, most perfect enlightenment of all buddhas arise from this sutra."[381] This diamond prajñā-wisdom is the Ground of Original Nature. The *Sutra of Complete Enlightenment* says, "All purity, suchness, enlightenment, nirvana, and perfections flow from perfect enlightenment."[382] Perfect enlightenment is the Ground of Original Nature. The *Lotus Samādhi Sutra* states, "The Thirty-seven Honored Ones of the Diamond Realm dwell in the castle of the mind."[383] The mind-castle is the Ground of Original Nature. Mahāvairocana Buddha, Vajrasatta, and all of the other Thirty-seven Honored Ones spoken of in the esoteric teachings dwell in the castle of the mind. Know that the marvelous principle of suchness and all buddhas and bodhisattvas depend upon the Ground of Original Nature. How much more inseparable from it, then, are all sentient beings and all worlds both pure and defiled.

Question: If Original Nature is not to be found in either mundane forms or supramundane principles, how can one possibly attain it?

Answer: This concern, common among people who wish to practice Zen, is based on an inadequate understanding of what the term "Original Nature" signifies. For example, if Original Nature were described to you as something like a worldly art, you would naturally wonder if you were talented enough to learn it; if it were described as a transcendental doctrine, you would worry whether you were intelligent enough to grasp it. However, having heard that Original Nature has nothing to do with either the mundane or the supramundane, it is senseless to wonder how to reach it.

Reaching the Ground of Original Nature is not like traveling from the countryside to the capital, or from Japan to China. Rather, it is as though you were asleep in your home, dreaming of enduring the sufferings of hell or enjoying the pleasures of paradise, then having a friend who is not sleeping tell you, "The hell and the paradise that you are seeing are nothing but illusions in your dreams. In your own actual home, neither of them exists." If upon hearing these words you continued to believe that the events in your dreams were real, then you would pay no heed to your friend. Instead, you would continue trying to escape your dream-sufferings and prolong your dream-pleasures.

In this way, you would remain under the influence of your dream experiences and never awaken to Original Nature. Even if, in your dreams, a good teacher convinced you that you had a peaceful home of your own, you would still remain within the overall dream, unable to let go of what you experience there. Thus you might ask the teacher how to reach this home of yours. "Should I get there by climbing these mountains and fording the rivers beyond? Should I learn to fly, then cross the mountains and rivers through the air?" Or you might ask, "Is this home of mine part of the natural world or separate from it? Should I consider the mountains, rivers, and earth to be this home just as they are?" Such questions all arise because you haven't yet awakened from the overall dream.

However, even if you haven't awakened from this dream, if you realize that everything you see and do are simply images in a dream, and therefore see as though blind and hear as though deaf and give rise to no thoughts of choice or discrimination, then you are basically the same as a person who *has* awakened. You are someone who has attained faith in the realm of reality.

The Buddhadharma is similar to this. In Original Nature there are no traces of sacred or mundane, no domains of pure or defiled. It is only because the dream of karmically conditioned consciousness arises through the agency of ignorance that the realms of "pure" and "defiled" appear in the midst of formlessness, and that distinctions between "sacred" and "mundane" are perceived in the midst of the unconditioned. If we regard ourselves as deluded we run about from east to west seeking fame and fortune, and we are overcome with sorrow if we fail to find them. If we regard ourselves as wise we become arrogant and look down upon everyone else. Deceived by these perverted views, we have no faith in Original Nature. The false domain of the dream world has, in other words, confused our minds so that we cannot accept the realm of reality.

In the midst of all this, there are occasionally people of superior capacities who, although recognizing that notions like "sacred" and "mundane" or "pure" and "defiled" are nothing but ephemeral forms floating in karmic consciousness[384] and that none of these things exist in Original Nature, are nevertheless susceptible to deception by illusory appearances since they have yet to attain the great awakening. Because they haven't let go of the self-attachments that cause them to regard themselves as deluded beings, they long for enlightenment and aspire to eloquence and supernatural powers. They end up arguing over which methods of training are correct and judging who bested whom in *mondō*, like dreaming men who, while aware that everything in their dreams is itself a dream, can't stop talking of right and wrong, gain and loss. This is because they haven't awakened from the overall dream and are thus taken in by the world it creates.

People of the highest capacities, even if they hadn't experienced great enlightenment, clearly perceive that all calculations involving self and other or body and mind are nothing but the deluded workings of karmic consciousness, and thus they neither disdain transmigration nor seek emancipation. Those who view things in this way are people of true insight. However, they, too, fall into error if they rest content in this insight. The *Sutra of Complete Enlightenment* says:

> They take the four great elements to be the attributes of their bodies and the impressions of the six sense objects to be the attributes of their minds. This is like an injured eye that sees flowers in the sky, or a second moon.... It is because of this that beings remain heedlessly caught in the samsaric realm. This is why it is called ignorance. This ignorance has no true substance. It is like a man who appears in a dream—the man has reality in the dream, but when the dreamer awakes the dream-man no longer exists.[385]

The *Śūraṅgama Sutra* says, "The subtle nature is perfectly clear and beyond all names and forms. From the beginning, neither the world nor sentient beings exist."[386] All of the Mahayana sutras speak in the same way. Why then do you not believe this and instead exhaust yourselves rushing about in external seeking?

Although ordinary people are unable to foretell the twists and turns of fortune, they trust the prophecies of seers and fortune-tellers, and if they act in accordance with these prophecies they may have occasion to benefit. Similarly, although Original Nature is immanent in everyone, those who have not realized it remain unaware of its presence despite using it every day. For that reason the buddhas and patriarchs, in their great compassion, indicate it to us with meticulous care. Even if our shallow karmic roots prevent us from directly realizing Original Nature, if we have faith in the teachings of the buddhas and patriarchs, just as we do in the words of oracles, and if we apply ourselves to practicing these teachings, how can we fail to benefit?

THE TRUE MIND

Question: Whether our social status is high or low, our bodies are all subject to birth, aging, sickness, and death. They are indeed just like phantoms. The mind, however, has no shape or form and must therefore be eternal and not subject to destruction. Why then do you say that both body and mind are like illusions? Certain passages in the sutras state the mind is illusory, while other passages explain that the mind is eternal and imperishable. Which of these explanations is correct?

Answer: In Japanese the character for "heart" or "mind," 心, pronounced *kokoro* or *shin*, is used in a number of different meanings.[387] When the surface layers of a dead tree have entirely rotted away, the sound, undecayed wood that remains is known as the *shin* of the tree. The Sanskrit word for this is *hṛdaya*, transliterated into Sino-Japanese as *kenritsuda* 乾栗駄 or *kenritsudaya* 紇栗陀耶. In the esoteric schools this term refers to the heart as a physical organ, as it does in the *Record of the Source Mirror*, where it is transliterated as *kiridaya* 紇利陀耶.[388] In addition, the word *shin* can indicate the spirit that imbues certain trees or rocks of great antiquity (this concept, too, is expressed in Sanskrit by the word *hṛdaya*).[389]

Shin is similarly seen as the agent of discriminative thinking, possessed by all conscious beings. In this case the corresponding Sanskrit word is *citta*. *Shin* as *citta* is mind as usually conceived of by the ordinary person. *Shin* in the same sense is what is referred to as "mind" in Hinayana Buddhism. The esoteric teachings sometimes use *citta* to mean *bodhicitta*. This is not *citta* as the discriminating mind of the ordinary person.

The Sanskrit word *ālaya-vijñāna* refers to what is called the storehouse consciousness; this is the so-called eighth consciousness. The Sanskrit *mano-vijñāna* is the defiled consciousness; this is the seventh consciousness. Both of these levels of consciousness, which denote mental phenomena present in all sentient beings, were not known in secular philosophy and Hinayana thought but were first identified by Mahayana thinkers. The eighth consciousness is where ignorance and Dharma-nature come together, so its nature is neither complete delusion nor complete truth. Some Mahayana schools view the eighth consciousness as the Mind King,[390] while others postulate the existence of a ninth consciousness above the eighth. For these schools the ninth consciousness—called *amala-vijñāna* in Sanskrit and indicating the "pure and undefiled consciousness"—is the fundamental mind of all sentient beings. Even amid delusion it is not tainted by delusion, and for that reason it is referred to as pure and undefiled.

Because of these various considerations, the overall mind is provisionally divided into two portions, "true" and "deluded." The discriminative thinking of the ordinary person is entirely of the deluded mind. The forms that temporarily appear when the four elements combine are utterly lacking in substance, and thus they are compared to phantoms or to flowers in the sky. Similarly, when for a time the deluded mind comes into existence through the action of the true mind it has no real existence. It is like the second moon that an injured eye sees when it looks at the actual moon. Two moons don't actually exist—it is just that the person with the injured eye speaks of a second moon in accordance with what he perceives. Similarly, two minds don't actually exist—it is just that the deluded person regards as "my mind" something that is not real. Thus it is called the "phantom mind" or the "mind of birth-and-death."

In truth, however, there is no deluded mind to arise and pass away. As the sages see it the mind is everlasting and imperishable, and thus they call it the true mind. To make this distinction clear, Sanskrit writers, when referring to the true mind, always use the word *hṛdaya*, explaining that just as the heart of the tree is hard and durable, so the true mind of sentient beings is strong and not subject to destruction. This is why, whenever the terms "inherent mind" or "subtle mind" appear in the Chinese translation of the *Laṅkāvatāra Sutra*, one always finds the gloss 乾栗馱, meaning *hṛdaya*,[391] written beside the character 心, "mind." Similarly, it is said that in the Sanskrit version of the *Heart Sutra* the word used for "mind" is *hṛdaya*. In the *Record of the Source Mirror* it is explained that there are several categories of mind, but that the hṛdaya mind is the source of them all.[392]

That which the ordinary person regards as mind has no color or form; it appears and disappears from one instant to the next and is never still, like flowing water or a flickering flame. Just like the physical body, it shows the four aspects of all phenomena: generation, duration, transition, and destruction. Thus, to think that the body undergoes birth and death while the mind is eternal is a non-Buddhist view. When the mind is said to be eternal, this refers to the mind in the sense of the One Mind that is the essence of the Dharma realm, in which sacred and profane are the same and the body is not separate from the mind. Thus the enlightened person never regards the mind alone as eternal but sees the body too as eternal. The doctrine that the body is mortal and the mind eternal is not a Mahayana teaching. A commentary on the *Mahāvairocana Sutra* says, "The body and mind of all sentient beings are absolute reality, and from the very beginning they comprise the universal wisdom body of Vairocana Buddha."[393]

In ancient times the National Teacher Nanyang Huizhong asked a monk, "Where did you come from?" "From the south," answered the monk. "And what did your teacher in the south tell his students?" asked Nanyang. "He said that although the body decays, the mind is everlasting and imperishable," replied the monk. Nanyang said, "That is the non-Buddhist teaching of the eternal soul, or ātman." The monk then asked Nanyang, "What do you teach?" "I teach that the body and mind are one," replied Nanyang.[394]

There once lived a layman named Feng Jichuan.[395] Seeing a painting of a corpse on a wall, he composed a verse about it:

> The corpse is there, but where is the person?
> I see that the spirit is not with the skin-bag.

This verse, in which "spirit" means "mind" and "skin-bag" means "body," indicates that Feng hadn't yet transcended the notion of an ātman. Feng's teacher, Dahui, disapproved of the verse and wrote one of his own:

> This corpse itself is the person.
> The spirit is the skin-bag; the skin-bag is the spirit.

Feng's verse is easy to understand, but how are we to interpret Dahui's? Even taking his words at face value would not be out of accord with his meaning, since the unity of body and mind is a universal principle of Mahayana thought. But how many grasp what Dahui truly had in mind? It is unlikely that the understanding of most people goes beyond that of Feng.

The difference between the true mind and the deluded mind is discussed at length in texts such as the *Sutra of Complete Enlightenment* and the *Śūraṅgama Sutra*, so I will not consider it further here.

THE ETERNAL SOUL
AND THE ONE MIND

Question: What is the concept of the eternal soul?

Answer: The non-Buddhist Indian philosophical school known as Sāṃkhya classified all of the world's phenomena into twenty-five principles. The first of these principles is prakṛti, translated as the "obscure principle." This principle precedes the separation of heaven and earth, is untouched by distinction, and is imperceptible to the senses. It cannot be described in words and so it is called the obscure principle for convenience sake. Prakṛti is regarded as eternal, and thus not subject to the four forces of generation, duration, transition, and destruction. The twenty-fifth principle is that of ātman, translated as the "spirit-self principle"; this is what is ordinarily regarded as the mind or soul. Sāṃkhya thought regards the ātman, too, as eternal.

The twenty-three principles between the first and the twenty-fifth principles comprise the various ever-changing forms—good and bad, weal and woe—in the world. These are the saṃskṛta, the conditioned phenomena. According to Sāṃkhya thought, if the ātman gives rise to discriminatory feelings the underlying principle of prakṛti manifests the corresponding forms. Thus, if the ātman conceives the notions of long or short, square or round, prakṛti then transforms to produce them. Thus the permutations of the world's conditioned phenomena are caused entirely by the ātman, giving rise to feelings. If the ātman did not do so but, instead, rested in prakṛti, then the transformational changes of conditioned phenomena would forever cease and the peaceful ease of the unconditioned would naturally ensue.

Sāṃkhya thought says that the physical body may be destroyed but the ātman endures, as a house may burn down while the master departs. This is the concept of ātman that National Teacher Nanyang was criticizing. The Taoist philosophy of Laozi and Zhuangzi[396] that was popular in ancient China had concepts similar to Sāṃkhya thought. Laozi's "nothingness" and Zhuangzi's "great Tao of nondoing," for example, correspond to prakṛti.

Even now there are students of the Mahayana who hold such views. The *Sutra of Complete Enlightenment* says:

> The pure maṇi jewel[397] reflects the five colors as they appear before it, yet the ignorant see the maṇi as actually possessing the five colors.... Although the pure nature of Complete Enlightenment likewise manifests as body and mind..., the ignorant speak of the pure Complete Enlightenment as having intrinsic characteristics of body and mind. For this reason body and mind are said to be illusory and defiled.[398]

The Great Teacher Yongjia says, "The loss of Dharma wealth and the destruction of merit are all due to the conscious thinking mind."[399] The Zen master Changsha[400] said, "That students do not know the True is solely because they have always recognized only the thinking mind."

When beginning students, practicing what they believe to be *zazen*, look inside and perceive the formless, boundless, and luminously spiritual space of the mind, they think they have experienced the Master or the Original Face. The ancient masters dismissed such understanding as "playing with the spirit, reifying the thinking mind." This is what the *Sutra of Complete Enlightenment* means when it speaks of "adopting a thief as your son."[401]

The Buddha said, "The three realms are just one mind; outside of mind there is nothing."[402] The term "one mind" is understood in different ways by the various Buddhist schools. Hinayana schools regard "one mind" as comprising the discriminative consciousness, the sixth of the six consciousnesses.[403] Some Mahayana schools posit the existence of two further forms of consciousness, the seventh and the eighth,[404] which are subtler than the sixth consciousness. These schools see all phenomena as permutations of the eighth conscious-ness, and thus teach that everything in the three realms is just one mind, with the Mind King being the eighth consciousness. The Mahayana thinkers who propose an even higher, ninth level of con-sciousness see all phenomena as manifestations of this ninth level,[405] which is their interpretation of the teaching that everything in the three realms is just one mind.

Students of Hinayana Buddhism are not aware of these subtler forms of consciousness, so they believe that they have reached the Absolute if thoughts of attachment and discrimination do not arise in relation to the objective world. Recently there are Mahayana prac-ticers who think the true mind consists of not discriminating with regard to any phenomenon—of seeing a mountain *as* a mountain, water *as* water, a monk *as* a monk, and a layperson *as* a layperson without clinging to notions of good and bad, right and wrong. This is not the true mind, however, but simply the functioning of the first five of the six consciousnesses.

Mind-nature is beyond the conceivable. Though it spans the sky it is not large; though contained in a tiny mustard seed it is not small. Beyond all forms yet encompassing all forms, displaying infinite vir-tue yet not defined by infinite virtue, it cannot be characterized as true or false nor described as coarse or fine. When one is still in the grip of delusion, however, true and false or fine and coarse are not the same. Thus those who have yet to transcend false views come up with their own interpretations when they hear the words "this very mind is buddha" and proclaim that joy, anger, and all the deluded feelings are themselves the Buddha-mind. Though what they say bears some resemblance to the Buddhadharma, their view is false. The reasons why are explained in the sacred texts for the sake of just such people as this. If you clearly understand the reasoning behind these explanations, then even if you have not attained enlightenment you will at least never mistake a fish eye for a pearl.

Those born in the Latter Age have shallow karmic roots, so those who follow the scholarly path believe that the ultimate goal consists of mastering the various doctrines expounding the principle of mind-nature, and thus they fail to realize the source of mind-nature itself. People who enter the path of Zen tend to regard such doctrines as something for scholars to discuss, and nothing for Zen practicers to bother about. Sincerely abandoning both mundane delusions and supermundane teachings and wholeheartedly striving toward Supreme Enlightenment—this is truly what the Zen school encourages. But is it not a great error to avoid studying the doctrinal meaning of the sutras and treatises and indulge instead in false thinking based on your own mental biases, thereby confusing the thinking consciousness for the Original Mind?

True Mind and Deluded Mind

Question: If what you say about the mind is correct, would it not be a mistake to seek the true mind apart from the deluded mind?

Answer: It is very difficult to explain the difference between the true mind and the deluded mind. Saying they are alike and saying they are different are both incorrect.

The false mind is something like the illusory second moon, separate from the true moon, that you see when you press a finger against the side of your eye. As long as you continue this pressure the second moon will be visible in front of you, even though it doesn't actually exist as an entity separate from the real moon. If you don't wish to see this illusory moon, it is useless to simply decide to have it disappear and see the true moon instead—you have to stop pressing the side of your eye with your finger, and then the true moon will be the only one there. You will never rid yourself of the illusory second moon as long as you press. On the other hand, some people might take a liking to this illusory moon, claiming that it is the only real moon. This, too, is a great error.

People who never press their finger against their eye never see a second moon in the first place. What, then, is the point of arguing whether this illusory moon should be eradicated or not eradicated?

Discussing whether or not the deluded mind and the true mind are the same is simply pressing the "eye" of Original Nature with the "finger" of delusion.

THE TWO FOUNDATIONS OF THE TRUE MIND

Question: Just as something crooked can be reshaped to make it straight, so too the biased, deluded mind of the ordinary person, if disciplined and rectified, should become the Buddha-mind. Why then disdain the deluded mind and liken it to an illusory second moon? If so, would it not be impossible for an ordinary person to become a buddha?

Answer: This is a question asked by Bodhisattva Samantabhadra in the *Sutra of Complete Enlightenment*,[406] and by Ānanda in the *Śūraṅgama Sutra*.[407] In the latter sutra the Buddha says to Ānanda, "Having lost the true mind, you believe your mind is the mind that conceptualizes and discriminates. But this is not your mind." Ānanda, doubting this, replied, "Rebirth in the six realms depends on this mind, and the realization of Buddhahood must also depend on this mind. Therefore, if this mind is not my mind, with what should I engage in practice and attain the fruit of Buddhahood? If this mind does not exist, how would I differ from earth, trees, tiles, and stones?" The Buddha answered, "I am not saying that you should suppress mind and try to convince yourself that it doesn't exist. But if what you think of as mind truly does exist, then it must be located somewhere. Where is it?" Ānanda at first replied, "It is in my body." When the Buddha explained to Ānanda why the mind cannot be in the body, Ānanda next said that it was outside the body. The Buddha showed why this too couldn't be, so Ānanda proceeded to successively name seven other places where the mind might exist. Finally he said, "My mind is neither inside my body nor outside my body, nor is it in between. My mind is that with absolutely no attachment." None of these answers met with the Buddha's approval, however, so Ānanda was at an utter loss as to what to think. The Buddha then said:

> The reason that sentient beings have from the beginningless past wandered vainly in the realms of birth and death is because they have lost the true mind and identified themselves with the mind that conceptualizes and discriminates. Even if they happen to practice the Buddhadharma, they do not know the two fundamentals and therefore practice mistakenly, causing them to fall into the realms of the celestial demons, non-Buddhists, and Two Vehicles.... The first of the two fundamentals is the primally pure essence of the originally enlightened mind. This is the source of the mind of every sentient being, but this fundamental has been forgotten. The second fundamental is that of beginningless transmigration. This is the mind that conceptualizes and discriminates, and that you have taken to be your very own mind. If this is the mind that you practice with, then, though you may generate further life-and-death karma, you will never realize the original source. It is like trying to cook rice by boiling sand—no matter how many eons go by, you get only hot sand and never cooked rice.

Master Nanyue Huisi,[408] in his work *On Śamatha and Vipaśyanā According to the Mahayana*,[409] says, "Practicers of śamatha and vipaśyanā must at first align the discriminative mind with the [inherent] pure mind. If they attempt to practice using the samsaric mind they will not attain realization."[410]

A commentary on the *Mahāvairocana Sutra* says, "Not only are ordinary people, the Two Vehicles, and non-Buddhists unaware of the mind beyond birth and death, but they also do not know even the mind of birth and death.... The nature of the mind is beyond all thought and cannot be known through conjecture."[411] The *Sutra on Divining the Effects of Karma*[412] says, "The mind takes two forms: true and deluded. The nature of the true mind is suchness—pure and perfect, pervading the entire phenomenal world and giving rise to all things. The deluded mind is the mind of discrimination and knowledge. It has no substance and it gives rise to all falsehood."[413]

Question: Sages such as Confucius and Laozi, said to be manifestations of the bodhisattvas, teach the path of disciplining the thinking mind. Similarly, the doctrinal schools, despite their respective differences, all teach with regard to the thinking mind that our usual wicked thinking should be transformed into true wisdom. Why then do the *Sutra of Complete Enlightenment* and the *Śūraṅgama Sutra* speak of this mind as though it were nonexistent?

Answer: All phenomena, both physical and mental, are differentiated according to whether they arise as the result of causal conditioning or of the spontaneous functioning of nature. The temporary forms that come into being through the interaction of related causes exist by virtue of causal conditioning, while the innate qualities of the tathāgata-garbha exist by virtue of the spontaneous functioning of nature.

Although the physical phenomenon of ordinary, causally produced fire lacks any real substance, it functions in accordance with conditions. When fire is skillfully employed it yields great benefits, such as warding off cold and cooking food; when unskillfully employed it causes great harm, such as destroying houses and other property. Thus it benefits society to instruct people how to use fire in a way that causes no harm. However, even if you know how to use fire skillfully, you still don't know the natural, unconditioned, all-pervading fire-nature.[414] If you wish to know fire-nature, you must avoid concerning yourself with the effects of conditionally generated fire.

The same is true of mental phenomena. The causally conditioned illusory mind has no permanent substance, but if it acts wrongfully it falls into the evil realms and undergoes all manner of suffering, and if it acts rightfully it is born into the higher realms and enjoys all types of favorable circumstances. It is because they understand this basic principle that even ordinary people and non-Buddhists often discipline the mind and refrain from evil actions.

However, even if you manage to control the conditioned, deluded mind, the only benefit this brings is rebirth in the human or celestial realms. Since you have yet to know Original Mind, you will not escape the realm of samsara. Even the bodhisattvas of the Three Worthy States and the Ten Holy Stages, who have rectified the biases of the deluded mind and attained an illusory form of wisdom, have not yet realized Original Mind and are thus unable to transcend transformational samsara.[415] All of this is at the same level as properly utilizing ordinary conditioned fire so as not to cause harm. Thus the *Sutra of Complete Enlightenment* and the *Śūraṅgama Sutra* explain that, just as fire-nature exists only apart from conditioned fire, true mind exists only apart from the conditioned mind.[416]

Buddhist schools other than Zen teach that one should cultivate illusory wisdom for a time to put an end to delusion, and that afterward one will naturally accord with Original Mind. This is what the *Sutra of Complete Enlightenment* and the *Śūraṅgama Sutra* mean when they say that, after doing away with delusion through the cultivation of illusory wisdom, one will attain the realm of that which is not illusion, where objects and knowledge are forgotten.[417] Nevertheless, certain immature students think that this illusory wisdom constitutes the true intention of the buddhas and ancestors. The *Sutra of Complete Enlightenment* says:

When the illusory body is extinguished, the illusory mind is also extinguished. When the illusory mind is extinguished, the illusory sense objects are also extinguished. When the illusory sense objects are extinguished, the illusory extinguishing is also extinguished. When the illusory extinguishing is extinguished, that which is not illusory is not extinguished. It is similar to how, when the dust is polished off a mirror, the brightness appears.

Virtuous man, you should know that body and mind are both illusory dust. When the form of this dust is wiped away, purity pervades the universe.[418]

Certain people who have not yet awakened to Original Mind misunderstand this passage, taking it to mean that the complete extinguishing of body and mind is the true teaching of the Buddha. This view, however, is the samādhi of extinction taught by the Two Vehicles, or the imageless samādhi taught by non-Buddhists. It is like hearing that conditioned fire is to be rejected as not true fire, then concluding that true fire is the darkness that results from extinguishing all conditioned fire.

The references to cultivating the illusory mind that are found in Confucianism, Taoism, Hinayana, and provisional Mahayana Buddhism are all expedient teachings.

70

MIND AND NATURE

Question: The ancient masters said that Bodhidharma came from the West in order to directly indicate the human mind with no reliance on words and letters, so that people might see their true nature and attain Buddhahood. Since all Mahayana schools teach that our own mind is buddha, why does Zen say "see one's own true *nature* and attain Buddhahood" rather than "see the *mind* and attain Buddhahood"?

Answer: In ancient times there was a monk who, troubled by this same question, called upon Nanyang Huizhong and asked the difference between mind and nature. Nanyang answered, "It is similar to how water crystallizes into ice when it is cold, and ice melts into water when it is warm. When one is deluded, then nature solidifies to form mind; when one is enlightened, mind dissolves to form nature. Mind and nature are the same, but there is a difference between the two with regard to delusion versus enlightenment."[419] Nanyang is explaining the distinction between mind and nature in a figurative fashion, and this should not be understood too literally.

The single word "nature" has a number of meanings, at least three of which are elucidated in the Buddhist doctrines. The first is nature as that which is immutable in a thing, as when the respective natures of pepper and licorice are said to account for why pepper can never be sweet and licorice can never be spicy. The second is nature as that which differentiates one thing from another, as with the distinct essential natures of animate and inanimate objects. The third is nature as Dharma-nature, that is, the nondual original source that is the intrinsic nature of everything that exists. Non-Buddhist texts and the Hinayana sutras do not refer to Dharma-nature but discuss the meaning of "nature" only in terms of immutability and differentiation. In the Mahayana tradition the various schools have different teachings on the significance of Dharma-nature.

The basic position of the Zen tradition is that of "a separate transmission outside the teachings." Although Zen speaks of seeing one's own nature, you should know that this "nature" does not mean the "Dharma-nature" of which the doctrinal schools speak, much less the "nature" referred to in non-Buddhist texts. That which is fundamental to every human being cannot be labeled as either "mind" or "nature." Nevertheless, it is by means of the words "mind" and "nature" that people are made aware of the fundamental, and therefore it is sometimes called "mind" and sometimes called "nature."

To regard "direct pointing to the human mind...to see true nature and attain Buddhahood" as referring to the ordinary deluded person's mind is like making a second moon. It is in order to inform people of this that the word "nature" is used instead of "mind" in "to see true nature." To speak of "seeing true nature" does not mean seeing it with the eyes, nor does it mean comprehending it with the intellect.

Similarly, "attaining Buddhahood" does not imply that you become a new buddha radiating light and manifesting all the distinguishing characteristics of a tathāgata. It is more like a drunk man coming to his senses when the effect of the alcohol finally wears off. When everyday delusion suddenly vanishes and we directly realize Original Nature, this is called "seeing true nature and attaining Buddhahood." Zen Master Dahui said, "When eyeless masters of the Zen school teach people they distort this, pointing to the human mind and speaking of 'nature' and representing this as the attainment of Buddhahood."[420] There are many teachers nowadays who simply teach people the principles of "mind" and "nature" and believe that so doing represents "direct pointing to the human mind." There are many students, too, who believe that understanding these principles constitutes attainment of the Dharma. This should be called "*explaining* nature," not "*seeing* nature."

71

DELUSION AND TRUTH

Question: Certain passages in the sutras say that all phenomena are unreal, while other passages say that all phenomena represent eternal truth. Which of these is true?

Answer: In Original Nature there are no notions of unreality or eternality. It is simply that, from their respective points of view, ordinary people speak of things as unreal while sages see them as eternal. However, the truly awakened do not hold to the views of ordinary people or sages. Thus all talk of either unreality or eternality is simply expedient teaching.

The *Laṅkāvatāra Sutra* says, "A non-Buddhist philosopher asked the Buddha, 'Are all phenomena impermanent?' The Buddha responded, 'Your question is mere sophistry.' The philosopher then asked, 'Are all phenomena permanent?' The Buddha replied, 'This question, too, is mere sophistry.'"[421] The *Vimalakīrti Sutra* says, "Do not use the birth-and-death mind to speak of the true nature of things."[422]

It is sophistry when someone whose views are no different from those of deluded people speaks of the meaning of ultimate reality. This is what is meant when it is said that if a person who is false preaches the true Dharma, the true Dharma becomes the false Dharma, and if a person who is true preaches the false Dharma, the false Dharma becomes the true Dharma.

ORDINARY PEOPLE AND SAGES

Question: What is the difference between the views of ordinary people and those of sages?

Answer: The Zen school does not discuss such issues, since it focuses on the direct realization of Original Nature. The Buddhist teachings, however, contain various explanations. The *Śūraṅgama Sutra* describes seven universal elements: earth, water, fire, wind, space, perception, and consciousness. All seven elements, as qualities inherent to the tathāgata-garbha, pervade the entire Dharma-realm and freely penetrate all things. These universal elements are referred to as fire-nature, wind-nature, and so forth. The Shingon (esoteric) school intends the same thing when it says that the substance of all phenomena is composed of six interpenetrating elements, consisting of the six senses—sight, hearing, etc.—as all-pervasive forces; these are the same elements as in the *Śūraṅgama Sutra*, but without the element of perception. In the Shingon system the six elements comprise the substance of the phenomenal universe; in the *Śūraṅgama Sutra* system the tathāgata-garbha comprises the substance of all phenomena, since the seven elements are all innate qualities of the tathāgata-garbha. Both systems are expedient teachings of the Tathāgata.

The six elements spoken of by Shingon are not the elements in

their conditioned form—conditioned water, conditioned fire, etc.—
but the elements in their essential form, as in the *Śūraṅgama Sutra*. In
Shingon it is the four mandalas that deal with conditioned phenomena. Thus in Shingon it is said that the six elements are the substance,
the four mandalas are the form, and the three mystic practices are the
function.

For each of the seven elements there is a distinction between the
element as an inherent quality and the element as a conditioned phenomenon. If you fully understand one of the elements, then all of
the other elements can be similarly understood. For example, the fire
produced by rubbing sticks or striking flints is conditioned fire, lacking any independent existence—that is, it cannot burn without the
proper conditions, such as the presence of fuel like wood or oil. Conditioned fire exists only when, and for as long as, all of the necessary
conditions are present. Thus it is said to be unreal and without true
substance. All of the exoteric and esoteric sutras teach the insubstan-
tiality of conditionally generated phenomena.

Fire-nature, on the other hand, permeates the universe. It never
burns and is never extinguished. Ordinary people see only conditioned fire and know nothing of fire-nature. If you truly understand
fire-nature then you need not reject conditioned fire, since conditioned fire is simply a function of fire-nature.

As it is with the fire element, so it is with the other elements,
including the element of consciousness. The consciousness element
refers to the conscious mind of sentient beings. The mind, as ordinary
people generally conceive of it, is the conditionally generated mind
and is referred to as such in the sutras. This mind is without true
substance; its functions of sight, hearing, and cognition temporarily
appear owing to the conditions associated with the six objects of sensation.[423] In this it is the same as conditionally generated fire, which
burns for a time when the necessary conditions, like fuel, are present.

Deluded people recognize only the conditioned mind and know
nothing of mind-nature. When the non-Buddhist texts and Hinayana teachings speak of the mind they are invariably referring to the

conditioned mind. Even the ālaya-vijñāna, the eighth consciousness spoken of in Mahayana Buddhism, is still within the realm of the conditioned mind. Because of this the highest Mahayana teachings recognize a ninth consciousness, in order to inform people of the existence of the consciousness element as an inherent quality.[424]

There are two types of phenomena: physical phenomena and mental phenomena. Among the seven elements, the element of consciousness is a mental phenomenon and the other six are physical phenomena. However, since all seven universal elements are inherent to the tathāgata-garbha and freely interpenetrate each other, there is no distinction between physical and mental; this is known as the true Dharma-realm.[425] Although there is no distinction between physical and mental, the two do not intermix. Thus in the true Dharma-realm the physical is not subject to the forms of generation and annihilation, prosperity and decline, while the mental does not undergo the dynamic of movement and stillness, arising and extinction. When the sutras speak of all things in their true aspect being eternal, this is what is meant.

When people give rise to false views, the tathāgata-garbha produces various forms of mental and physical phenomena in accordance with the conditions generated by those views. Because false views are always changing, the various phenomena associated with them are also always changing. It is similar to how the shore seems to move when seen from a drifting boat, or to how the air seems full of lights appearing and disappearing when seen with abnormal eyes. This is why it is said that all phenomena are unreal.

Therefore, although it is sometimes taught that all phenomena are unreal and sometimes taught that all phenomena are eternal, the essence of the phenomena themselves[426] is the same despite the seemingly contradictory statements. Those who do not understand the Buddha's meaning, seeing the difference in the two teachings, accept one and reject the other. This is no more than worldly logic. It is as if someone with abnormal eyes and someone with normal eyes are looking at the same patch of sky; the former sees numerous lights appearing and disappearing, while the latter sees just the sky and has no need to wonder about lights.

All of this applies to other apparently contradictory statements like "the deluded passions are enlightenment," "samsara is nirvana," and "all things, just as they are, are the mysterious." It is also in this sense that teachings such as "form is the Way" and "phenomena are identical with truth" are meant.

However, it would be a great error to understand this to mean that ordinary deluded views, just as they are, are equal to the wisdom of a buddha. If this were true, for what purpose did the buddhas appear in the world? What problems are the masters of the exoteric and esoteric schools attempting to address when they urge their students to engage in spiritual disciplines? For what reason did the great teachers of the past establish monasteries away from populous places, prohibit the entrance of women, and forbid the drinking of alcohol and the eating of meat?

THE EYE OF THE BUDDHA

Question: Doesn't the eye of the Buddha see all conditionally generated phenomena in the same way as the eye of an ordinary person?

Answer: The Buddhist teachings mention the "five types of eye." These five types of eye are explained in various ways, but for the present I will confine myself to just one of these explanations.

The first type of eye is the physical eye, signifying the vision of ordinary people. However, those who have attained complete purity of the six sense organs can see the entire chiliocosm with the physical eye.[427] Second is the divine eye, signifying the vision of the deities. With this vision one can see through walls and beyond mountains and rivers. This, too, is an unawakened form of vision. When sages see with the divine eye the entire chiliocosm is visible to them.

Third is the eye of wisdom, signifying the vision that sees the nonsubstantiality of all phenomena. This type of vision is attained only when one reaches the bodhisattva stage, although to some degree it is available to śrāvakas and pratyekabuddhas as well. Fourth is the Dharma eye, signifying the vision that sees the phantasmal nature of all things. This type of vision, too, is attained only when one reaches the bodhisattva stage.

These four types of vision, though differing with regard to whether they are mundane or supramundane, are all the same in that they consist of various ways of seeing causally generated phenomena.

Fifth is the buddha eye, signifying the wisdom of the buddhas' inner realization. This type of vision cannot be known by beings up to and including bodhisattvas. However, the *Nirvana Sutra* says, "Although śrāvakas have divine eyes, they employ them as physical eyes. Although people who study the Mahayana have physical eyes, they use them as buddha eyes."[428] If it is as the sutra says, then we must not regard the buddha eye as possessed only by tathāgatas and unavailable to ordinary beings. An ancient master said, "The four eyes and the two wisdoms belong to the phenomenal world; the omniscient wisdom of the buddha eye is truly empty and utterly void."[429] However, because buddhas possess all five eyes they can see mundane forms just as ordinary people do and can perceive the nonsubstantiality of all phenomena and the phantasmal nature of all conditionally generated things, just as bodhisattvas do. Although they see as ordinary people do, the forms of generation and annihilation, past and future, do not catch them. Although they share the understanding of bodhisattvas, they do not abide in the realm of emptiness.

Thus it is only from the perspective of unenlightened nature that the differences between the five eyes are spoken of. From the standpoint of Buddha-wisdom there is no separation between deluded and enlightened or absolute and relative, and no difference between essence and form or phenomena and principle. To an ordinary person, precious metals, stones, water, fire, and plants are all qualitatively different. Buddhas, however, can turn metal into stone and fire into water, and therefore they feel no heat upon entering fire and no coolness upon entering water. Similarly, to them gold and silver are no better than tiles and stones, and tiles and stones are no worse than gold and silver. For those who have not yet attained such freedom, it is wrong to equate water and fire or to say that gold and stones are the same. So, too, is it wrong for people who have not yet awakened to Buddha-wisdom to say there is no difference between delusion and enlightenment or form and essence.

Question: What do the doctrinal schools mean when they say there are differences between the Mahayana and Hinayana traditions, and between the provisional and true teachings?

Answer: In the pure Dharma teachings there are no distinctions between "Mahayana" and "Hinayana," "provisional teachings" and "true teachings." However, since there are differences in the capacities of students, so too are there differences in the doctrines they can understand. In the *Lotus Sutra* it is written:

> The Dharma preached by the Tathāgata is of a single form and flavor, but because the natures and inclinations of sentient beings differ, the teachings they understand also differ. It is similar to how, when the same rain falls from the sky, the various herbs and trees absorb the moisture differently according to the sizes of their roots, stems, branches, and leaves.[430]

75

CAPACITIES

Question: Differences in the Dharma teachings exist because of differences in the natures of the students. For what reason, though, are the natures of the students not the same?

Answer: In the Dharma-realm of absolute suchness there are neither people nor objects. People and objects are provisionally differentiated on account of the deluded passions. Sentient beings have natures of various types, but, generally speaking, there are five basic kinds. The first is śrāvaka nature, the second is pratyekabuddha nature, the third is bodhisattva nature, the fourth is indeterminate nature, and the fifth is icchantika nature.

The Two Vehicles of the śrāvaka and the pratyekabuddha follow different paths, but both seek liberation for themselves only and have no interest in benefiting others, and they are thus said to be of the Hinayana mind. The bodhisattva is one who desires to benefit all sentient beings and thus follows the Mahayana path. Indeterminate nature characterizes people who are sometimes of the Hinayana mind and sometimes of the Mahayana mind, while icchantika nature is the nature of those who have no faith in the Buddhadharma.

The differences between the five natures come into being for a time when an instant of delusion arises within the equal, undifferentiated nature. In view of the differences between the respective natures they are clearly not the same, and thus each of the five natures has its own Dharma gates. The *Sutra of Complete Enlightenment* says:

> Desire being inherent in all sentient beings, sentient beings give rise to ignorance and manifest the differences between the five natures.... The intrinsic nature of perfect enlightenment is devoid of the five natures, but, in accordance with the five natures, gives rise to the distinct forms. In absolute truth there are no bodhisattvas or any sentient beings. Why? Because bodhisattvas and sentient beings are all like illusory transformations. [431]

The *Sutra for Resolving Doubts during the Age of the Semblance Dharma* says:

> The Tathāgata is neither being nor nonbeing, he neither appears nor disappears, he is neither form nor not-form; from the time of his enlightenment to the time of his final nirvana he preached not a word of the Dharma. However, ignorant people think that he appeared in the world, taught the Dharma, and liberated people. The realm of the Tathāgata is beyond understanding. It cannot be known through consciousness; it cannot be known through wisdom.... The physical aspect of sentient beings is like an illusory transformation, like an image in a mirror or the reflection of the moon on water. The mental aspect of sentient beings is also beyond understanding. It neither comes nor goes, it is neither being nor nonbeing, it is neither internal nor external. Nevertheless, sentient beings in their confusion become deeply attached to the view of an existent self, and therefore needlessly undergo transmigration. [432]

The *Laṅkāvatāra Sutra* says, "From the beginning at the Deer Park until the end at the River Hiraṇyavatī, the Buddha spoke not a single word."[433] The *Avataṃsaka Sutra* says, "In the realm of true purity there is neither Buddha nor sentient beings."[434] The *Commentary on the Treatise on Mahayana* says, "The nondual Mahayana is independent of nature and doctrine."[435] The nondual Mahayana is that which existed prior to the separation of the Mahayana and Hinayana traditions and the provisional and true teachings.

It is because people refuse to believe holy teachings such as these that they take up the practice of upāya, that they talk of Mahayana, Hinayana, and provisional teachings, and that they distinguish superior, intermediate, and inferior capacities among practicers. As a result some become arrogant and fall into the way of the demons, while others become discouraged and return to the byways of delusion. Can such people be considered wise?

Question: The teachings speak of there being "no form of buddha and no form of ordinary beings."[436] Is this not what Zen speaks of when it refers to "the place prior to the separation of buddhas and ordinary beings"?

Answer: When the teaching schools speak of there being no forms of "sacred" and "profane," they mean that in the realm where sacred and profane are already separate, the essential natures of both are free of distinguishing forms. This is not what Zen means by "the place prior to the separation of buddhas and deluded beings"; one should not assume that Zen and the doctrinal schools are the same just because there are certain similarities in the words they use. A general description of the human face—"Below the forehead is a pair of eyebrows, each with an eye underneath, and between the eyes is a nose with a mouth below"—applies to everyone, whether highborn or lowborn, male or female. Yet when you actually look at individual faces you see they are quite different. The doctrinal traditions rely on words and reason to convey the Buddhadharma, and thus they classify the traditions into Mahayana or Hinayana, provisional or true, according to the nature of their teachings. Zen, however, is "a separate transmission outside the teachings, not relying on words and letters." Therefore, to compare Zen and the doctrinal schools on the basis of the words of the Zen masters is to miss the mark.

Certain Zen practicers today, noticing that the sayings of the Zen masters often differ from the teachings of the doctrinal traditions, regard this as proof of Zen's superiority. If one says that Zen is superior because of its differences from the doctrinal traditions, by the same logic the doctrinal traditions are superior because of their differences from Zen. The fundamental truth of the separate transmission outside the teachings is utterly unrelated to any similarities or differences it might have with doctrinal explanations.

Sometimes people say, "The doctrinal traditions all speak from the standpoint of words and reason, while not getting involved in words and reason is the fundamental position of the Zen school." However, there are Dharma gates in the doctrinal schools, too, that do not rely upon words and letters. Would one call these Zen?

Occasionally followers of the scholarly schools complain that Zen cannot claim it does not rely on words and letters, since Zen masters often use words and letters in their teaching. Although Zen masters do indeed quite frequently use words, their purpose is not to have people study the concepts expressed in those words but to awaken them to the fact that the true principles of the Buddhadharma are not to be found in words. Saying this, however, does not mean that simply cutting off the paths of talk or sinking into silent nihility represents the true teaching of the Zen school.

The ancient masters asserted that Bodhidharma came from the West, not in order to transmit a particular teaching, but simply to point out that which everyone already possesses in complete perfection.[437] If it is already possessed by everyone, how can it be said to be limited to followers of Zen and to be lacking in followers of the doctrinal schools? Nor is it perfectly present only in the followers of Zen and the doctrinal traditions—it may be discerned in the labors of the farmer cultivating his fields and in the blacksmith and carpenter exercising their crafts. The essential point is that everything living beings do—seeing, hearing, thinking, knowing, walking, standing, sitting, reclining, playing, and talking—is without exception an expression of the Mysterious Principle of the coming from the West. How much more so does this apply to the actions of those who, following the Buddha's teachings, perform all manner of meritorious deeds?

However, not being aware of this Mysterious Principle, most people are deceived by the illusions of the world and squander their existence in the cycle of birth and death. The Buddha expounded various teachings intended to help people escape from this deluded thinking, but people then became attached to these teachings and again obscured the Mysterious Principle. Therefore the Patriarch came from the West and revealed Original Nature. This revelation is called "the Mysterious Principle outside the teachings that is transmitted by mind to mind."[438] This Mysterious Principle is not simply another type of Dharma gate transmitted in the same way as the various doctrinal traditions. If it were just another teaching passed on through words, then it would be no more than an unusual teaching method and could not be called "a separate transmission outside the teachings."

After the Sixth Patriarch the Zen lineage divided into the Five Houses, each in its own characteristic way seeking to awaken people to what they already possess. However, practicers nowadays, instead of awakening to the Mysterious Principle, simply copy down and memorize the explanations of the masters, ponder the relative merits of the Five Houses, and compare the strengths and weaknesses of their various approaches to teaching. Are they not missing the point of the Patriarch's coming from the West?

Many years ago, when I was on an excursion with seven or eight other monks, we visited a place called West Lake not far from Mount Fuji. Everything we saw amazed us, and it seemed as if we had entered the enchanted realm of the Taoist immortals. Meeting a fisherman by the shore, we hired him to take us out in his boat. With each new inlet he sculled us to we were met by scenes of the rarest beauty. The monks, unable to contain their delight, slapped the side of the boat and shouted with joy. The old fisherman, who had lived by the lake since childhood and had viewed its scenery from dawn to dusk every day, did not share in our reaction. Seeing the monks' excitement, he asked, "What is it that makes you cry out like that?" The monks answered, "We are struck by the beauty of the mountains and the wonderful views of the lake." The old man couldn't understand, and finally he asked, with a skeptical look on his face, "You mean to say that you came all the way here just to see the scenery?"

I said to the other monks, "If this old fisherman asks us to explain what it is that so moves us about this place, how could we convey it to him? If we pointed to the scenery and told him that *that* is what we find so moving, the old man would say he has seen the same scenery his entire life and observed nothing remarkable about it. However, if we tried to correct this misunderstanding by telling him that what delights us is something different from what his eyes are seeing, he might conclude that we were somehow viewing a place of great beauty somewhere apart from West Lake and therefore dismissing what he sees."

The meaning of "the special transmission outside the teachings" is like this. It does not differ from the acts and deeds of living beings, nor does it differ from the words and teachings of the Buddhist and non-Buddhist scriptures. However, those who are unaware that the Mysterious Principle is *within* these things entertain various misunderstandings when they hear about this separate transmission. Some people think that the Mysterious Principle consists of giving free rein to the three poisons,[439] while others equate it with the teachings of Taoism and Confucianism. Still others see it as no different from a thorough understanding of the various schools of doctrinal Buddhism, or of the respective natures of the Five Houses of Zen. All of these interpretations are like the old fisherman of West Lake thinking that what the monks were so excited about was the same old scenery he was accustomed to seeing every day.

When Zen masters attempt to disabuse students of such misconceptions by changing tack and saying that the Buddhist and non-Buddhist teachings do *not* express the Mysterious Principle, and that the acts and deeds of living beings are nothing but delusion, then foolish people look for a separate transmission apart from the Buddhist and non-Buddhist teachings, and seek the Mysterious Principle somewhere else than in the everyday activities of life. This is like the old fisherman concluding that the Zen monks were excited about some place of wonderful beauty somewhere apart from West Lake.

The difference between the monks and the old man had nothing to do with the mountains, trees, water, and rocks that they were seeing, but with whether or not they were affected by the sight of them. The experience of being moved is not something that one learns through explanation. When the time is ripe and one's heart is open to being moved, only then does one experience it for oneself. The same is true of Original Nature. One knows this Ground only when one approaches it with an open spirit. Although crystal clear when one knows it, it cannot be grasped and shown to someone else. Thus, although all inherently possesses it, when one is not in accord with it everything one does simply generates more samsaric karma. This is what an ancient master meant when he said that one either knows it completely or knows it not at all.[440] It is because people are not awakened to the Mysterious Principle of Bodhidharma that they compare the words and phrases of the scriptures with those of the Zen masters, seeking similarities and differences and judging which is superior.

Question: Does the fact that the Zen school is divided into the Five Houses indicate that there are various levels in the attainment of the Dharma?

Answer: The division of Zen into Five Houses occurred not because there are various levels in the attainment of the Dharma but because there are various different ways of guiding students to Original Nature. This is not the same as the way in which the scholastic schools teach different doctrines in accordance with their respective interpretations of the Dharma. In the Zen school, attainment of the Dharma signifies the direct realization of the Ground of Original Nature, not the thorough understanding of the doctrinal teachings of the buddhas and patriarchs.

Consequently the words used by Zen masters are not teachings aimed at such understanding but are expedients for bringing their students directly to enlightenment. The Zen teacher's words are sometimes directed toward attainment of the ultimate principle and sometimes employed as an expression of this principle. In either case they are beyond the understanding of the deluded consciousness, and they are thus referred to as "the barriers of the Zen ancestors."

Zen Master Dahui said, "Even with true awakening and true

attainment, if one has not yet realized the complete Dharma, then one blinds others by teaching on the basis of one's own personal awakening and attainment."[441] Know, therefore, that the guidance of clear-eyed teachers of the Zen school is not based on personal awakening and attainment.

In ancient times a government official called upon Wuzu Fayan[442] and asked what characterized the Zen school. Wuzu answered that the nature of the Zen school cannot be grasped with the deluded mind, but that a general sense of what it is about can be gained from the following poem:

> I try to express my feelings but I am not able.
>> Here in this back chamber I convey my sadness
> By repeatedly calling my maid Little Jade, for no other reason
>> Than to have my man hear my voice.[443]

"My man" refers to the lover of the young woman who wrote the poem. One day when he was near her residence she wished to let him know that she was there. Careful of her reputation, however, she repeatedly called out to her maid Little Jade, asking her to raise the paper screens or lower the bamboo blinds, all for no other purpose than to let her lover hear her voice and know of her presence.

The methods used by the Five Houses are similar to this. All are expedient devices, like the calling of Little Jade. However, ranking the respective schools according to the relative merits of their oral and literary traditions simply reveals that one has not understood the intent of the schools' founders.

THE REASON FOR PRAISE AND CENSURE

78

Question: The stories and *mondō* of the ancient masters contain many examples of them praising or censuring each other. Why, then, is it considered wrong for students to criticize others?

Answer: Praise and criticism are used by the Zen masters as expedient devices, like the calling of Little Jade. This is known in Zen as "encouraging and suppressing, praising and censuring." It is not the same as judging people on the basis of human emotion and selfish attachments.

As the *Song of Enlightenment* says, "Whether it is right or whether it is wrong, people do not know; whether the going is rough or whether the going is smooth, even the heavens cannot tell."[444]

79

THE TRUE MEANING
OF THE BUDDHA'S TEACHINGS

Question: Did the Buddha ever employ such methods in his teachings?

Answer: The way Zen sees it, all of the Buddha's teachings throughout his entire career were expedient devices, just like calling Little Jade. Sometimes he taught that all things are impermanent and sometimes that all things are eternal. Sometimes he explained that all things are unreal and sometimes that all things are absolute reality. Sometimes he said that the Buddhadharma has nothing to do with the written word and sometimes that verbal explanations are the very body of the absolute Dharma. All of these teachings are like calling out to Little Jade and asking her to raise or lower the paper screens.

The true intention of the Tathāgata does not lie in the words and phrases. Nevertheless, people who know nothing of the Buddha's meaning take up the intellectual content of what he said, believe those particular things that suit their deluded views, and think of them as expressing what the Buddha was truly attempting to communicate. This is similar to believing that the woman's instructions to Little Jade to raise and lower the screens expressed what was really on her mind.

Some people think that the Tathāgata's teachings were not fixed because he realized that the Dharma has no set form. According to this view, when the Buddha spoke of formlessness it was because the noumenal ground of absolute reality is free of even the slightest impurity; when he said that all forms are distinct it was because the totality of conditioned phenomena consists of the ten realms with their individual beings and their environments.[445] Although people who think in this way are superior to those who are biased toward a particular teaching of the Buddha, they still haven't grasped the Buddha's true intention. It is as though, upon hearing the story of Little Jade, they interpret it to mean, "The woman has the screens closed to keep out the wind and has them opened when the room needs ventilating. In this way there are no fixed positions and things shouldn't be taken at surface value." Such interpretations also miss what the woman truly intended.

The *Sutra of the Arising of the World* says, "When the god of fire enters water then even water becomes fire, and when the god of water enters fire then even fire becomes water."[446] The Buddhist teachings are similar to this. When the doctrinal teachings are viewed with the eye of Zen they align with Zen understanding. When Zen understanding is viewed with the eye of the doctrine, it is no different from the doctrinal teachings. This is true not only of the doctrinal teachings and Zen but also of Buddhism and worldly affairs. If one has realized the enlightened understanding of the Dharma, then the affairs of the world all partake in the Buddhadharma. But if one remains caught in the worldly passions, then even what one takes to be the profound and subtle principle is simply another worldly concern.

Question: The Buddha had two ways of preaching the Dharma. One way is called "adapted teaching," in which the Buddha preached in accordance with the capacities of his listeners. The other way is called "direct teaching," in which the Buddha directly expressed his true intentions. In the Zen school, is the device referred to as "calling Little Jade" regarded as a form of adapted teaching?

Answer: To categorize certain of the Tathāgata's sermons as "adapted teachings" and others as "direct teachings" is the approach of the doctrinal schools. When Zen masters take up the Buddha's teachings they may refer to them as "adapted" or they may refer to them as "direct," but these terms are simply expedients, like calling Little Jade. There are in Zen no fixed categories. Thus it may be that a teaching of the Buddha referred to today as direct will be referred to tomorrow as adapted. This is the case not only with these two terms but also with similar pairings, such as "superficial teachings" versus "profound teachings" and "false teachings" versus "true teachings."

As an ancient master said, the Zen way of teaching is different from that of the doctrinal schools, in which an inch is always an inch and a foot is always a foot. Śākyamuni Buddha never defined himself as a teacher of doctrine, just as he never labeled himself a teacher of meditation. Nor when he taught did he ever differentiate between meditation teachings and doctrinal teachings, because the Tathāgata's inner realization was never limited to just meditation or just doctrine. The distinction between doctrine and meditation only arose when the mysterious functioning of the Tathāgata's inner realization would respond in accordance with the individual needs of the listeners. Thus the *Vimalakīrti Sutra* says, "The Buddha preaches the Dharma with a single voice, but each living being understands it in his or her own way."[447]

While the Buddha was still in the world there was no division of his disciples into "doctrinal monks" and "meditation monks," even though they interpreted his teachings in different ways. It was only after the Buddha's passing that the separation of doctrine and meditation occurred, along with the division into the exoteric and esoteric teachings in the doctrinal tradition, and the division into the Five Houses in the Zen tradition.

These divisions arose because eminent teachers further developed the Buddha's teaching methods, devising expedient means suited to the temperaments and preferences of various individuals in order to convey the Buddha's central teaching of Original Nature. These wise and virtuous figures became the doctrinal authorities and meditation masters who, themselves having broken through their deluded biases and transcended the split between meditation and doctrine, extended a hand to lead other beings to the Ground of Original Nature. In other words, the true objective of genuine doctrinal masters does not lie within doctrine, nor does the true objective of clear-eyed meditation masters lie within meditation. The reason the tenets preached by these masters are different is that all are expedients like calling Little Jade. In this Latter Age of the Dharma, followers of the meditation and doctrinal schools for whom sectarian biases come first end up sinking in the sea of right and wrong and thus obscuring the true objective of the buddhas and patriarchs.

The *Sutra for Resolving Doubts during the Age of the Semblance Dharma* states, "To understand the meaning of a sutra only on the basis of its words is to harm all buddhas in the past, present, and future."[448] Clear-eyed masters of the Zen school do not have a prepared set of teachings that they have memorized. Rather, they respond in accordance with the situation, letting the words come as they will. There are no set strategies. If someone asks about Zen, masters may answer with the words of Confucius, Mencius, Laozi, or Zhuangzi. Sometimes they may use doctrinal teachings or popular sayings, or point to something nearby. Or they may wave their stick, give a loud shout, raise their finger, or hold up their fist. These are the methods used by Zen masters; they are the vital functioning of Zen. Those who have not yet reached the Ground of Original Nature cannot fathom it with either senses or intellect.

TEACHING THROUGH PRINCIPLE, TEACHING THROUGH DEVICES

Question: What do the expressions "teaching through principle" and "teaching through devices" mean?

Answer: If one is speaking from the standpoint of Original Nature there is nothing to refer to as "teaching through principle" or "teaching through devices." However, when utilizing expedient means to further the message of Zen, the expression "teaching through principle" is applied to those methods that employ reason as a way to encourage students, while the expression "teaching through devices" is applied to those methods that do not employ reason, that is, methods such as the stick, the shout, and the koan. In either case these are no more than expedients, like calling Little Jade.

An ancient master said:

> Prior to Mazu and Baizhang, many teachers utilized the "teaching through principle" approach and few used the "teaching through devices" approach. Subsequent to Mazu and Baizhang, many teachers utilized the "teaching through devices" approach and few used the "teaching through principle" approach. In so doing, their policy was to "watch the wind and set the sails accordingly."[449]

Present-day students who like teaching through principle tend to dislike teaching through devices, and those who like teaching through devices tend to dislike teaching through principle. Neither type of student understands the methods of the founding masters. If you say that teaching through devices is the superior method, would you then say that all of the masters prior to Mazu and Baizhang lacked the Zen eye? If you say that teaching through principle is superior, would you say that Linji and Deshan did not know the true meaning of Zen?

During the course of his fifty years of teaching, Śākyamuni preached on more than three hundred occasions. And yet the *Laṅkāvatāra Sutra* says, "From the beginning at the Deer Park until the end at the River Hiraṇyavatī, the Buddha spoke not a single word." If one understands the point of this statement, are there any teachings to be dismissed as "teaching through principle"?

Fayan Wenyi[450] once asked Juetiezui, "I heard that your teacher, Zhaozhou, was asked the meaning of Bodhidharma's coming from the West and answered, 'The juniper tree in the garden.' Is this true?" Juetiezui replied, "My late teacher never said such a thing—don't slander him!"[451] Juetiezui was a top disciple of Zhaozhou [so he would have known that Zhaozhou *did* speak of a juniper tree]. Why then did he answer as he did? It was because Juetiezui would never have countenanced anyone who conceptually interpreted Zhaozhou's words.

This applies not only to this koan but also to every other koan expressed by the masters. A koan is simply an upāya; if one imposes interpretations upon the different expressions of this upāya, one obscures what the masters are truly attempting to convey. A completely liberated person can take gold and transform it to dirt and can take dirt and transform it to gold. When such people hold something in their hands, how can you possibly know whether it is dirt or gold? It is no different with the teachings. When a clear-eyed master expresses a teaching, it is impossible to define it either as "teaching through principle" or "teaching through devices."

82

EASY PRACTICE, DIFFICULT PRACTICE

Question: Followers of the Pure Land teachings say, "People in this Latter Age of the Dharma cannot attain enlightenment even if they practice the Mahayana. Therefore people should engage in the practice of *nenbutsu*, gain rebirth in the Pure Land, and thereupon enter the Mahayana. They also say that, regardless of what Age of the Dharma one is in, the Dharma gate of *nenbutsu* is the highest of all teachings. This is because it does not disapprove of evildoers, nor is it closed to the foolish; all who chant the name of Amitābha Buddha will attain rebirth in the Pure Land, where they will eventually attain true enlightenment. For this reason the Pure Land teaching is known as the path of easy practice, or the World-Transcending Vow. Consequently, following the path of difficult practice is futile." Is there anything to this point of view?

Answer: Those who encourage the Pure Land teachings are followers of Śākyamuni's teachings. Are not all of the various Mahayana sutras the teachings of Śākyamuni? Among the Mahayana sutras are those that were preached for the sake of Mahayana followers in the Latter Age. None of these sutras say that sentient beings in the Latter Age should abandon practice of the Mahayana and engage only in recitation of the *nenbutsu*. This does not mean, however, that belief in the *nenbutsu* teachings should be disparaged, since people have various dispositions and some lack the karmic propensity for Mahayana practice. It is for the sake of such people that the Tathāgata preached this particular path.

Even among those who possess the karmic propensities to practice the Mahayana, there are those who, while following the Mahayana teachings, are filled with deluded thoughts and are unable to realize their true minds. Some such people say that even if they were to practice their entire lives they would never escape the evil consequences certain to befall them, and that they should therefore rely on the Original Vow of Other Power[452] and aspire to rebirth in the Pure Land.

These people do not understand the essential message of the Mahayana, even as they study the Mahayana teachings. Aspiring for a Pure Land separate from the evil realms, distinguishing Self Power from Other Power, arguing about the path of easy practice versus the path of difficult practice—none of this partakes of the fully revealed teachings of the Mahayana. Those who believe in the essential message of the Mahayana, even if they have yet to attain a clear awakening, should not let the arising of deluded thoughts discourage them, or, still less, cause them to talk of evil realms and the Pure Land or separate Self Power from Other Power. The distinction between the evil realms and the Pure Land is nothing more than a momentary image arising from a passing thought.

The *Sutra of Complete Enlightenment* says, "All of the buddha realms are like flowers in the sky."[453] If you have faith in the essential message of the Mahayana and keep it in mind throughout your activities, you will surely avoid falling into the evil realms even if you are unable to immediately attain enlightenment. And should a person whose karmic burden is heavy and whose capacity to practice is weak fall into the evil realms, it is still possible to attain sudden liberation through unshaken faith in and understanding of the Mahayana.

Evidence for this is provided by the *Lotus Sutra* story of the Dragon King's daughter, who, though born in the realm of the animals, was able to attain sudden true enlightenment at the age of eight.[454] King Ajātaśatru committed the mortal sin of patricide, yet he was able to attain awakening upon meeting Śākyamuni just before the Buddha entered nirvana.[455] At that time the Buddha said to Ajātaśatru, "You and I were students together under Vipaśyin Buddha[456] and awakened to the Mahayana mind at the same time. However, you neglected your practice and have therefore failed to attain the Buddha Way. Nevertheless, because the power of your faith in the Mahayana has never weakened, since the time of Vipaśyin you have never fallen into the evil realms but have always been born into the families of kings and ministers. It is because of the fruition of your karmic tendencies from these former lives that, despite having committed a mortal sin in your present existence, you were able to meet me and attain realization."[457]

A sutra says, "Falling into hell for slandering the Mahayana is preferable to erecting a hundred thousand stupas. It is like the ground causing a person to stumble and the ground enabling that person to arise."[458] What this means is that even if you fall into hell for a time as a result of slandering the Mahayana, the fact of having encountered the Mahayana will eventually result in your liberation; all the more so for those who never forget the essential message of the Mahayana and practice in accordance with its forms.

Various practices have been established for those who believe in the unity of sacred and profane in the Mahayana but who have yet to clearly understand this truth. Though these Mahayana practices take disparate forms, they all differ from the Hinayana approach of seeking nirvana apart from samsara and from the provisional teachings' approach of seeking the true mind apart from the deluded mind. This is what is meant when the Mahayana talks about "practicing without practicing, and awakening without awakening."[459]

If you keep in mind the essential message of the Mahayana and in that spirit read the sutras, recite the mantras, and chant the name of Amitābha Buddha, none of these practices will hinder you in any way. Those who, deceived by ignorance and deluded thinking, believe that Mahayana practice is too difficult and that one must therefore depend upon Other Power cannot rightly be called students of the Mahayana. Indeed, if one says one knows the Mahayana teachings but advocates *nenbutsu* practice because the Mahayana path is too difficult, one is a slanderer of the Mahayana. However, if one says one knows nothing of the Mahayana teachings and therefore focuses on *nenbutsu* practice, that is acceptable as far as it goes.

There are those who say, "The Dharma gate of *nenbutsu* is the ultimate teaching because it does not condemn evildoers nor abandon the foolish, and because anyone who chants the name of Amitābha Buddha will attain rebirth in the Pure Land and immediately attain Buddhahood. All other teachings are paths of difficult practice, and are therefore inferior." If it were true that even the evil and the foolish could immediately attain true enlightenment by merely chanting the name of Amitābha Buddha, this would be a Dharma gate appropriate not only for people of inferior capacities in the Latter Age of the Dharma but also for people of superior capacities in earlier ages of the Dharma. Teaching such people the path of difficult practice would have been completely superfluous. Yet the great majority of sutras preached by Śākyamuni during his lifetime teach the difficult path so disdained by the Pure Land tradition. Sutras that teach the path of rebirth in the Pure Land through practice of the *nenbutsu* are few in number. The only texts that truly teach the Pure Land practices are the three Pure Land sutras.[460] Would the Tathāgata have been so ignorant as to teach so many nonessential and difficult Dharma gates?

FULLY REVEALED AND
PARTIALLY REVEALED TEACHINGS

83

Question: Some people say that the *nenbutsu* teachings are also of the Mahayana. Why is this?

Answer: In *nenbutsu* samādhi there is no form of "Hinayana" or "Mahayana." There are, however, distinctions based on the various understandings of people of differing capacities. Sutras such as the *Nirvana Sutra* and the *Sutra of the Great Treasure Collection* have passages stating that the Buddha's teachings are of two types, the fully revealed sutras and the partially revealed sutras, and that sentient beings in the Latter Age should rely on the teachings of the fully revealed sutras. Teachings such as "the Buddha exists apart from deluded beings" or "the Pure Land is separate from the world of defilement" are those of the partially revealed sutras, they say, explaining that the fully revealed sutras see no distinction between the sacred and the profane or the pure and the defiled.[461]

If such passages are correct, then the Pure Land school, which posits the existence of a Pure Land separate from the realm of defilement and of buddhas separate from ordinary people, cannot be regarded as a fully revealed teaching of the Mahayana. Furthermore, the *Sutra on the Contemplation of Eternal Life* says that among those who practice the *nenbutsu* and are reborn in the Pure Land, those of the lowest grade of the lowest class[462] will pass twelve great kalpas[463] in the buds of lotus blossoms, after which they will hear the supremely profound Mahayana teachings preached by the bodhisattvas Avalokiteśvara and Mahāsthāmaprāpta[464] and will for the first time arouse bodhicitta.[465] Thus it is not the case that those reborn in the Pure Land immediately attain true enlightenment. If the practice of *nenbutsu* is indeed the ultimate teaching of the Mahayana, why then does the sutra say that one does not awaken to bodhicitta until hearing a second, separate communication of the Mahayana doctrines following rebirth in the Pure Land?

Know that the "single practice" of the *nenbutsu* is advocated in order to guide those who lack the karmic roots for Mahayana practice, so that they might first be helped toward rebirth in the Pure Land and then awakened to the Mahayana. Or it may be recommended to those Mahayana practicers for whom severe impediments and deficient wisdom make enlightenment difficult, so that with the protective mental forces of the buddhas as a support they might more rapidly accomplish the Mahayana bodhisattva practices. If someone of superior capacities engages in the concentrated practice of *nenbutsu*-with-form he should quickly attain the samādhi of formless *nenbutsu*. This is the teaching of the *Samādhi of Beholding the Buddhas Sutra.*[466] Even if one can accomplish this, however, it is not the supreme, fully revealed gate to the Dharma.

THE FULLY REVEALED
MAHAYANA NENBUTSU

Question: From ancient times there have been proponents of the fully revealed teachings of the Mahayana who have practiced the *nenbutsu*. There are also many Zen masters who praise this practice. Why then do you disparage it?

Answer: Chanting the name of Amitābha Buddha is not necessarily a partially revealed teaching. The *Nirvana Sutra* says, "All speech both coarse and fine returns to the ultimate principle."[467] The *Lotus Sutra* states that "earning a living and producing things never transgresses the True Law."[468] If you awaken to the true principle of the Mahayana, then every word and action in the world becomes the fully revealed Mahayana. No one, then, could possibly claim that recitation of the Buddha's name is Hinayana in nature.

Although they themselves understood the profound principles of the Mahayana, the founders of the Pure Land school provisionally differentiated the Pure Land from the defiled realm and Self Power from Other Power in order to guide the unlearned. One should not say, therefore, that they were lacking in wisdom—theirs was the compassionate upāya of the bodhisattvas, even if those believers who recite the *nenbutsu* hoping for rebirth in a Pure Land outside the defiled world cannot be considered followers of the fully revealed Mahayana.

The Buddha himself preached partially revealed teachings, which served as expedients for guidance and thus cannot be regarded as useless. The reason that the partially revealed teachings are disparaged in the *Nirvana Sutra* and other texts is to emphasize the fact that the Buddha's true message is expressed in the fully revealed teachings.

The Shingon school has an esoteric *nenbutsu* practice, which they understand differently from the way Pure Land Buddhists do their *nenbutsu*. Zen people also say the *nenbutsu*, but with a different intent than that of the usual Pure Land follower. In Zen there are no fixed forms of practice. The recitation of dhāraṇīs such as the *Laṅkāvatāra Dhāraṇī* and the *Great Compassion Dhāraṇī* is a recent introduction. In Zen there are no set conventions enjoining worship of a particular buddha or other object of devotion; those who have faith in Avalokiteśvara or Kṣitigarbha,[469] for example, recite for themselves the names of these bodhisattvas. If someone who has faith in Amitābha Buddha wishes to chant his name, what harm could there be in that?

Certain Zen believers nowadays distance themselves from the Pure Land tradition, regarding the *nenbutsu* as a Hinayana teaching and *nenbutsu* devotees as ignorant. Such people do not understand that the central truth taught by the Zen masters is inherent in everyone. The *Questions of Viśeṣacinta Brahmā Deva Sutra*[470] says:

> There are people who hear the Mahayana teachings but reject them in disbelief. This is like a fool objecting to the existence of space and attempting to remove himself from it. Anyone seeing this who took pity on the fool and tried to call him back into space would be just as foolish. It is the same with people who take pity on those who reject the Mahayana and attempt to bring them into it.[471]

Question: If it is as you say, wouldn't that mean belief in the *nen-butsu* is fine just as it is, since it is fully in line with the intent of the patriarchs?

Answer: Those who have faith in the message of the patriarchs know that everything one does is in accord with that message, and thus at times they say the *nenbutsu* or recite dhāraṇīs. *Nenbutsu* practice done in this spirit is fine. However, among ordinary *nenbutsu* devotees there are some who insist that calling the Name is the only correct practice and that all other practices are useless. This viewpoint goes against the true principles of the Mahayana and cannot be said to agree with the central teaching of the patriarchs.

It would be equally mistaken for followers of the Zen school to declare that the only true practice is *zazen* and that all other practices are a waste of time. Nevertheless, it is helpful for beginning Zen students to set aside other methods for a time and concentrate solely on *zazen*, singling out this practice though fundamentally nothing is rejected. It is in this sense that the eminent priests who established the Pure Land school set aside the "other practices" and aspired to "the samādhi of the single practice [of *nenbutsu*]"; it was not that they condemned the other methods. Similarly, the intent of clear-eyed

Zen masters when they criticize *nenbutsu* is never to condemn this practice. This is the case not only with criticisms directed toward the Pure Land school but also with those directed toward all other traditions. Even when non-Buddhists and celestial demons engage enlightened masters in discussion, the masters do not regard themselves as superior and their adversaries as inferior. Rather, they criticize their challengers only in order to disabuse them of their biased notion that "our views are better than the teachings of the Buddha"— a notion based on their failure to see that there is not a hairbreadth of difference between a sage and an ordinary person. The *Sutra of Complete Enlightenment* says, "The Dharma attained by bodhisattvas and by non-Buddhist practicers is the same bodhi."[472] In the *Lotus Sutra*, Bodhisattva Never Disparaging would bow to everyone without discriminating between celestial demons, non-Buddhists, evil people, and good people, saying, "I have great reverence for you and would never disparage you, because all of you are practicing the bodhisattva path."[473]

Only after penetrating to the ground attained by Never Disparaging and starting to utilize upāya should students of the Mahayana provisionally distinguish right from wrong where there is no right and wrong, criticize people, and argue against other doctrines. Anyone speaking of right and wrong who still has strong attachments to self and objects is not a true disciple of the Buddha. How could such behavior be in accord with the truth?

Question: Some people say that when clear-eyed Zen masters slander the buddhas and censure the patriarchs, or praise the buddhas and revere the patriarchs, this is a Zen technique known as "encouraging and suppressing, praising and censuring" and does not involve praise and censure of the buddhas and patriarchs themselves but rather of the correct and false views of the learners. Is this explanation true?

Answer: When enlightened masters praise or censure the buddhas and patriarchs, this is not directed toward the buddhas and patriarchs but is intended as an expedient to benefit their students. The ancient masters said that we do not differ a hairbreadth from the buddhas and patriarchs. Before a clear-eyed person there are no buddhas and patriarchs to revere, no deluded beings to disdain. It is in order to help people reach the stage where there is no separation between sacred and mundane that the masters employ various expedients. Sometimes they praise and sometimes they censure, but their true intention never lies in the praise or censure itself. Foolish students fail to realize this, and, taking the masters at their word, become happy when praised and angry when scolded. Even if their reactions don't go as far as anger they still wonder what they did that caused them to be admonished and attempt to correct their error.

Present-day teachers may understand the notion that there is no separation between sacred and mundane, but if they have not themselves actually reached this stage then they will praise or censure their students on the basis of appearances of right and wrong. The *Sutra of Complete Enlightenment* says, "In the Latter Age of the Dharma, people cultivating bodhi who have partial realizations and do not root out the traces of self will be pleased with those who believe in their teaching and angry with those who criticize it."[474]

KEEN STUDENTS, DULL STUDENTS

Question: Why do you say that there is not a hairbreadth of difference between sages and ordinary people when you speak of some teachers as clear-eyed and others as blind, and of some students as keen and others as dull?

Answer: Assessments of people as keen or dull are not made according to ordinary logic. For example, even a person who has mastered the entire body of teachings is considered dull if he is unaware that he differs in no way from the buddhas and patriarchs. This does not mean, however, that there exist "ignorant people" who are fundamentally different from the buddhas and patriarchs. It is similar with the division of masters into those who are clear-eyed and those who lack the eye. A teacher who lacks the eye is one who discusses the teachings while still attached to self and objects, regarding himself as enlightened and his students as deluded and failing to see that there is no real difference between bodhi and avidya. But this is not to say that there are inherently ignorant and unenlightened people who are inferior to clear-eyed masters.

These teachings are not subject to understanding by the ordinary deluded consciousness; only when one has reached the stage [of realizing that there is no difference between bodhi and avidya] can they be grasped.

Question: There are those who say that a Mahayana practicer need not necessarily observe the precepts. Is this correct?

Answer: The teachings of the buddhas are infinite, yet all of them are contained within the three disciplines: the precepts, meditation, and wisdom. These three disciplines are inherent in the One Mind of sentient beings. Thus if one penetrates to the source of this One Mind one attains all of the marvelous virtues of the three disciplines. It is like obtaining the maṇi, the wish-fulfilling jewel that manifests all other treasures. Therefore the investigation of the source of the One Mind is the essence of Mahayana practice. This is what is meant when it is said that the form of the precepts need not necessarily be observed. The *Nirvana Sutra* says, "Observing the precepts consists of diligent application to the practice of the Mahayana."[475]

Nevertheless, it is wrong to say that Mahayana practicers need not keep the precepts. Since the time of the Tathāgata (and, needless to say, during his lifetime as well), the teachers of doctrine and meditation who have spread his Dharma have all fully maintained the precepts. While the Buddha was alive there were no such things as meditation monks, scholastic monks, and precept monks distinguished by appearance and dress. Externally they all behaved in accordance with the rules of conduct and deportment, while internally they all cultivated meditation and wisdom.

In the present Latter Age of the Dharma, however, those able to combine all three disciplines are rare, so it is not unreasonable that the followers of the respective disciplines would divide into distinct schools. It is mistaken, however, for each school to criticize the others, insisting that the discipline it focuses on is first in importance. In the *Sutra for Resolving Doubts during the Age of the Semblance Dharma* the Buddha says:

> In the Latter Age of the Dharma, meditation monks, scholastic monks, and precept monks will separate from one another and eventually destroy my Dharma with their mutual condemnations. They are like parasites in a lion who eat away at its flesh.[476]

Monks of this sort behave in this way because they have failed to extinguish their deluded passions and thus remain attached to their egos. One wonders, however, how even such monks as they can call themselves disciples of the Buddha and still transgress the rules laid down by him.

Buddhism first entered China at the time of Emperor Ming of the Later Han dynasty.[477] At that time, and for several centuries thereafter, the appearance of the monks was much as it was at the time of the Buddha. From the time of the Tang-dynasty master Dazhi of Baizhang,[478] however, Zen monks started to live apart from Vinaya temples. They established their own monasteries and followed rules of conduct different from those of the Vinaya monks. Baizhang explained these developments by saying:

> In the Latter Age of the Dharma people's capacities are dull, and they are unable to simultaneously follow all three disciplines of precepts, meditation, and wisdom. If they reside in Vinaya temples, practicers of meditation can get

so involved in learning the minutiae of the precepts[479] that
they forget the One Great Purpose of the Buddha. Thus
I have established a separate monastery for meditation.[480]

Baizhang did not intend that Zen monks should not maintain
the precepts. Indeed, in his *Pure Rule* for monastic life he explains in
great detail the code of conduct proper to monks of the meditation
tradition.

Question: Every Buddhist tradition has teachings on meditation. Why then do you say that the Zen school is a separate transmission outside the teachings?

Answer: Meditation is practiced not only in Buddhism but also in the non-Buddhist traditions. The power of meditation is used, for example, to attain rebirth in the realms of pure form and formlessness;[481] this is what the four meditations and eight samādhis[482] are concerned with. Non-Buddhists employ these meditations, regarding them as supreme.

Although "Zen school" literally means "meditation school," meditation as practiced in the Zen school is not the same as that taught in the other Buddhist schools. Furthermore, in this Latter Age of the Dharma the meditation methods of the other schools, while they continue to be taught on a theoretical level, are seldom actually engaged in. Only the followers of the Zen school continue their cultivation of *zazen*, and thus Zen has come to be known by people both inside and outside the tradition as "the school that practices meditation." However, if there is no more to the Zen school than the practice of meditation, then Bodhidharma's coming from the West would lose its meaning.

Four types of meditation are mentioned in the *Laṅkāvatāra Sutra*.[483] The first is the meditation practiced by non-Buddhists and the deluded, who believe that meditation means not arousing thought and discrimination. The second type is the meditation of observing forms and meanings; this is the meditation of Hinayana practicers and bodhisattvas of the Three Worthy States, who investigate the principles of the teachings. The third type is the meditation of perceiving reality as it is; this subtle practice free of effort is the meditation of the bodhisattvas of the Ten Stages of Development, who abide in the true reality of the Middle Way.[484] The fourth type is the pure meditation of the Tathāgata, the meditation of those who have reached the Tathāgata stage in which one attains the uncaused universal wisdom of the Dharma realm.[485] This is the "Tathāgata Zen" referred to by the descendants of Bodhidharma. However, an ancient master once told a disciple, "You have attained only Tathāgata meditation—you haven't yet realized Patriarch meditation."[486] Know from this that though "Zen school" literally means "meditation school," Zen meditation is not meditation as it is spoken of in the other schools.

The term *zen* originally comes from the Sanskrit word *dhyāna*, which transliterates into Sino-Japanese as *zen'na*; *zen* is the shortened form of this. The basic meaning of dhyāna is "right mindfulness" or "quiet contemplation." The *Sutra of Complete Enlightenment*, in its explanation of the three contemplations, identifies dhyāna as a contemplation different from the other two, that is, samādhi and wisdom.[487] The Zen master Guifeng Zongmi[488] called it the contemplation of the absolute mind.[489] In his *Anthology of Essential Writings on the Origins of Zen*, Guifeng wrote that "only the Way transmitted by Bodhidharma corresponds to the true dhyāna, and hence his Way is called 'the Zen (that is, the Dhyāna) school.'"[490]

RECOGNIZING THE TRUE DHARMA

Question: Those who have realized true enlightenment can accurately distinguish between true and false, and they are thus undeceived even if celestial demons and non-Buddhists come to them preaching their various doctrines. But how can unenlightened people know true from false, since the statements of the ancient masters often seem contradictory and the teachings of present-day guides are disparate? On what basis should beginners judge?

Answer: In this Latter Age of the Dharma false teachings abound, greatly confusing the true Dharma. In secular pastimes like wrestling, horse racing, and card games there are clear rules for winning and losing, and so there is seldom any confusion about results. In civil disputes and criminal trials it is sometimes difficult to judge who is right and who is wrong, but decisions can eventually be reached through appeal to the higher authorities.

In Buddhism, however, there are no preestablished standards for ranking the teachings. Thus individuals, on the basis of their own understanding, think the tradition they follow is best, regardless of what other people think. Buddhism is not like the courts, so there are no higher authorities to appeal to. The texts people cite in support of their positions may be the words of the Buddha and the ancient masters, but since the interpretation of passages varies according to one's point of view they do not suffice as evidence. People also seek support for their positions in the sanction of their teachers, but the sanction of individuals with vested interests is hardly worthy of trust.

When deluded people, on the basis of their own false beliefs, place their faith in any one teaching (it doesn't matter which), they tend to reject all other teachings. Some people, having selected a teacher for themselves, are unwilling to even listen to other teachers' doctrines, regarding them all as inferior. Such people are the most foolish of all. Other people, seeing that the doctrines of the various schools and teachers are all different, are unable to make up their minds and end up "neither putting out to sea nor heading for shore."

People such as these cannot grasp the import of the separate transmission outside the teachings. Even unenlightened people, if they understand the meaning of "outside the teachings," know that the true Dharma is ineffable. Thus they avoid a rigid, exclusive adherence to the words of a master and are not confused by the fact that different teachers have different teachings.

The various types of food are characterized by different flavors. Can one of these flavors be designated the most essential of all? Because people have different constitutions, some like their food sweet while others prefer it spicy. It would be foolish to declare that one's favorite flavor is the best and dismiss all others as unnecessary. It is no different with the Buddhist teachings. Because the natural inclinations of people differ, it is perfectly reasonable that a certain individual would feel a special affinity for a particular teaching. However, if that individual regards his preference as absolute, his chosen faith as the one true doctrine, and all other teachings as erroneous, then his outlook is mistaken.

The *Lotus Sutra* says, "The Dharma King, destroyer of being, when he appears in the world accords with the desires of living beings, preaching the Law in a variety of ways."[491] We should realize that all of the Tathāgata's various teachings were provisionally expounded in accordance with the deluded inclinations of sentient beings. If those who have turned directly toward the Original Nature that precedes the separation of buddhas and sentient beings happen to hear a variety of teachings, why should they trouble themselves trying to decide which is best? An ancient master said, "All the Buddha's teachings were expounded to liberate minds. In me there is no trace of mind—what use have I of any teachings?"[492]

A SEPARATE TRANSMISSION
OUTSIDE THE TEACHINGS

Question: In the doctrinal schools they criticize Zen, saying, "Zen's 'separate transmission outside the teachings' neither follows the Buddha's discourses nor investigates the doctrines. It is no more than Zen's own arbitrary outlook and is unworthy of trust." Is there any merit to this criticism?

Answer: Those who make such criticisms know only the letter of the doctrine and not its spirit. If they understood the Buddha's true intention in expounding the teachings then they would surely believe in the separate transmission outside the teachings. Those who do understand are the ones who deserve to be called "true students of the doctrine."

The *Laṅkāvatāra Sutra* says, "From the beginning at the Deer Park until the end at the River Hiraṇyavatī, the Buddha spoke not a single word."[493] Given this passage, is there anything that the Buddha taught during his lifetime that should be adhered to as unchanging and real? The *Sutra for Resolving Doubts during the Age of the Semblance Dharma* states, "To understand the meaning of a sutra only on the basis of its words is to harm all buddhas in the past, present, and future."[494] How, then, could discussing doctrine solely on the basis of the words of the sutras and commentaries possibly be in accord with the true intention of the Buddha?

The *Sutra of Complete Enlightenment* says, "The teachings of the sutras are like a finger pointing at the moon."[495] The reason one uses a finger to point to the moon is to indicate the moon to other people. If these people look only at the finger they cannot see the moon. If they then proceed to discuss the length of the finger and argue over whether it is large or small, surely that is the height of delusion.

The great doctrinal masters of the past were all awakened to the true intention of the Buddha, so they were not concerned with the "finger" of the teachings. However, they utilized this "finger" for the sake of those of medium and inferior capabilities who were unable to directly perceive the "moon" of the Buddha's true intention. In an attempt to indicate this intention, all of the doctrinal schools have established Dharma gates that go beyond expression in words and conception in thought. Thus the Hossō school has the teaching it calls "abolish verbal explanations to express the tenet," the San-ron school has its teaching of "sacred silence," the Tendai school the "subtle tenets" teaching, and the Kegon school has its teaching of the ineffability of the buddha-fruit of enlightenment. The Shingon school dismisses the exoteric practice of "no words, no teachings" as a mere mind-purification technique and emphasizes instead "absolute words."[496]

Absolute words transcend the level of verbal and nonverbal; they are secret and wondrous words that are eternally expressed throughout past, present, and future. They must not be understood in the same way as words based on deluded attachments. Thus there is a passage in a sutra in which the Tathāgata says that in the realm of the ultimate mystery, "Fundamentally I have no words; it is solely for the benefit of sentient beings that I preach."[497] A commentary on the *Mahāvairocana Sutra* states, "In the realm of enlightenment realized by the Tathāgata there is nothing for an observer to see or any words for a speaker to say. It cannot be conveyed to someone through language."[498]

Kōbō Daishi,[499] in his letter responding to Dengyō Daishi's request to borrow and transcribe the *Commentary on the Principle of Wisdom*

Sutra,[500] emphasizes that "the secret tenets cannot be discussed in writing but only transmitted from mind to mind; written words are no more than dregs and rubble." Clearly the true meaning of the scriptures does not lie in their words and letters. How can one claim that the separate transmission outside the teachings is nothing but Zen's "arbitrary outlook"?

In his work *The Lineages of the Innerly Realized Buddhadharma*,[501] Dengyō Daishi has chapters entitled "The Lineage of Teachers in Bodhidharma's Dharma Transmission," "The Lineage of Teachers in the Tendai Lotus School Transmission," "The Lineage of Teachers in the Tendai Perfect Teaching Bodhisattva Precepts Transmission," and "The Lineage of Teachers in the Womb and Diamond Mandalas Transmission."[502] From this it is clear that Dengyō Daishi transmitted the Zen school to Japan.

At the time of Emperor Saga[503] the Japanese monk Egaku[504] was sent to Tang-dynasty China by the imperial court in order to study Buddhism and help its dissemination in Japan. Egaku studied Zen under the master Yanguan Jian[505] and succeeded to his Dharma. He then invited another of Yanguan's students, the Chinese Zen master Yikong,[506] to return with him to Japan. In Kyoto, Yikong resided at the subtemple Sai-in of Tō-ji. When Kōbō Daishi informed the imperial court of Yikong's presence, both the emperor and the empress arranged meetings with him. Owing to the maturation of karma from her previous lives, the empress was awakened to the transmission outside the teachings. She then had the temple Danrin-ji[507] built in the Saga district west of Kyoto and invited Yikong to take up residence there (for this reason she is known as Empress Danrin).[508]

Yikong said, "In this land the time is not yet ripe for the widespread dissemination of the Zen school. For that reason earlier priests have confined themselves to spreading the doctrinal teachings, and have not attempted to transmit the Supreme Vehicle. For me, too, it would be of little benefit to remain here." He therefore returned to China after about three years. Later, however, desiring that in the future the Japanese should know of these matters, he had a stele shipped from

China and placed near the temple Tō-ji. The inscription, written by the monk Qiyuan of the temple Kaiyuan si,[509] was entitled, "An Account of the First Transmission of Zen to Japan." If Zen were of no importance, why would Kōbō Daishi have bothered to recommend Master Yikong to the imperial court?

Jikaku Daishi[510] established a meditation hall on Mount Hiei and promoted the practice of contemplation. In *A Comparison of the Teachings of the Various Schools*[511] Chishō Daishi[512] wrote:

> In Japan there are eight Buddhist schools, including the six Nara schools (the Kusha, Jōjitsu, Ritsu, Hossō, Sanron, and Kegon schools) and the two Kyoto schools (the Tendai and Shingon schools). The Kusha and Jōjitsu schools are both Hinayana, while the Ritsu teachings are common to both Mahayana and Hinayana. All of the remaining five schools are Mahayana. In addition there is the Zen school, which is unrelated to any of the other schools but which the great teachers of Mount Hiei have all received transmission in.

How many people have ever excelled Dengyō Daishi, Kōbō Daishi, Jikaku Daishi, and Chishō Daishi in their mastery of the deep inner truths of exoteric and esoteric Buddhism? If the teachings of the Zen school are nothing more than arbitrary opinions, why then did these teachers reach beyond the exoteric and esoteric traditions and show such great respect for it?

In his *Classification of the Teachings and Periods*,[513] the priest Annen[514] praises Mount Hiei above all other monastic institutions, saying, "Our mountain offers training in the three schools of Zen, Shingon, and Tendai. I have heard of nothing similar in India or China."

Prince Shōtoku was a reincarnation of the Chinese Zen master Nanyue Huairang.[515] Because Nanyue had succeeded to the teachings of Bodhidharma, when Prince Shōtoku was promoting the spread of

Buddhism the sage Bodhidharma manifested in the form of a beggar on Mount Kataoka in Nara. Seeing the beggar, who had collapsed by the side of the road, Prince Shōtoku placed his robe around him and said:

> How sad you must be,
> O fallen traveler without parents,
> starving for something to eat on Mount Kataoka.

Bodhidharma responded with his own poem:

> O Ikaruga![516]
> Only if your precious stream runs dry
> would I forget the name of my sovereign.

Not long afterward the beggar died. The prince, together with his retainers, hauled rocks and made a burial mound, in which they laid the dead man's casket. The retainers were upset by this behavior toward a mere beggar, so later the prince said, "If that is how you feel, go dig up the grave and remove the casket." When the retainers had done so, they opened the casket and found only the robe that the prince had placed around the beggar; his body was nowhere to be seen. Marveling at this, the retainers respectfully reburied the casket.

This grave exists even today. Later Gedatsu Shōnin[517] erected a shrine over it sheltering images of Bodhidharma and Prince Shōtoku. Prince Shōtoku, in his *Treatise on the Clear Eye of Teaching the Dharma*,[518] wrote, "I was told by the Patriarch of South India that if one seeks a swift release from samsara one should follow the fundamental One Vehicle, and that the true essence of the One Vehicle is Buddha-mind." He also wrote, "The Patriarch of South India divides Buddhism into two types: the type that relies on the teachings and the type that does not rely on the teachings." Bodhidharma was a prince of the South Indian kingdom of Pallava, which is why Prince Shōtoku refers to him as "the Patriarch of South India." If Zen is truly of no value, why would Prince Shōtoku, who first promulgated Buddhism in our land, have shown such respect toward Bodhidharma?

Dengyō Daishi, in his comparative classification of the teachings of the various Buddhist schools, has not a word of criticism regarding the relative merits of the Zen school. In his *Treatise on the Ten Stages of Mind*,[519] Kōbō Daishi categorizes the differences between exoteric and esoteric Buddhism and even explains the teachings of the Two Vehicles and the non-Buddhist schools, yet he offers no criticism of the Zen school. This is because he realized that the fundamental meaning of the separate transmission outside the teachings is beyond all logical analysis.

This is what Chishō Daishi, too, intended when he commented that the Zen school is unrelated to all other schools. The Chinese Zen master Zhijue Dashi[520] said, "If you do not know that Zen is in the teachings, then you are not a true student of the teachings; if you do not know that the teachings are in Zen, then you are not a true student of Zen."[521] Thus followers of the doctrine who criticize Zen have failed to understand not only Zen but the doctrine as well, and followers of Zen who criticize the doctrine have failed to understand not only the doctrine but Zen as well. These are the types of people that Tiantai Dashi was referring to when he spoke of "word-and-letter Dharma teachers" and "dark-enlightenment meditation masters."[522]

According to Nanyang Huizhong, "A student of the Zen school must honor the words of the Buddha. The fully revealed teachings of the Mahayana all penetrate to the source of the innate mind. The partially revealed teachings are like warring parasites in a lion's body."[523] The vinaya tells us that disciples of the Buddha should take time every day to study non-Buddhist thought, because if they are unfamiliar with such thought they run the risk of unknowingly falling into similar views themselves. Moreover, in order to effectively argue against non-Buddhist teachings they must know what those teachings are.

One might also say that a scholastic who is tempted to censure Zen should first study under a good meditation teacher and awaken to the true meaning of the practice. Similarly, a Zen adept who wishes to criticize the doctrine should first attain a thorough understanding of the teachings. In this way all disputes would naturally come to an end. If the two sides remain ignorant of each other's positions they can argue on forever, red in face and loud in voice, without ever reaching a conclusion. Not only that, but they will surely invite karmic retribution for defiling the Dharma. Nothing could be more senseless than this.

REGARDING THE PUBLICATION OF THESE EXCHANGES

Question: I have taken the liberty of jotting down in Japanese script the contents of our discussions after each of our regular meetings. Would you mind if I prepared a clean copy of this manuscript to show to laywomen and other people with an interest in the Way?

Answer: The guidance of a Zen monk is not like that of scholastics, who teach doctrines they have memorized or written down on paper. The Zen monk simply expresses in a direct and immediate way whatever the situation calls for. This is known as "face-to-face guidance." As with a bolt of lightning or a spark struck from flint, it is useless to seek its traces. An ancient master said, "Even realizing the meaning behind the words is already to have fallen into the realm of the secondary."[524] How much worse is it, then, to write down those words and show them to others! For this reason the ancient masters all forbade the recording of their statements. However, if nothing were ever to be written down, then the paths of guidance would be severed. Thus the Zen school has resigned itself to publishing the records of the ancients, though this is not its true intention.

The ancients generally began their Zen practice only after a broad education in the Buddhist and non-Buddhist classics. Hence they were not biased in their understanding. Nowadays, however, there are Zen followers who have yet to discern the principle of cause and effect or perceive the difference between the true and the false. Even such people as these, however, if they remain ardent in the Way and tirelessly investigate the Original Nature beyond all words and understanding, are far superior to pedants with their shallow knowledge.

Looking around, one sees people neglectful of their meditation and unlearned in the sutras, treatises, and sacred teachings; people who, having meditated a bit and attained a level of understanding no greater than that of non-Buddhist or Hinayana practicers, imagine that, since their understanding resulted from *zazen*, they are now fully enlightened. Or they intuitively grasp the teachings preached by a lecture master and assume that, since they are Zen monks, their understanding reflects the deepest tenets of the Zen school.

It is in an attempt to correct such errors that I regularly lecture on the sutras and treatises. Nevertheless, few people grasp my intended meaning when I speak on textual or doctrinal matters, or even on more specific subjects like cause and effect or true versus false. Everyone interprets what I say in their own way, praising me or criticizing me in accordance with the way they understand me. Thus neither the praise nor the criticism has anything to do with what I have actually been attempting to express. I feel that recording our "dream conversations" will be of even less benefit.

However, if by considering my words people gain a deeper connection—whether positive or negative—with the teachings of Buddhism, how can I refuse to let them do so?

93 A KOAN GIVEN TO ASHIKAGA

Question: Master, what, truly, is the Dharma that you teach people?

Answer: At midnight in Silla the sun shines bright!

POSTSCRIPT BY ZHUXIAN FANXIAN

O NE DAY Zen Master Kosen Ingen[525] of Tōji-ji called upon me. Holding the manuscript of this book, he spoke as follows:

"This is a record of National Teacher Musō's answers to questions posed to him by the General of the Left, Layman Kozan,[526] over the course of the latter's study of Zen. It is intended as a guide for everyone, both lay and ordained, including women intent on following the Way and people of all levels of learning. For ease of reading it has been transcribed in the Japanese *kana* syllabary, and its title is *Dialogues in a Dream*. Musō's lay disciple Lord Ōtaka of Iyo made the arrangements for publication.[527] Could I impose upon you to write a few words of commentary for a postscript?"

I answered, "I am at a loss as to how the Buddhadharma can be conveyed to people, barring the appearance of a buddha capable of guiding sentient beings by employing wisdom and upāya in infinitely varied ways and in all possible circumstances. Even Śākyamuni, a buddha of all-encompassing wisdom, could liberate only people with whom he had the right karmic connections, and he was unable to reach those who lacked such connections. He was a master of explaining all manner of things through the use of parables, but parables are incapable of expressing the Buddhadharma itself. The Buddhadharma is inconceivable; it is where the ways of knowledge are exhausted and the paths of language do not reach.

"Nevertheless, that which the sutras and śāstras are unable to fully express may, even if only to a limited extent, be communicated through the expedient use of words and letters. The Buddha said, did he not, 'I do not preach using expedient means, except when I employ provisional names in order to conduct and guide sentient beings.'[528] This is what he meant. Unfortunately, since the Buddha's passing there has been no one to succeed him in this upāya preaching. What else, though, can one call the present manuscript than a reappearance of the Buddha's [expedient] teaching?"

Regrettably, my inability to read this *kana* manuscript prevents me from plumbing its true meaning and tasting its true flavor, so that I cannot "feel its contours and sense its subtleties." That being the case, one might ask how I can understand the contents well enough to praise it as "a reappearance of the Buddha's teaching." I would answer, "What does Heaven ever say? Yet the four seasons come in turn and living beings continue to grow." This is what is meant when it is said that all know the Way of Heaven, even the deaf and the blind. It is just that there are only few who know what makes the Way what it is. It is the same with the Way of National Teacher Musō. I have been acquainted with his Way for some time and would have known of it even without this book. With it, of course, I know it better, though I still do not understand it in detail.

The word "buddha" means "awakened one." The Buddha was called such because he was himself thoroughly awakened to the Way and was skilled at awakening others. This is what I intended earlier when I mentioned skill in "guiding sentient beings employing wisdom and upāya." Those who awaken earlier awaken those who awaken later; by employing the Way, people are brought to awakening. "[Earlier or later,] the principle is the same."[529] This Way is vast, extending throughout the ten directions and encompassing the three periods of time. Is there anything in the infinity of existence that does not partake of it? It is inherently present, perfect and complete, in all people and all things. How could the National Teacher alone possibly know it? If you have yet to see it, it is simply because "awakened" and "not yet awakened" are so extremely close.

It is lacking in no one. If you have yet to attain a first awakening I would say to you that you are, just as you are, a buddha. If, at this very moment, you rid yourself of the nonawakened—that is, if you bring it to awakening—then what is there to doubt? Or one might say that those who doubt have yet to awaken and therefore do not know this. But why doubt in the first place? Why not just take it as a matter of faith?

It is often said that when the Buddha was in the world he had no dreams. One might therefore ask why a text by an enlightened teacher would be entitled *Dialogues in a Dream*. I would answer, "You have heard but you have yet to understand. When it is said that 'a buddha has no dreams', 'has no' does not refer to the same type of 'having' as ordinary 'having' and 'not having,' since a dream is not a dream. This is not something you should be asking. I will not speak of this again, for, as the old saying has it, 'One mustn't speak of a dream in front of a fool.'"

It is similar to Śāriputra asking if preaching the six pāramitās in a dream is the same as preaching them while awake. Subhūti answered, "Your question is too subtle and profound; I cannot answer it. There is in the Sangha the bodhisattva Maitreya. Please put your question to him."[530] If I were to be asked about *Dialogues in a Dream* in the same manner as Śāriputra questioned Subhūti, I would reply, "Your question is too subtle and profound to answer. Go pay your respects to the National Teacher."

POSTSCRIPT TO THE REVISED EDITION

NEARLY THREE YEARS have now passed since I wrote the postscript to this text. One day the senior monk of the assembly came to me, produced the present text, and said, "We have this superb manuscript, along with the postscript you wrote earlier. If this cooperative effort of two buddhas—dissimilar in their appearance but identical in spirit, different in their approach but the same in their goal, the two together comprising front and back—is not for the purpose of educating all sentient beings, for what purpose does it exist? Nevertheless, I wonder if the master [Zhuxian] truly understands Lord Ōtaka's intentions in having this text published."

I replied, "I have known for years that Lord Ōtaka is an awakened man, but to be honest I do not know his reasons for publishing this book. Might he not have been rather too eager to help other people? What other purpose might he have had?"

The head monk said, "Lord Ōtaka, precisely because he is, as the master says, an awakened man, perceived the true quality of this manuscript and therefore determined to make it public. At first the National Teacher refused to permit this, but Lord Ōtaka reasoned with him in the following way:

If this manuscript had never existed the National Teacher's position would cause no problems. However, the fact is that it does exist, with the result that people are making copies and summaries of their own and all sorts of scribal errors are appearing.[531] Even minor discrepancies can lead to differences as great as heaven and earth. If publication isn't permitted then such errors will simply multiply, one mistake leading to the next, until finally we will be left with various fault-filled, conflicting texts.

People will be confused, yet not know where to find the National Teacher's original words. How incongruous that a work intended to benefit people could end up leading them astray! It is true that the National Teacher's answers to questions posed by the shōgun Ashikaga Tadayoshi, intended solely for his ears, were the origin of this work. However, the Buddha's discourses, which were also initially intended for certain people at specific times and places, have proved to be of benefit to infinite beings throughout the ages.

If the Buddha's disciples had not convened after his death and codified and memorized his teachings, how could they have survived until this day?

"The National Teacher accepted Lord Ōtaka's position and permitted the book to be published. As a result people now know the original text and can practice the Great Way in confidence, without wasting their time following misleading paths."

"So that is how it was," I said. "Indeed, could the buddhas and masters of the three periods of time possibly have regarded that Great Way, so clearly manifest, as nothing but sleep-talking?"

The head monk said, "Please write that and append it to this book."

"I have no objections," I replied. "I will write an additional postscript." The head monk also said, "Lord Ōtaka is known as Kaigan Koji (Layman Seacoast). He has entered deeply into the gates of the

Dharma and resembles the sea in the vastness of his mind. In manner he is similar to the layman Vimalakīrti and has ceaselessly continued his efforts to benefit all sentient beings. In the spring of this year he was promoted to lord of Wakasa Province."[532]

1. Myōan Eisai (Yōsai) 明庵榮西 (1141–1215) was the first Japanese monk to successfully transmit Rinzai Zen to Japan. In 1168, after studying the Tendai teachings for many years on Mount Hiei, he traveled to China for six months to learn more about Tendai doctrine and meditation. In 1187 he went to China again, hoping to make a pilgrimage to India through China and Central Asia. When the Chinese government denied him permission to do so, he practiced Rinzai Zen under the master Xuan Huaichang 虚庵 懷敞 (J., Koan Eshō; n.d.). After returning to Japan in 1191 Eisai founded the monastery Shōfuku-ji 聖福寺 on the island of Kyūshū, Jufuku-ji 壽福寺 in Kamakura, and Kennin-ji 建仁寺 in Kyoto, where he taught a combination of Zen meditation and esoteric ritual. Although Eisai's lineage died out after several generations, he was instrumental in laying the foundations of Zen monasticism and meditation in Japan. His honorary title is National Teacher Senkō 千光國師.

2. Shun'oku Myōha 春屋妙葩 (1311–1388), Musō's nephew, was born in the province of Kai (present Yamanashi Prefecture). At the age of seven he entered Kokei-an 古谿庵, a temple founded by Musō in 1313 in the province of Nōshū 濃州 (present Gifu Prefecture), where he stayed until his return to Kai at the age of twelve to continue his temple studies. Upon Musō's assumption of the abbacy of Nanzen-ji 南禪寺 in 1325 Myōha went to Kyoto to receive ordination from him. He then trained under the masters Gen'ō Hongen (see note 43, p. 378), Zhuxian Fanxian (see note 68, p. 382), and Qingzhuo Zhengcheng (see note 54, p. 380), after which he practiced exclusively with Musō. He is said to have experienced enlightenment while reading the *Sutra of Complete Enlightenment*. In 1357 the shogun, Ashikaga Takauji, appointed him abbot of Tōji-ji 等持寺, from which he oversaw the reconstruction of Tenryū-ji 天龍寺 and Rinsen-ji 臨川寺 following major fires at those temples in 1358 and 1361, respectively. He later served as abbot of several other major temples, including Tenryū-ji. Disturbances between the Zen temple Nanzen-ji and the Tendai temple Enryaku-ji 延暦寺 in 1369 led to his exile two years later, but he was called back to Kyoto in 1379 and appointed abbot of Nanzen-ji. He established a number of temples, notably the Ashikaga family temple Shōkoku-ji 相國寺 (designating Musō Soseki as honorary founder), and served as the first *sōroku* 僧録 (Registrar General of Monks; see p. 45) in charge of all the *gozan* temples in Japan (see note 61, p. 381).

3. A collection of talks by Musō, edited by Shun'oku Myōha and published in 1353.

4. Martin Colcutt, "Musō Soseki," in *The Origins of Japan's Medieval World: Courtiers, Clerics, Warriors, and Peasants in the Fourteenth Century*, ed. Jeffrey P. Mass (Stanford: Stanford University Press, 2002), 261–94.

5. The Minamoto 源, or Genji 源氏, were one of the imperially descended clans that dominated the government of Japan from the late Heian period (794–1185) until the end of the Edo period (1600–1868). The Minamoto fought the Taira clan in the Genpei War of 1180–1185, which ended in the defeat of the Taira. Subsequently Minamoto Yoritomo 源頼朝 (1147–1199), the leader of the Minamotos, founded the Kamakura Shogunate, which ruled Japan between 1185 and 1333.

The Taira 平, or Heishi 平氏, another of the imperially descended clans, was particularly influential in the late Heian period. The clan lost power following its defeat by the Minamoto in the Genpei War.

6. The Hossō 法相 school is a philosophical school of Japanese Buddhism that taught the doctrines of Yogācāra thought, which hold that all things experienced exist only as processes of cognition and do not have a reality as objects outside the mind.

7. The Tendai 天台 school is a Mahayana tradition founded in China by Zhiyi (see note 201, p. 393) and based on Madhyamaka school philosophy and the *Lotus Sutra* teachings. It was brought to Japan in 805 by Saichō (see note 107, p. 386) as an eclectic teaching incorporating doctrinal study, meditation, *nenbutsu*, and esoteric teachings.

8. The Shingon 眞言 school is the main esoteric school of Japanese Buddhism, transmitted to Japan from China in the early 800s by Kūkai, also known as Kōbō Daishi (see note 148, p. 389). Its practices center on the use of mantras, mandalas, and the visualization of buddhas and bodhisattvas.

9. Bodhidharma (d. 528? 536? 543?) is regarded as the twenty-eighth patriarch of the Indian Zen lineage and the first patriarch of the Chinese Zen lineage. According to legendary accounts of his life, he was the third son of a king in southern India. Some years after finishing his training under his teacher Prajñātara he made the long sea voyage to China, where he remained the rest of his life spreading the teachings of Zen. He first visited the land of Liang in southern China, then journeyed north and settled at Shaolin si 少林寺, where for nine years he meditated in a cave. According to some accounts he finally returned to India.

10. Sushan Guangren 疎山光仁 (837–909) was a native of Ganyang 淦陽 in present-day Jiangxi 江西. He first studied Buddhist doctrine at Donglin si 東林寺 on Mount Lu 廬, but he later turned to Zen. After visiting a number of well-known Zen masters he became a disciple of Dongshan Liangjie 洞山良价 (J., Tōzan Ryōkai; 807–869) and eventually succeeded to his Dharma. After Dongshan's death Sushan resided for the rest of his life on Mount Su 疎 in Fuzhou 撫州.

11. Shitou Xiqian 石頭希遷 (700–791) was a native of Gaoyao 高要 in present-day Guangdong 廣東. At age twelve he met the Sixth Patriarch, Huineng (see note 33), and studied under him until the master's death a year later. After taking the full precepts on Mount Luofu 羅浮 in 728 he joined the assembly under Qingyuan Xingsi 青原行思 (J., Seigen Gyōshi; d. 740). In 742 Xiqian took up residence at the monastery Nan su 南寺 on Mount Heng 衡. There he built a hermitage for meditation on top of a large rock east of the temple, thus receiving the name Shitou, meaning "Stonehead." From 764 he resided in Liangduan 梁端, present Hunan. Xiqian left several important heirs, and his lineage

gave rise to three of the Five Houses of Chinese Zen. His teaching is summarized in the expression "This very mind, just this is buddha."

12. Shinchi Kakushin 心地覺心 (1207–1298) became a Shingon monk at age eighteen, took the full precepts at Tōdai-ji in Nara at twenty-nine, and subsequently studied esoteric Buddhism at the Shingon headquarters on Mount Kōya 高野. From 1239 he practiced Zen meditation under the Rinzai master Taikō Gyōyū 退耕行勇 (1163–1241) at Kongō-zanmai-in 金剛三昧院 on Mount Kōya and, from 1341, at Jufuku-ji in Kamakura. In 1249 he sailed for China, where he studied under Wumen Huikai 無門慧開 (J., Mumon Ekai; 1183–1260), from whom he received sanction in just six months. Kakushin returned to Japan in 1254 with a copy of the koan collection *Wumen guan* 無門關 (J., *Mumonkan*), compiled by his teacher Wumen. In Japan, Kakushin resided at the temple Saihō-ji 西方寺 (later called Kōkoku-ji 興國寺) in the town of Yura 由良. He was often called to the capital to lecture before the emperors Kameyama 龜山 (r. 1259–1274) and Go-Uda 後宇多 (r. 1274–1287) and was designated abbot of the temples Zenrin-ji 禪林寺 and Myōkō-ji 妙光寺 by the court. Following his death he received the title National Teacher Hottō Enmyō 法燈圓明國師 from Emperor Go-Daigo 後醍醐 (r. 1319–1339). Kakushin established an influential lineage known as the Hottō 法燈 (also pronounced Hattō) line, and he is also honored as the founder of the Japanese Fuke school 普化宗 of *shakuhachi* flute-playing itinerants.

13. Muin Enban 無隱圓範 (1230–1307) was born in Kii 紀伊 (present-day Wakayama Prefecture). After beginning his training under the Chinese master Lanxi Daolong (see next note) Muin went on pilgrimage to China, resuming his study under Lanxi following his return. From 1293 to 1299 he served as abbot of Kennin-ji, then went to Kamakura to serve as abbot of Kenchō-ji 建長寺 and Engaku-ji 圓覺寺.

14. Lanxi Daolong 蘭溪道隆 (J., Rankei Dōryū; 1213–1278) was born in what is presently the Sichuan region of China. After becoming a monk at age thirteen he trained under the masters Wuzhun Shifan 無準師範 (J., Mujun Shihan; 1177–1249), Chijue Daochong 癡絶道冲 (J., Chizetsu Dōchū; 1169–1250), and others before receiving the sanction of Wuming Huixing 無明慧性 (J., Mumyō Eshō; 1162–1237). He traveled to Japan in 1246, residing for a time on the island of Kyūshū before moving to Kamakura. There, in 1253, the regent Hōjō Tokiyori 北条時頼 (1226–1263) appointed him founding abbot of Kenchō-ji, which Lanxi ran according to the strict codes of Song-dynasty Zen. Lanxi later served as abbot of Kennin-ji, where he replaced Eisai's part-Zen, part-Tendai training with Song-style Zen. After reforming Kennin-ji he returned to Kamakura to serve as abbot of Zenkō-ji 禪興寺 and, once again, Kenchō-ji. In 1265 he was accused of spying for the Mongols and subsequently exiled on two occasions, but he was eventually exonerated and allowed to return to his post at Kenchō-ji. Following his death he received the title Meditation Master Daikaku 大覺禪師.

15. Mukyū Tokusen 無及德詮 (n.d.) trained at Kenchō-ji under Lanxi Daolong. After completing his training he did further study in China, returning to Japan in 1279 with the Chinese master Wuxue Zuyuan (see note 39, p. 378). He later served as abbot at Zenkō-ji 禪興寺 and Tōzen-ji 東漸寺.

16. Ikō Dōnen 葦航道然 (1219–1301) was born in Shinano 信濃 (present-day Nagano Prefecture) and trained under Lanxi Daolong. He served as head monk at Kenchō-ji when Wuxue Zuyuan assumed the abbacy there. Later he became the sixth abbot of Kenchō-ji and the fifth abbot of Engaku-ji.

17. Chōkei Tokugo 挑谿德悟 (1240–1306), a native of western Kyūshū, studied esoteric Buddhism before joining the assembly at Kenchō-ji under Lanxi Daolong. After succeeding to Lanxi's Dharma he traveled to China and practiced under Wanji Xingmi 頑極行彌 (J., Gankyoku Gyōmi; n.d.), returning to Japan in 1279 with Mukyū Tokusen and the Chinese master Wuxue Zuyuan. He later became abbot of Shōfuku-ji, Engaku-ji, and Tōzen-ji.

18. Chidon Kūshō 癡鈍空性 (d. 1301?) was born in Nara and trained under Lanxi Daolong. After receiving Lanxi's sanction he became the fourteenth abbot of Kennin-ji and, subsequently, the eighth abbot of Kenchō-ji. He also established three temples in the northern part of Honshū: Reizan-ji 靈山寺, Fumon-ji 普門寺, and Zenpuku-ji 禪福寺.

19. Yishan Yining 一山一寧 (J., Issan Ichinei; 1247–1317) first studied the Vinaya and Tiantai teachings, then turned to Chan meditation. He trained under a number of masters and eventually succeeded to the Dharma of Wanji Xingmi 頑極行彌. He had a distinguished career in China, serving as the abbot of several temples in China and receiving the title of Great Teacher Miaoci Hongji 妙慈弘濟大師. In 1299, at the age of fifty-two, he was sent by the Yuan court to Japan as part of a diplomatic delegation. Although detained at first on suspicion of spying, Yishan soon won the respect of the Kamakura regent Hōjō Sadatoki 北条貞時 (1271–1311) and was asked to serve as abbot of several of the great Zen temples in Kamakura, notably Kenchō-ji and Engaku-ji, where he gained renown for his Zen teaching and proficiency in poetry and the other arts associated with Zen. His reputation grew when Emperor Go-Uda called him to Kyoto in 1313 to assume the abbacy of Nanzen-ji 南禪寺. He was honored after his death with the title National Teacher Issan 一山國師.

20. Kōhō Kennichi 高峰顯日 (1241–1316), a son of Emperor Go-Saga 後嵯峨 (1220–1272), received the tonsure at age sixteen from Enni Ben'en 円爾辯圓 (1201–1280), the founder of Tōfuku-ji 東福寺. He entered Kennin-ji in 1260 to practice under Wuan Puning 兀菴普寧 (J., Gottan Funei; 1197–1276), eventually serving as the master's attendant. He then secluded himself in the mountains near Nasu 那須, to the north of what is now Tokyo. Followers in the area eventually built the temple Ungan-ji for him. When the Chinese master Wuxue Zuyuan assumed the abbacy of Kenchō-ji in 1279, Kōhō went to Kamakura to practice under him. After receiving Wuxue's sanction he returned to Ungan-ji, where he remained until 1300, when he was called to serve as abbot at Jōmyō-ji 淨妙寺 in Kamakura. He later assumed the abbacy of the temples Manju-ji 萬壽寺, Jōchi-ji 淨智寺, and Kenchō-ji, before returning in his final years to Ungan-ji. He is usually referred to by his honorary title, National Teacher Bukkoku 佛國國師.

21. The Five Houses 五家 were the five main teaching lines of Chinese Zen. They were: (1) the Linji 臨濟 (J., Rinzai) school, established by Linji Yixuan 臨濟義玄 (J., Rinzai Gigen; d. 866); (2) the Guiyang 潙仰 (J., Igyō) school, established by Guishan Lingyou 潙山靈祐 (J., Isan Reiyū; 771–853) and his disciple Yangshan Huiji 仰山慧寂 (J., Kyōzan Ejaku; 807–883); (3) the Caodong 曹洞 (Jap., Sōtō) school, established by Dongshan Liangjie 洞山良价 (J., Tōzan Ryōkai; 807–869) and his student Caoshan Benji 曹山本寂 (J., Sōzan Honjaku; 840–901); (4) the Yunmen 雲門 (J., Unmon) school, established by Yunmen Wenyan 雲門文偃 (J., Unmon Bun'en; 864–949); and (5) the Fayan 法眼 (J., Hōgen) school, established by Fayan Wenyi 法眼文益 (J., Hōgen Mon'eki; 885–958).

22. This is an expression found in many Zen texts, notably the *Blue Cliff Record*, Case 5, commentary on the case (T 48: 145a).

23. Found in the *Blue Cliff Record*, Case 15, commentary on the verse (T 48: 156a).

24. Zen describes its central purpose as "the investigation and clarification of the matter of self" 己事究明.

25. Okushū 奥州 was the region north of the Kantō Plain, corresponding to today's Miyagi, Yamagata, and Fukushima prefectures.

26. 佛果圜悟眞覺禪師心要 (x 69: #1357). Yuanwu Keqin 圜悟克勤 (J., Engo Kokugon; 1063–1135), also known by his honorary title Foguo 佛果 (J., Bukka), began his study of Zen when a serious illness made him despair of resolving the problem of samsara through the mastery of doctrine alone. He practiced under Wuzu Fayan and eventually became his Dharma heir. He delivered the lectures on koans that later formed the great Zen literary work *Blue Cliff Record* (*Biyan lu* 碧巖錄). His two most important disciples were Dahui Zonggao (see following note) and Huqiu Shaolong 虎丘紹隆 (J., Kukyū Jōryū; 1077–1136).

27. 大慧書 (T 47: #1998A). Dahui Zonggao 大慧宗杲 (J., Daie Sōkō; 1089–1163), also known as Dahui Pujue, became a monk at the age of sixteen and, after receiving the full precepts a year later, set out on a pilgrimage that took him to a number of masters before he joined the assembly under Yuanwu Keqin. After receiving Dharma transmission from Yuanwu he succeeded him as master of the temple Tianning Wanshou si 天寧萬壽寺. Later, after the invasion of China by the Jurchen, he moved south with Yuanwu and resided at the temple Zhenru yuan 眞如院. He later served as abbot of several other temples before being defrocked in 1141 owing to his involvement with an official who advocated armed resistance to the Jurchen. After receiving an imperial pardon in 1155 he taught at the temple Nengren Chanyuan 能仁禪院 on Mount Jing 徑. Dahui is known especially for his criticism of "silent illumination Zen" and his support of "koan-introspecting Zen."

28. 林間錄 (x 87: #1624). Juefan Huihong 覺範慧洪 (J., Kakuhan Ekō; 1071–1128) was a native of Ruizhou 瑞州 in what is now Jiangxi 江西. He entered the clergy at the age of fourteen and soon revealed his intellectual abilities, being able, it is said, to memorize an entire book at a single reading. After taking the full precepts and studying the Madhyamaka and Yogācāra teachings, he became a disciple of the Zen master Zhenjing Kewen 眞淨克文 (J., Shinjō Kokubun; 1025–1102). After succeeding to Zhenjing's Dharma he lived at the temple Qingliang si 清涼寺 in Ruizhou. Subsequently he went to Xiangxi 湘西 and devoted himself to scholarship. In addition to the *Zen Forest Records*, his notable works include the *Biographies of Monks of the Zen School* 禪林僧寶傳 and the *Biographies of Eminent Monks* 高僧傳.

29. Mazu Daoyi 馬祖道一 (J., Baso Dōitsu; 709–788), one of the greatest of the Tang-dynasty Zen masters, was the sole Dharma heir of Nanyue Huairang 南嶽懷讓 (J., Nangaku Ejō; 677–744), an important disciple of the Sixth Patriarch. Mazu is said to have produced 139 Dharma heirs, the most important of whom were Baizhang Huaihai, Nanquan Puyuan, and Damei Fachang.

30. 五燈會元 3; x 80: 85b. Translation based on *Sun Face Buddha*, by Cheng Chien Bhikshu (Berkeley: Asian Humanities Press, 1992), 76–77.

31. 大慧普覺禪師宗門武庫 (T 47: #1998B).

32. T 47: 949a.

33. Huineng 慧能 (J., Enō; 638–713) is honored as the Sixth Patriarch of Chinese Zen and the master who gave the school its distinctive Chinese character. Traditionally

said to have been an illiterate woodseller who became interested in Zen upon hearing someone read a passage from the *Diamond Sutra*, Huineng practiced under Hongren 弘忍 (J., Gunin; 600–674) on Mount Huangmei 黄梅. After succeeding to Hongren's Dharma, Huineng taught at the temple Baolin si for thirty-five years. Among Huineng's important disciples were Nanyang, Heze Shenhui 荷澤神會 (J., Kataku Jinne; 670–762), the main proponent of the Southern school; Qingyuan Xingsi 青原行思 (J., Seigen Gyōshi; d. 740), whose descendants founded the Caodong, Fayan, and Yunmen schools of Zen; and Nanyue Huairang, whose descendants founded the Linji and Guiyang schools.

34. These two expressions are found in separate places in the same passage of the *Record of the Source Mirror* 宗鏡錄 (T 48: 898b–c).

35. In Mahayana Buddhism there is a belief that 5,670,000,000 years in the future the bodhisattva Maitreya—presently meditating in the Tushita Heaven—will become the next buddha and descend to earth to save all sentient beings.

36. Usuba 臼庭, presently Kitaibaraki-shi Usuba 北茨城市臼庭, was a town in present Ibaraki Prefecture on Japan's Pacific coast.

37. Even following enlightenment, residual karmic forces and the seeds of former habits remain.

38. The clan head at the time may have been Nikaidō Sadafuji 二階堂貞藤 (1267–1335), who was later to be one of Musō's most important patrons and supporters. Nishiyama, however, reports that the evidence on the clan head's identity is inconclusive.

39. Wuxue Zuyuan 無學祖元 (J., Mugaku Sogen; 1226–1286) was, like Wuan Puning, a successor of the Chinese master Wuzhun Shifan. After coming to Japan in 1279 at the invitation of the Kamakura regent, Hōjō Tokimune 北条時宗 (1251–1284), he served as abbot of Kenchō-ji and later became founding abbot of Engaku-ji. He was the teacher of Musō Soseki's teacher, Kōhō Kennichi.

40. Nāgārjuna (150?–250?) was one of the greatest Buddhist thinkers and a founding figure of Mahayana Buddhism. Most Mahayana schools include him in their ancestral lineages; in Zen he is honored as the fourteenth patriarch of Indian Zen. He is said to have been born to a South Indian Brahmin family and to have studied the Hinayana teachings in his youth. His thought was central to the development of the śūnyatā philosophy and Middle Way doctrine of the Madhyamaka school.

41. I was unable to locate a source for this passage. Baizhang Huaihai (J., Hyakujō Ekai 百丈懷海; 720–814) was a Dharma heir of the Zen master Mazu Daoyi. After leaving Mazu he established a monastery on Mount Daxiong 大雄, where he is said to have formulated the first monastic code for Zen temples, *Pure Rules for the Zen Community* 禪林清規. One of the central elements of monastic life for Baizhang was manual labor, as expressed in his famous dictum, "A day of no work—a day of no eating."

42. Yinshan Longshan 隱山龍山 (Inzan Ryūzan; n.d.) was a disciple of Mazu Daoyi who, after his training, spent the rest of his life deep in the mountains.

43. Gen'ō Hongen 元翁本元 (1282–1332) was a native of Mikawa 三河 in Nōshū who became a monk and trained under Kōhō Kennichi, then followed Musō to Jōko-ji and later Kokei-an. When Musō was called to Nanzen-ji in 1325 Gen'ō accompanied him to the capital, where he dwelt in the outlying temples of Enryaku-ji 延暦寺 and Daigo-ji 醍醐寺 in order to escape the bustle of the city. Later he accepted the post of abbot at important

temples in Kamakura and Kyoto, including Manju-ji, Nanzen-ji, and Rinsenji 臨川寺. At the end of his life he returned to Kokei-an.

44. The name "Kyūkō-an" 吸江庵 (Swallowing-the-River Hermitage) has its origins in a famous koan involving Layman Pang and Mazu Daoyi: "Layman Pang Yun called upon Mazu and asked, 'Who is it that doesn't get caught up in the ten thousand things?' Mazu answered, 'I'll tell you when you swallow the water of the West River in a single gulp.'"

45. Hakusen-an 舶船庵 (Boat Mooring Hermitage) was located on the side of Mount Hakusen, a hill overlooking Tokyo Bay on what is presently the grounds of the U.S. Yokosuka Naval Base. A stone monument on the site reads, in part: "Musō Kokushi, a famous Zen Buddhist priest of Japan, lived here from 1319 until 1323. During this period he established Hakusen-an (hermitage).... With the establishment of Yokosuka Iron Works in 1865, much of the local tableland including Mt. Hakusen was removed."

46. Lingshan Daoyin 靈山道隱 (J., Reizan Dōin; 1255–1325) was a native of Zhejiang 浙江 in China who studied under the master Xueyan Zuqin 雪巖祖欽 (J., Setsugan Sokin; d. 1287). He traveled to Japan in 1319 and at the invitation of Hōjō Takatoki became the eighteenth abbot of Kenchō-ji. In 1324 he assumed the abbacy of Engaku-ji and later built the subtemple Shōju-an 正受庵 at Kenchō-ji.

47. The Ocean-Imprint Samādhi 海印三昧 is "a kind of meditation expounded in the [*Avataṃsaka Sutra* in which] all phenomena of the three existences of past, present, and future are clearly observed in the mind, just as all things are reflected on the calm surface of the ocean" (*The Soka Gakkai Dictionary of Buddhism*, 470).

48. Translation based on Martin Collcutt, "Musō Soseki," 276.

49. A detailed explanation of Go-Daigo's actions can be found in *Kenmu: Go-Daigo's Revolution*, by Andrew Edmund Goble (Cambridge: Harvard University Asia Center, 1996), particularly chapter 2, "Moves and Setbacks, 1321–1324."

50. Shūhō Myōchō 宗峰妙超 (1282–1338) became a monk at age eleven and studied Tendai doctrine. He studied under Kōhō Kennichi at Manju-ji until 1304 (and may have encountered Musō at that time), then went to Kyoto in 1304 to practice under Nanpo Jōmyō (see next note). When Nanpo moved to Kenchō-ji in 1308 Shūhō accompanied him; just ten days after arriving in Kamakura he attained enlightenment with the koan "Yunmen's 'Barrier'." Shūhō returned to Kyoto after Nanpo died several months later and lived in seclusion at Ungo-ji 雲居寺 in eastern Kyoto. Zen legend has it that while there Shūhō begged near the Gōjō Bridge for twenty years until discovered by Emperor Hanazono. The historical record shows that Shūhō was known much earlier, however. Although twenty years would have put him among the beggars until 1329, in fact Daitoku-ji 大徳寺 was established for him in 1319. Shūhō lived there for the rest of his life, serving as the teacher of not only Zen monks but also the emperors Hanazono and Go-Daigo. He is best known by his honorary title, Daitō Kokushi 大燈國師.

51. Nanpo Jōmyō 南浦紹明 (1235–1309) began his Zen training at Kenchō-ji at the age of eighteen. There he studied under Lanxi Daolong until 1259, when he journeyed to China to practice under Xutang Zhiyu 虚堂智愚 (J., Kidō Chigu; 1185–1269), from whom he received the seal of transmission in 1265. After returning to Japan in 1267 he studied further under Lanxi, then in 1270 he went to Kyūshū to serve as abbot of Kōtoku-ji 興徳寺 and, three years later, of Sōfuku-ji 崇福寺. He remained there for thirty-three years.

In 1305 he was appointed abbot of Manju-ji in Kyoto, and in 1307 he became master of Kenchō-ji, where he died in 1309. He is usually referred to by his posthumous title, Daiō Kokushi 大應國師.

52. See Martin Collcutt, "Musō Soseki," 276.

53. Mingji Chujun 明極楚俊 (J., Minki Soshun; 1262–1336) was a native of Zhejiang 浙江 in China. He was ordained at the age of twelve and later studied under Huyan Jingfu 虎巖淨伏 (J., Kogan Jōjō; n.d.). After succeeding to Huyan's Dharma and heading a number of important temples he was invited to Japan by the Shogunate in 1329. He arrived in the country together with Zhuxian Fanxian (see note 68, p. 382), and served as abbot of Kenchō-ji, Nanzen-ji, and Kennin-ji. He also founded Kōgon-ji 廣嚴寺 in what is presently Hyōgo Prefecture and built the subtemples Shōrin-ji 少林寺 in Nanzen-ji and Untaku-an 雲澤庵 in Kenchō-ji.

54. Qingzhuo Zhengcheng 清拙正澄 (J., Seisetsu Shōchō; 1274–1339) was born in what is presently Fujian 福建. He became a monk at the age of fifteen and received the precepts the following year. He studied widely under various masters, including Yuji Zhihui 愚極智慧 (J., Gukyoku Chie; n.d.) and Huyan Jingfu. In 1326 Hōjō Takatoki invited him to Japan and appointed him abbot of Kenchō-ji. This was followed by postings to Jōchi-ji, Engaku-ji, Kennin-ji, and Nanzen-ji. Qingzhuo also founded Kaizen-ji 開善寺 in what is presently Nagano Prefecture and the subtemple Zenkyo-an 禪居庵 in Kenchō-ji.

55. The Five Mountain literary movement (*gozan bungaku* 五山文學) was a tradition of Chinese-language prose and poetry associated with the Five Mountain Zen temples (see note 61, p. 381). The movement was at its height during the fourteenth and fifteenth centuries, but it continued through the seventeenth century. The facility in Chinese literature of the Five Mountain Zen monks (both Chinese émigrés and Japanese who had studied in China) helped win them the support of the Kamakura and Muromachi governments, as the warrior leaders saw in Chinese prose and poetry a counterweight to the Japanese-language literary culture of the imperial court and the established sects of Tendai and Shingon. The government also employed the monks' literary skills for drafting official documents and conducting diplomacy with the continent. The Five Mountain literary movement was instrumental in introducing more sophisticated forms of Chinese prose and poetry to Japan and in introducing new forms of Chinese thought (e.g., Neo-Confucianism).

56. Kengai Kōan 巉崖巧安 (1252–1331) was born in what is presently Nagasaki Prefecture. He was ordained as a Tendai monk but later changed to the Zen school and studied at Kenchō-ji under Daxiu Zhengnian (see note 185, p. 392). After receiving Daxiu's sanction he served as abbot of a number of temples, including Kennin-ji, Engaku-ji, and Kenchō-ji.

57. The Genkō 元弘 era lasted from 1331 to 1334.

58. See Martin Collcutt, "Musō Soseki," 278. Collcutt refers to Tamamura Takeji's 玉村竹二 book *Musō Kokushi: Chūsei Zenrin Shuryū no Keifu* 夢窓國師—中世禪林主流の系譜 (Kyoto: Heirakuji Shoten 平樂寺書店, 1958).

59. Martin Collcutt, "Musō Soseki," 280.

60. Mukyoku Shigen 無極志玄 (1282–1359), a native of Kyoto and a fourth-generation descendant of Emperor Juntoku 順徳 (r. 1210–1221), studied esoteric Buddhism at Tō-ji 東寺 prior to beginning Zen practice under Mui Shōgen 無爲昭元 (1245–1311) at Tōfuku-ji. When Mui moved to Engaku-ji, Mukyoku accompanied him and served as

head monk. Later he studied under Musō at Nanzen-ji. In 1337 he became abbot of Rinsen-ji when Musō retired to the Rinsen-ji subtemple San'e-in. He also succeeded Musō at Tenryū-ji when the latter vacated the abbacy there in 1346.

61. Five Mountain temple systems, based on a similar system in China, ranked Japan's major government-supported Zen temples. At the top were the respective *gozan* 五山 (Five Mountains) of Kyoto and Kamakura. As finally classified by the Muromachi Shogunate, the Kyoto Five Mountains were, in order from the top, Tenryū-ji, Shōkoku-ji, Tōfuku-ji, Kennin-ji, and Manju-ji, while the Kamakura Five Mountains were Kenchō-ji, Engaku-ji, Jufuku-ji, Jōmyō-ji, and Jōchi-ji. Nanzen-ji was placed above them all as "the first Zen temple in the land." Next in importance to the *gozan* were the *jissetsu* 十刹 (Ten Temples) and the *shozan* 諸山 (Various Mountains). The entire system consisted of about three hundred temples. The temples developed into centers of cultural and political activity and are best known for their association with the Five Mountain literary movement (*gozan bungaku*).

62. Translation from *Zen Buddhism: A History, Japan*, by Heinrich Dumoulin (New York: MacMillan Publishing Company, 1990), 162.

63. Gyōki 行基 (668–749), a monk of the Hossō school, is revered in Japan as a living bodhisattva who dedicated his life to propagating Buddhism and helping the populace. Born in Kawachi Province in what is presently Osaka Prefecture, he became a priest at the age of fifteen and studied Buddhist doctrine in Nara. At the age of thirty-six he left his official post and began traveling throughout central Japan teaching Buddhism and agricultural techniques, constructing roads, bridges, and reservoirs, and establishing temples that also functioned as hospitals. Although his activities were at first viewed with suspicion by the government, he later won the respect of Emperor Shōmu 聖武 (701–756). During the construction of Tōdai-ji 東大寺, famous as the site of the Great Buddha of Nara, the authorities obtained his help in raising the necessary funds. He died shortly before the temple's completion.

64. Translation based on the *Blue Cliff Record*, trans. Thomas Cleary (Berkeley: Numata Center for Buddhist Translation and Research, 1998), 103–4.

65. Sugawara no Michizane 菅原道眞 (845–903) was an important official, scholar, and poet who was exiled to the remote government outpost of Dazaifu on the island of Kyūshū after running afoul of a powerful member of the governing Fujiwara family. Following his death several years later the capital was struck with plagues and a series of storms that caused fires and floods. A number of imperial princes and members of the Fujiwara family died, leading the court to believe that the angry spirit of Michizane was responsible. It therefore restored his positions and titles and established the Kitano Tenmangū Shrine 北野天滿宮 to honor his spirit, deified as the god Tenjin 天神.

66. Kosen Ingen 古先印元 (1295–1374), born in Satsuma in southern Kyūshū, entered Engaku-ji in Kamakura at the age of eight and was ordained at thirteen. He trained with various Japanese masters, then went to China in 1318 and studied under Zhongfeng Mingben (note 292, p. 400). After succeeding to Zhongfeng's Dharma he continued his practice in China, finally returning to Japan in 1326 with the Chinese master Qingzhuo Zhengcheng (see note 54, p. 380) when the latter was invited to Japan by the Hōjō authorities. In 1327 Kosen served as head monk at Kenchō-ji under Qingzhuo, then, in 1338, he entered Tōji-ji 等持寺 in central Kyoto (Tōji-ji, full name Hōōzan Tōji-ji 鳳凰山等持寺, is not to be confused with Mannenzan Tōji-in 萬年山

等持院, an important Five Mountain temple northwest of central Kyoto that was founded by Musō in 1341). In 1339, at Musō's request, Kosen served as nominal abbot of Erin-ji, though he continued to live in the capital. From 1350 he departed Kyoto for eastern Japan and was later designated abbot of several important temples there, including Engaku-ji and Kenchō-ji in Kamakura. His honorary title is Meditation Master Shōshū Kōchi 正宗廣智禪師.

67. One *kan* 貫 was the equivalent of one thousand copper coins (*mon* 文).

68. Zhuxian Fanxian 竺仙梵僊 (J., Chikusen Bonsen; 1292–1348) was born in Zhejiang 浙江 in China and entered a temple at the age of ten. After taking the precepts at age eighteen he went on pilgrimage and visited a number of masters, including Zhongfeng Mingben. He finally received transmission from Gulin Qingmao 古林清茂 (J., Kurin Seimo; 1262–1329). While visiting Mount Jing 徑 in 1329 he met Mingji Chujun (see note 53, p. 380), who had just been invited to Japan by the Shogunate. Zhuxian decided to accompany him, and a year after arriving in Japan was appointed head monk of Kenchō-ji. He subsequently served as abbot of a number of important temples, including Jōmyō-ji, Jōchi-ji, Nanzen-ji, and Kenchō-ji. Both Ashikaga Takauji and Ashikaga Tadayoshi held him in the highest regard and became his disciples.

69. Dongling Yongyu 東陵永璵 (J., Tōryō Eiyo; 1285–1365) was a Dharma successor of the Caodong (Sōtō) master Yunwai Yunxiu 雲外雲岫 of Tiantongshan 天童山. In 1351, after serving as master of Tianning si 天寧寺 he traveled to Japan, where he served as abbot of Tenryū-ji, Nanzen-ji, Kenchō-ji, and Engaku-ji.

70. Gidō Shūshin 義堂周信 (1325–1388) was born in Tosa (modern Kōchi Prefecture) on the southern island of Shikoku. He entered Enryaku-ji at the age of fourteen and received the precepts. At seventeen he began his Zen practice at Rinsen-ji under Musō. Following Musō's death he attempted to go to China but was prevented from doing so by illness. He therefore entered Kennin-ji for further Zen training, then spent twenty-two years in various Kamakura temples. In 1379 (by some accounts 1380) he was appointed abbot of Kennin-ji by the shogun Ashikaga Yoshimitsu 足利義滿 (1358–1408); in 1386 he became abbot of Nanzen-ji. Gidō was one of the greatest poets of the Five Mountain literary movement; as a Zen monk he stressed the virtues of frugality and the practice of meditation. With Zekkai Chūshin, he is honored as one of the "two jewels" of the Five Mountain literary movement.

71. Zekkai Chūshin 絶海中津 (1336–1405) was born in the province of Tosa and with Gidō Shūshin was known as one of the "two jewels" of the Five Mountain literary movement. At the age of thirteen he entered Tenryū-ji and studied under Musō. After taking the precepts he practiced at Kennin-ji and at monasteries in the eastern part of Japan. In 1368 he traveled to China and studied under Litan Zongle 李潭宗泐 (J., Ritan Sōroku; 1318–1391) and other masters. Returning to Japan in 1378, he served as head monk at Tenryū-ji before being appointed abbot of Erin-ji in Kai. He later headed a number of the great monasteries of Kyoto, including Tenryū-ji, Shōkoku-ji, and Nanzen-ji. His skill in the Chinese language helped him become one of the finest poets of the Five Mountain literary movement. Owing to his literary skills, Zekkai was also employed by the Shogunate to write state documents.

72. The figure for the number of students comes from Musō's tomb inscription; the figure for the number of Dharma successors from the *Zengaku daijiten* 禪學大辭典 (lineage chart no. 45).

73. Hakuin Ekaku 白隠慧鶴 (1686–1769), venerated in Japan as the great reviver of Rinzai Zen, is known for the severity of his practice and the depth of his awakenings. Hakuin's admiration for Musō is expressed in his biographical work *Wild Ivy* (*Itsumadegusa*), in which he relates a story he once heard about the master. One summer Musō climbed Mount Kentoku in Kai with a supply of dried persimmons, having decided to train in seclusion and eat no more than a single persimmon a day. Not long after he reached the mountain a young monk appeared and offered to serve Musō throughout the summer if the master would share half of his daily persimmon. Musō agreed, and the monk cheerfully cleaned, drew water, and performed various other tasks for the entire time the master was there.

At the end of the summer Musō showed his appreciation by giving the young monk his surplice. The monk thanked him, then quickly ran off. Musō gathered his few belongings and descended to the foot of the mountain. As he was eating a meal at the home of a believer, another villager appeared and reported that he had just seen a young monk run into the village shrine, straight through the wooden lattice door. When Musō and the villagers examined the shrine, they saw a statue of Kṣitigarbha Bodhisattva in the corner wearing the same surplice that Musō had given the young monk that morning. Realizing that the monk who had served him had in fact been Kṣitigarbha, Musō broke into tears and pressed his palms together in gratitude. The village people were deeply impressed, and people from all over the district came to pay their respects at the shrine. Hakuin, however, states in *Wild Ivy* that what truly impressed him about the story was not the miraculous occurrence with Kṣitigarbha but "Musō's deep faith and steadfastness of purpose. I envy his pure dedication to the Way. I want to do as he did, find a pure, consecrated spot, quiet and secluded, where no one ever comes." (*Wild Ivy*, trans. by Norman Waddell [Boston: Shambhala Publications, 1999], 60)

74. Kawase Kazuma 川瀬一馬, *Muchū Mondō shū* 夢中問答集 (Tokyo: Kōdansha, 2000).

75. Nakamura Bunpō 中村文峰, *Gendaigo yaku Muchū Mondō* 現代語訳夢中問答 (Tokyo: Shunjūsha, 2000).

76. Karaki Junzō 唐木順三, *Zenke goroku shū* 禪家語錄集 (Tokyo: Chikuma Shobō, 1969), 95–172.

77. Nishimura Eshin 西村惠信, *Muchū Mondō* 夢中問答 (Tokyo: Nihon Hōsō Shuppan Kyōkai, 1998).

78. Musō Soseki, *Dream Conversations on Buddhism and Zen*, trans. and ed. by Thomas Cleary (Boston: Shambhala, 1994).

79. Kenneth L. Kraft, "Dialogues in a Dream," *The Eastern Buddhist* 14/1 (Spring 1981): 75–93.

80. W. S. Merwin and Sōiku Shigematsu, *Sun at Midnight* (San Francisco: North Point Press, 1989).

81. The "evil realms" 惡道 (lit., "evil paths") are the realms of the animals, pretas (hungry spirits), and hell-dwellers. See also note 91, p. 384, and note 290, p. 399.

82. This probably refers to the disaffection among the warrior class regarding the reapportionment of land following the Kenmu Restoration (see p. 34).

83. Sudatta, also called Anāthapindada ("Supplier of the Needy") for his generosity to the poor, was one of the richest merchants in Śrāvastī, the capital of the kingdom

of Kośala. After hearing Śākyamuni preach at the Bamboo Grove Monastery in Rājagriha, he became the Buddha's disciple and built the Jetavana Monastery as an offering. Śākyamuni and the Sangha subsequently spent the rainy seasons at Jetavana in retreat.

84. A *shō* 升 is a measure of volume of about 1.8 liters.

85. Śāriputra was one of the Buddha's ten great disciples, renowned for his wisdom.

86. Maudgalyāyana, also among the Buddha's ten great disciples, was renowned for his supernatural powers.

87. Māhākāśyapa, another of the Buddha's great disciples, was known for his strict observance of the rules of training.

88. Dāna is the practice of almsgiving.

89. The Three Treasures are the Buddha, the Dharma, and the Sangha.

90. The Latter Age of the Dharma is the third and final age before the destruction of Buddhism. The first age, that of the True Dharma, which lasted five hundred years or a thousand years depending on the source, was the era immediately after the time of the Buddha when the true Dharma was practiced and many people were able to attain enlightenment. The second age, that of the Semblance Dharma, which also lasted five hundred years or a thousand years, was an era in which the Dharma became formalized and few people attained enlightenment. During the Latter Age of the Dharma, which will last ten thousand years and is the age we are presently in, the Buddhist doctrines still exist but there is no longer any practice or enlightenment.

91. The realm of the pretas is one of the six realms or six paths (六道 or 六趣), the six states of incarnate existence into which sentient beings are born. The six states are: (1) the realm of the heavenly beings 天; (2) the realm of human beings 人; (3) the realm of the asuras 阿修羅 (titans, fighting deities); (4) the realm of the animals 畜生; (5) the realm of the pretas 餓鬼 (hungry spirits, beings condemned to insatiable hunger); and (6) the realm of the hell-dwellers 地獄.

92. A dhāraṇī 蛇羅尼 is a mantra-like formula recited to provide protection for and power to the reciter.

93. This is a paraphrase of a line from the *Lotus Sutra*, "Chapter on the Teacher of the Law" 法師功徳品; T 9: 50a.

> Moreover, Constant Exertion, if good men or good women accept and uphold this sutra after the Thus Come One has entered extinction, if they read it, recite it, explain and preach it, or transcribe it, they will acquire twelve hundred mind benefits.... If they should expound some text of the secular world or speak on matters of government or those relating to wealth and livelihood, they will in all cases conform to the correct Law. (*The Lotus Sutra*, trans. Burton Watson [New York: Columbia University Press, 1993], p. 263).

94. Tadayoshi (the questioner) uses the word 福業, lit., "prosperity karma." In the following discussion the word translated as "action" is generally "karma" 業 in the original, but in the sense of karma as any act that has an influence on one's later life. "Defiled" and "undefiled" translate 有漏 and 無漏, respectively. The 漏 of these terms translates the Sanskrit *āśrava*, which means "flow" or "leakage" and indicates the kleśa, the defiling passions, since the kleśa ceaselessly flow through the six sense organs. "Defiled" 有漏 is

the state in which such leakage is present; "undefiled" 無漏 is the pure state in which there is no flow of kleśa.

95. The śrāvaka and pratyekabuddha form the so-called Two Vehicles, the two paths that comprise the Hinayana (the "Small Vehicle," whose followers strive only for their own liberation and not for that of others). The śrāvaka ("listener") achieves enlightenment through hearing the words of a buddha; the pratyekabuddha achieves enlightenment through his or her own efforts.

96. The Ten Stages 十地 are the forty-first to fiftieth of the fifty-two stages through which the bodhisattva advances on the way to Buddhahood. The stages are: (1) the stage of joy at having partially understood the truth; (2) the stage of purity (freedom from all defilement); (3) the stage of luminosity (shining with the light of wisdom); (4) the stage of radiance (glowing with the wisdom that eradicates ignorance); (5) the stage of invincibility (overcoming the most difficult delusions); (6) the stage of manifesting wisdom; (7) the stage of reaching far (overcoming the limitations of the Two Vehicles and going everywhere freely); (8) the stage of immovability (dwelling firmly in the Middle Way); (9) the stage of excellent wisdom (attaining the wisdom allowing one to teach freely); and (10) the stage of the Dharma-cloud (spreading the Dharma everywhere).

97. The stage of Equivalent Enlightenment 等覺, the fifty-first of the fifty-two stages of the bodhisattva, is regarded as the initial stage of Buddhahood, at which a bodhisattva has attained an enlightenment nearly as complete as that of a buddha.

98. 悲華經 (T 3: #157). This sutra, translated into Chinese by Dharmakshema of the Northern Liang dynasty, compares Śākyamuni to the white lotus flower, the most beautiful of all flowers, since in his immeasurable compassion he chose to be born in the world of delusion in order to help people to liberation. The story of King No-Thought-of-Conflict is found in fascicles 2 and 3.

99. In Indian mythology the cakravartin ("wheel-turning kings") are ideal rulers who govern through wisdom and justice. These kings possess the thirty-two primary features of a buddha but lack the secondary characteristics of a buddha. They rule the four continents surrounding Mount Sumeru: Gold-Wheel Kings 金輪王 rule the northern, eastern, western, and southern continents; Silver-Wheel Kings 銀輪王 rule the eastern, western, and southern continents; Copper-Wheel Kings 銅輪王 rule the eastern and southern continents; and Iron-Wheel Kings 鐵輪王 rule the southern continent. See also note 118, p. 387. "Cakravartin" is often used as an epithet for Śākyamuni.

100. The seven treasures 七寶 are various precious substances mentioned in the sutras. In the "Treasure Tower" chapter of the *Lotus Sutra* these are listed as gold, silver, lapis lazuli, seashell, agate, pearl, and carnelian (T 9: 32b). The *Treatise on the Great Perfection of Wisdom* 大智度論 lists them as gold, silver, lapis lazuli, crystal, agate, cornelian, and red pearl (or rubies) (T 25: 134a).

101. The Great Vehicle, the expression of Buddhism in which one follows the Way and strives for enlightenment so that one may help save all sentient beings.

102. Amitābha Buddha is the Tathāgata of Immeasurable Light who presides over the Pure Land of Perfect Bliss in the west. He is the buddha central to the Pure Land Buddhist traditions.

103. Avalokiteśvara is the bodhisattva of compassion, known in Japan as Kanzeon 觀世音 or Kannon 觀音. Avalokiteśvara is regarded as the manifestation of Amitābha Buddha's

vow to save all sentient beings and is said to appear in thirty-three different forms for this purpose.

104. Mahāsthāmaprāpta is the bodhisattva who bestows the wisdom necessary to attain liberation. He and Avalokiteśvara are often shown as companions of Amitābha, with Mahāsthāmaprāpta representing Amitābha's wisdom power and Avalokiteśvara representing Amitābha's compassion power.

105. The Phantom City 化城 is a metaphor from the "Phantom City" chapter 化城品 of the *Lotus Sutra*, which compares the Buddha, in his efforts to lead sentient beings to the complete enlightenment of the One Buddha Vehicle 一佛乘, to a wise leader guiding a group of people to a faraway treasure. Halfway through the journey the exhausted group tells the leader that they wish to turn back, so the leader conjures up a phantom city as a resting place for them. Once the group has recovered, however, the leader causes the city to disappear and the rested travelers continue on to the treasure land. The Phantom City symbolizes the Three Vehicles and the various other upāya by which the Buddha leads people to their true destination: the one supreme vehicle of Buddhahood, represented by the treasure land.

106. These two terms refer to various stages of the development of a bodhisattva. Altogether there are fifty-two stages. The first ten stages are known as the Ten Stages of Faith 十信. These are followed by the Ten Stages of Security 十住, the Ten Stages of Practice 十行, and the Ten Stages of Devotion 十廻向, which together are known as the Three Worthy States 三賢. Next are the Ten Stages of Development 十地 (sometimes known simply as the Ten Stages or Ten Holy Stages; see note 96, p. 385), which are followed by the two highest stages, that of Equivalent Enlightenment 等覺 and that of Marvelous Enlightenment 妙覺.

107. Dengyō Daishi 傳教大師 is the title of the monk Saichō 最澄 (767–822), who is honored as the founder of the Japanese Tendai 天台 school. Saichō was ordained at the age of twelve and received the traditional precepts at Tōdai-ji in Nara in 785. In 804, after some years of study and practice on Mount Hiei to the northeast of Kyoto, he went to China and studied the Tiantai (J., Tendai) exoteric and esoteric teachings, which he transmitted to Japan upon his return in 805. He also attempted to establish a Mahayana ordination platform at his temple on Mount Hiei; permission was granted a week after his death.

108. Kōjō 光定 (779–858), also known by the title Bettō Daishi 別當大師, was one of Saichō's foremost disciples and the one who realized his teacher's dream of establishing a Mahayana ordination platform on Mount Hiei.

109. Jōshū 常州 corresponds to present-day Ibaraki Prefecture in northeastern Japan. For Usuba 臼庭, see p. 16 and note 36, p. 378.

110. The dragon kings 龍王 are regarded in East Asia as the rulers of the waters, with the power to bring rain.

111. Bhaiṣajya-guru (J., Yakushi 藥師) is the Buddha of Healing.

112. Samantabhadra (J., Fugen 普賢) is the bodhisattva who represents the principles of teaching, practice, and salvation.

113. The One Great Matter 一大事因縁 is a Buddhist term that derives from the following passage in the *Lotus Sutra*: "All the buddhas, the world-honored ones, appear in the world only for one great matter, one great cause" (T 9: 7a). That cause is to awaken all beings to Original Nature and induce them to attain it.

114. Saigyō 西行 (1118–1190), usually known as Saigyō Hōshi 西行法師 (Dharma Master Saigyō), was a Japanese monk of noble birth who is renowned especially for his poetry, much of it inspired by the long pilgrimages he made through northern Japan.

115. Musō gives a simplified version of a well-known story about Saigyō, in which the poet-monk, caught in a sudden rainstorm, asks for lodging at an inn run by a prostitute. When the woman refuses him a room, the two exchange the poems mentioned above. The poem and its answer play on the notion of a "temporary lodging," which refers not only to a single night's shelter but also, here, to the woman's body. The story relates that Saigyō found the woman's response so perceptive that, once she allowed him to stay, he ended up speaking with her throughout the night as she sadly told him the story of her life. Subsequently they maintained a correspondence, and the woman later wrote to him saying that she had become a nun.

116. There are three main sections of a sutra: the prefatory section, which explains the circumstances and purpose of the sutra's teaching; the teaching section, which presents the sutra's central message; and the transmission section, which explains the sutra's importance and urges its dissemination.

117. Kiyomizu-dera 清水寺 is a large, popular temple located in the southeastern section of Kyoto.

118. In ancient Indian cosmology, Uttarakuru is the continent to the north of Mount Sumeru, the enormous mountain at the center of the universe. The other continents are Pūrvavideha, to the east of Sumeru; Aparagodānīya, to the west of Sumeru; and Jambudvīpa (our human world), to the south of Sumeru. See also note 99, p. 385.

119. See note 99, p. 385.

120. The "seven treasures" 七寶 of the cakravartin are said to be: (1) a metal wheel (gold, silver, copper, or iron); (2) elephants, (3) horses, (4) jewels, (5) excellent ministers, (6) beautiful women, and (7) excellent generals.

121. The realm of desire 欲界 (kāmadhātu) is the lowest realm of the threefold world 三界, which consists of the realm of desire, the realm of form 色界 (rūpadhātu), and the realm of formlessness or pure consciousness 無色界 (arūpadhātu).

122. The Four Heavenly Kings are: Vaiśravaṇa (J., Bishamon-ten 毘沙門天), protector of the northern continent; Dhritarāṣtra (Jikoku-ten 持國天), protector of the eastern continent; Virūpākṣa (Kōmoku-ten 廣目天), protector of the western continent; and Virūdhaka (Zōchō-ten 增長天), protector of the southern continent.

123. The Heaven of the Thirty-three Gods 三十三天 is known in Sanskrit as Trāyastrimśa Heaven. It is the second of the heavens in the realm of desire, located on a plateau atop Mount Sumeru. The god Indra has his palace there, and at each of the four cardinal directions is a mountain where eight deities reside.

124. Śakra, or Indra (J., Taishaku-ten 帝釋天), is the king of the gods.

125. J., Take-jizai-ten 他化自在天, lit., "The Heaven of Freely Enjoying Things Conjured Up by Other [Gods]." The palace of the Demon King who rules the realm of desire is located in this heaven.

126. The five degenerations are the signs that mark the approaching end of the gods' lifetimes: (1) their flowery crowns wilt; (2) sweat appears in their armpits; (3) their robes become soiled; (4) their physical appearance fades; (5) they no longer enjoy sitting on their thrones.

127. The three calamities are destruction by water, destruction by fire, and destruction by wind. A kalpa of destruction is one of the four periods of time in Buddhist cosmology that, together, comprise a single major kalpa. The four periods are: (1) a kalpa of formation 成劫, (2) a kalpa of continuation 住劫, (3) a kalpa of decline 壞劫, and (4) a kalpa of destruction 空劫.

128. The Vast Fruit Heaven 廣果天 is known in Sanskrit as Bṛhatphalāḥ Heaven.

129. The four heavens in the realm of the formless are: (1) the Heaven of Boundless Empty Space 空無邊天, (2) the Heaven of Boundless Consciousness 識無邊天, (3) the Heaven of Nothingness 無所有天, and (4) the Heaven of Neither Thought nor No-Thought 非想非非想天.

130. T 9: 14c. Translation from *The Lotus Sutra*, Burton Watson, 69.

131. The five impurities 五濁 are: (1) era impurity 劫濁 (an era in which warfare, disease, and natural disasters are common), (2) view impurity 見濁 (in such impure eras false views prevail), (3) the impurity of desire 煩惱濁 (in such eras craving, aversion, and ignorance are strong), (4) the impurity of sentient beings 衆生濁 (in such eras the bodies and minds of sentient beings are weak), and (5) the impurity of life 命濁 (in such eras life spans are short).

132. Fixed karma 定業 is a deep form of karma that produces a specific, fixed result at a specific, fixed time.

133. Zhuangzi 莊子 (369–286 BCE) is considered, along with Laozi 老子, to be one of the founders of the philosophical school of Taoism. His most famous work, *Zhuangzi*, is named after him.

134. The passage is found in the esoteric text *Commentary on the Principle of Wisdom Sutra* 理趣釋 (T 19: 610b). See note 500, p. 411–12.

135. The term translated as "hear and respond" is 感應, which indicates the buddhas' ability to sense when a being has the aspiration to awaken the Buddha-mind and to respond appropriately to that aspiration.

136. King Prasenajit of the kingdom of Kośala requested a consort from the Śākya clan. The Śākyas were unwilling to do so, however, as they regarded themselves as royalty and the Kośalans as barbarians. A Śākya general named Mahānāma therefore suggested that they take the beautiful daughter of his maidservant and offer her to King Prasenajit, presenting her as Mahānāma's own daughter. The king accepted the woman as his queen, and their first son was Virūdhaka. Eight years later Virūdhaka was sent to learn archery in the Śākya's kingdom of Kapilavastu, where he was ridiculed for his mother's low birth. Insulted, Virūdhaka vowed revenge. He later usurped the throne from his father, and soon afterward set out for Kapilavastu. One week after destroying the country, he and all of his soldiers were killed in a flood during a storm. The story is found in the *Further Discourses of the Buddha* 增一阿含經 (T 2: #125; fascicle 26).

137. For Maudgalyāyana, see note 86, p. 384.

138. Qipo Bianque 耆婆偏鵲 was a semilegendary Chinese doctor said to have been born sometime in the fourth century BCE.

139. *Heihaku* may refer to offerings in general, or more specifically to offerings of strips of paper or silk tied to a stick.

140. This visit occurred in 1326, when Musō was fifty-one years old.

141. Emperor Kinmei 欽明 (509–571).

142. The Inner Shrine 内宮 of Ise is thought to have been established in the third century, and the Outer Shrine 外宮 in the fifth century. Buddhism first arrived in Japan in the mid-sixth century.

143. This is an expression of *honji suijaku* 本地垂迹 thought (Shinto/Buddhist syncretism), according to which buddhas and bodhisattvas (known as the *honji* 本地, the "original state") manifest themselves in the form of Shinto gods, or *kami* 神 (known as the *suijaku* 垂迹, the "manifestation"), in order to save sentient beings.

144. The offerings are of the glutinous form of rice known in Japanese as *mochi*. *Mochi* rice is usually put into a large mortar and thoroughly beaten with mallets until it is sticky and smooth.

145. The Usa Hachiman Shrine 宇佐八幡宮 was founded in the early eighth century on the spot where the deity Hachiman is said to have appeared in Buzen 豊前 (a region in northeastern Kyūshū, the westernmost main island of Japan). Hachiman is the guardian deity of warriors and the protector of the Japanese nation, and he is also worshipped as a god of agriculture. He is associated with the Japanese emperor Ōjin 應神, the fifteenth emperor in the traditional lineage, and thought to be the first historical emperor, though nothing is known of his life.

146. The province of Yamashiro 山城 corresponds to present-day Kyoto Prefecture; the deity was moved from Buzen to Otokoyama 男山 in 859.

147. Gyōkyō 行教 (n.d.) was a priest of Daian-ji 大安寺.

148. Kōbō Daishi 弘法大師 is the honorary title of the monk Kūkai 空海 (774–835), founder of the Japanese Shingon 眞言 school. Kūkai, after study at the government university in Nara, began Buddhist practice at the age of twenty-two. In 804 he joined a government-sponsored expedition to China in order to deepen his understanding of the esoteric *Mahāvairocana Sutra*. In 806, after receiving the final initiation into the esoteric teachings, Kūkai returned to Japan and commenced an active teaching career. He was eventually appointed head of Tōdai-ji in Nara and chief of the Office of Priestly Affairs. In addition to spreading the esoteric teachings he founded several important temples, principally Tō-ji 東寺 in Kyoto and the monastery on Mount Kōya 高野.

149. The Hōjō-e 放生會 (rite for release of sentient beings) is a ritual in which captured animals are purchased and then released back to their natural environment.

150. An upāya, usually translated as "expedient means," "skillful means," or "provisional means," is a method or stratagem, sometimes deceptive on the surface, for leading people to higher spiritual states and eventually to the final goal of Buddhahood.

151. *Jōbuku* 調伏 (the subduing of malevolent spirits) and *sokusai* 息災 (the elimination of misfortune) are two of the four esoteric practices, the other two being *zōyaku* 増益 (the promotion of happiness, prosperity, and well-being) and *keiai* or *kyōai* 敬愛 (the augmentation of the love or benevolence received from buddhas, gods, nations, or other people).

152. "Manifest attainments" 有相の悉地 are siddhi (attainments or powers) with form, as opposed to "formless attainments" 無相の悉地, siddhi without form. The siddhi are transcendent powers attained through spiritual practices. The manifest attainments are such mundane powers as clairvoyance, levitation, invisibility, and control over

the spirit world. Formless attainments relate to the supermundane siddhi of Supreme Enlightenment.

153. T 18: 54c.

154. The various Mahayana traditions divide the Buddhist teachings into expedient or provisional teachings 權教 and the true Mahayana teaching 實大乘教. The expedient teachings were used by Śākyamuni to guide people until they were capable of understanding the true Mahayana teachings, which were the direct expression of the Buddha's enlightened understanding. The Tiantai (Tendai) tradition regards the *Lotus Sutra* as representing the true Mahayana teaching; other traditions accord this position to the *Nirvana Sutra* or *Avataṃsaka Sutra*.

155. Musō is citing the *Notes on the Commentary on the "Stages of Mind" Chapter of the Mahāvairocana Sutra* 大日經住心品疏私記, T 60: 364a. The Samādhi of Great Emptiness, known as *daikū zanmai* 大空三昧 in Japanese, is the highest of the 108 levels of samādhi, the level in which one realizes that all things are intrinsically of the same Buddha-nature.

156. Dharma gate (*hōmon* 法門) refers to a Buddhist teaching regarded as an entrance to enlightenment.

157. That is, enlightenment. See note 152.

158. T 12: 384a.

159. Prince Shōtoku 聖徳太子 (574–622) was the second son of Emperor Yōmei 用明 (r. 585–587). When Empress Suiko 推古 (554–628) of the Soga family ascended the throne in 593, she appointed Shōtoku as her regent, making Shōtoku the de facto ruler of Japan. Shōtoku is historically important for his promotion of Buddhism and his initiation of many major governmental reforms.

　· After the death of Emperor Yōmei a power struggle broke out between the Soga clan, led by Soga no Umako 蘇我馬子 (d. 626), and the Mononobe clan, led by Mononobe-no-Moriya 物部守屋 (d. 587). The fifteen-year-old Shōtoku, at the time already a devout Buddhist, gave his support to the Sogas, praying to the Four Heavenly Kings for the Sogas' victory. The Sogas did prevail in battle against the Mononobes, killing Moriya and largely destroying the latter clan's political influence.

160. I have not been able to locate this passage in the *Nirvana Sutra*.

161. The Three Sovereigns and Five Emperors are legendary Chinese rulers, said to have lived between four and five thousand years ago, who are regarded as model rulers and moral paragons.

162. T 24: 1004b.

163. See the explanation of "hear and respond" 感應, note 135, p. 388.

164. 蘇香圓.

165. The five precepts are: (1) not to kill or injure sentient beings, (2) not to take that which has not been given, (3) not to engage in adultery, (4) not to lie, (5) not to take intoxicants.

166. The ten good actions are: (1) not to kill, (2) not to steal, (3) not to commit adultery, (4) not to lie, (5) not to use harsh words, (6) not to slander, (7) not to engage in idle talk, (8) to avoid greed, (9) to avoid anger, (10) to avoid false views.

167. *Treatise on the Great Perfection of Wisdom* 大智度論. An extensive commentary on the

Great Perfection of Wisdom Sutra, attributed to Nāgārjuna (ca. 150–250); Chinese translation by Kumārajīva (350–409) in the years 401–405. The text explains many important Mahayana concepts, including prajñā, śūnyatā, and the six pāramitās, and had a great influence on the development of East Asian Buddhist thought. Passages similar to what Musō cites appear in various places in the *Treatise*, including T 25: 410c and 416c.

168. The transference of merit is known in Japanese Buddhism as *ekō* 回向. Buddhist practices such as the recitation of sutras are believed to generate benefits or "roots of goodness" 善根 that can be transferred to other beings, even those who are dead, thus helping them on the path to enlightenment.

169. See, for example, the *Laṅkāvatāra Sutra* (T 16: 561b).

170. See note 95, p. 385.

171. See note 37, p. 378.

172. The term in the *Vimalakīrti Sutra* is 愛見の大悲 (T 14: 545a).

173. This saying is found in numerous texts, including Dahui Zonggao's *Treasury of the True Dharma Eye* 正法眼藏; x 67: 564c.

174. I have not been able to locate the source of this quote. For Baizhang, see note 41, p. 378.

175. The term *kaji* 加持 originally referred to the compassion that the Buddha bestowed upon living beings. In esoteric Buddhism it came to indicate rituals involving incantations, mudras, and other esoteric practices to obtain the buddhas' power for some purpose. Many *kaji* are conducted for the attainment of this-worldly benefits, but originally the ritual was intended to help the devotee realize Buddhahood by bringing his or her thoughts, words, and actions into accord with those of the buddhas and by evoking, through faith, an infusion of the buddhas' power into the devotee.

Kitō 祈禱 rituals are prayers offered to the gods and buddhas in order to obtain their aid in achieving secular or spiritual goals.

176. The ten realms as defined by Shingon are: (1) hell-dwellers; (2) pretas (hungry spirits); (3) animals; (4) humans; (5) asuras (titans or fighting demons); (6) deities (gods, heavenly beings); (7) śrāvakas (listeners); (8) pratyekabuddhas (individually enlightened buddhas); (9) bodhisattvas; (10) buddhas. The first five are regarded as the five mundane paths and the latter five as the five sacred paths. In the exoteric schools the first six are regarded as the six mundane paths and the final four as the four noble worlds.

177. Mahāvairocana Buddha represents the Dharmakāya 法身, the essential or absolute body of buddha. The Dharmakāya is buddha viewed as universal truth itself.

178. See note 152, pp. 389–90.

179. The six elements 六大 are earth, water, fire, wind, space, and consciousness.

180. The four universal mandalas 四種曼荼羅 are the Great Mandala 大曼荼羅, the Samaya Mandala 三昧耶曼荼羅, the Dharma Mandala 法曼荼羅, and the Karma Mandala 羯磨曼荼羅. Together they symbolize every form of existence that arises from the six elements. The Great Mandala depicts the realm of the buddhas' enlightenment; the Samaya Mandala their inner virtues and vows; the Dharma Mandala the expression of their enlightenment in writing; and the Karma Mandala the expression of their enlightenment in activity.

181. The three mysteries 三密 are the three esoteric mysteries of body, mouth, and mind. According to esoteric thought, all phenomena are manifested into being by Mahāvairocana Buddha and are thus emanations of Mahāvairocana, the universal

source. The bodies of all beings partake of its mystic body, the voices of all beings partake of its mystic voice (i.e., its mouth), and the thoughts of all beings partake of its mystic mind. However, because of our fundamental ignorance, the true nature of body, mouth, and mind are beyond our understanding, and they are thus mysteries to us. Through the three mystic practices, however, we can bring ourselves, in this very life, to a realization of our essential oneness with the Dharmakāya. The mystic practice of the body is the formation of mudras with the hands; the mystic practice of the mouth is the recitation of mantras; and the mystic practice of the mind is the contemplation of mandalas. The perfection of these practices is seen as the perfection of the formless powers (siddhi). For formless siddhi, see note 152, pp. 389–90.

182. Saimyōji 最明寺 was the Buddhist name of Hōjō Tokiyori 北条時頼 (1226–1263), the fifth regent of the Kamakura Shogunate.

183. See note 14, p. 375.

184. Wuan Puning 兀庵普寧 (J., Gottan Funei; 1197–1276) was a successor of the Chinese master Wuzhun Shifan 無準師範 (J., Mujun Shihan; 1177–1249). He held leading positions at several important Chinese monasteries, then came to Japan in 1260 to avoid the Mongol invasions of his homeland. After serving for several years as Lanxi's successor at Kenchō-ji he returned to China in 1265.

185. Daxiu Zhengnian 大休正念 (J., Daikyū Shōnen; 1215–1289) was a successor of Shixi Xinyue 石溪心月 (J., Sekkei Shingetsu; d. 1254). After arriving in Japan in 1269 he was designated founding abbot of Jōchi-ji by Hōjō Tokimune 北条時宗 (1251–1284). He later served as abbot of Zenkō-ji, Jufuku-ji, Kenchō-ji, and Engaku-ji.

186. See note 39, p. 378.

187. The Kōan 弘安 era (1278–1287) was the period in which the second, and larger, of the two Mongol invasions of Japan occurred.

188. Hōjō Tokimune 北条時宗 (1251–1284) was the eighth Kamakura regent and the leader of Japan at the time of the Mongol invasions in 1274 and 1281.

189. The *Dhāraṇī of Great Compassion* 大悲圓滿無礙神呪 (usually abbreviated to 大悲呪), the most frequently recited text in the Zen monastery, is the dhāraṇī section of the *Thousand-armed, Thousand-eyed Bodhisattva Avalokiteśvara's Sutra of Dhāraṇīs on the Vast, Perfect, and Unobstructed Mind of Great Compassion* 千手千眼觀自在菩薩廣大圓滿無礙大悲心陀羅尼經), which praises the marvelous qualities of Avalokiteśvara.

190. The *Śūraṅgama Dhāraṇī* 大佛頂萬行首楞嚴神呪 (usually abbreviated to 楞嚴呪) is the dhāraṇī portion of the seventh fascicle of the ten-fascicle *Śūraṅgama Sutra*.

191. *Hōsan* 放參 originally referred to occasions when evening interviews with the master were called off.

192. The *Avalokiteśvara Sutra* 妙法蓮華經觀世音菩薩普門品第二十五 (usually abbreviated to 觀音經) is the twenty-fifth chapter ("Chapter on the universal gate of Bodhisattva Avalokiteśvara") of the *Lotus Sutra* as translated by Kumārajīva.

193. 祝聖.

194. T 13: 363b. The "Moon Store" section of the *Great Collection Sutra* 大方等大集經月藏分 (abbreviated to 大集月藏經) comprises fascicles 46–56 of the 60-fascicle *Great Collection Sutra* 大方等大集經 (T 13: #397).

195. The term "field of merit" 福田 usually refers to the Buddha (who is the greatest "field of

merit") and the Sangha, since making offerings to these produces merit, just as a field produces food.

196. The twenty-eighth of the secondary precepts, "On issuing discriminatory invitations." Translation from the *Brahmā Net Sutra*, Sutra Translation Committee of the United States and Canada (New York, San Francisco, Niagara Falls, Toronto: 2000).

197. "Good friend" translates 善知識 (Skr., *kalyāṇa-mitra*), a wise guide or other person who helps one progress on the Way.

198. King Enma 閻魔王 is in Buddhist mythology the king of the hell realms and the judge of the dead.

199. This quote is found in the *Recorded Sayings of Meditation Master Dahui Pujue* 大慧普覺 禪師語錄 (T 47: 942a).

200. The *Sutra on Trapuśa and Bhallika* 提謂波利經 is an apocryphal sutra centering on a narrative of the brothers Trapuśa and Bhallika, who became disciples of the Buddha soon after his enlightenment. The text is concerned with how sentient beings should be taught following the passing of the Buddha.

201. Tiantai Zhiyi 天台智顗 (J., Tendai Chigi; 538–597) was the third patriarch and de facto founder of the Chinese Tiantai school.

202. The six stages of practice 六即 are: (1) the stage at which one is a buddha in theory, though not yet aware of the Buddha-nature inherent within all beings (理即); (2) the stage at which one learns of this inherent Buddha-nature through hearing the name and words of the Dharma (名字即); (3) the stage at which one begins the practice of meditation (觀行即); (4) the stage at which the sense-roots are purified, illusion is to a certain extent transcended, and a semblance of the Buddha's enlightenment is attained (相似即); (5) the stage of progressive awakening to true wisdom, in which one eliminates all illusion except fundamental ignorance and progressively advances toward full enlightenment (分眞即); and (6) the stage of full enlightenment, at which fundamental ignorance is eliminated and Buddha-nature is fully realized (究竟即).

203. The second of the six stages is regarded as the first stage of understanding, since it is at this stage that the awakening process begins (the first stage is the stage of the unawakened).

204. The six pāramitās are the "six perfections" by means of which one attains liberation from the world of birth-and-death. The six pāramitās are: (1) dāna (布施), charity or giving; (2) śīla (持戒), keeping the precepts, maintaining moral conduct; (3) kṣānti (忍辱), patience and forbearance; (4) vīrya (精進), zeal and devotion; (5) dhyāna (禪定), contemplation or meditation; (6) prajñā (智慧), transcendental wisdom.

205. The "Awakening Nature and Encouraging Good" 悟性勸善文 chapter of the *Essential Teachings of Meditation Master Foguo Yuanwu Zhenjue* 佛果圜悟眞覺禪師心要 can be found at x 69: 474a-c. For Yuanwu Keqin, see note 26, p. 377.

206. This sentence refers to Ashikaga Tadayoshi.

207. See Introduction, pp. 30-31, and note 57, p. 380.

208. The Seventeen Article Constitution 十七条憲法, issued in 604 CE, is a code of moral precepts attributed to the imperial regent Prince Shōtoku. The code outlined the general ethical principles by which the government and its subjects were expected to live in order to achieve a peaceful and harmonious society. It was firmly based on Confucian principles, with considerable influence from the Buddhist teachings.

209. See note 159, p. 390.

210. Emperor Wu 武帝 (464–549), founder of the Liang 梁 dynasty (502–556) of China, is generally remembered as a wise and benevolent ruler who emphasized education and stressed ethical behavior. He ruled according to Confucian principles but was also an ardent supporter of Buddhism, building numerous temples and ordaining many monks and nuns. Known as the Bodhisattva Emperor, he lived frugally, ate only vegetarian food, and even took the bodhisattva precepts. However, his lenience toward official corruption and his lessening involvement with state affairs during his later reign are believed to have contributed to the decline of the Liang.

211. Hou Jing 侯景 was a general of the Northern Wei, Eastern Wei, and Liang dynasties who rebelled against Emperor Wu in 548, capturing the capital Jiankang and laying siege to the palace. The emperor died a year later. Hou, reviled by history for his cruelty to both soldiers and civilians, died in 552.

212. The *Śūraṅgama Sutra* 首楞嚴經 is said to have been translated in 705 by Pāramiti, but is now generally regarded as a Chinese apocryph. It discusses such Yogācāra concepts as the tathāgata-garbha and the storehouse consciousness, and it also shows Tantric influences. The sutra stresses the importance of meditation, the precepts, and doctrinal knowledge for the attainment of full liberation, and emphasizes the power of the *Śūraṅgama Dhāraṇī* and Śūraṅgama samādhi.

213. The *Great Calming and Contemplation* 摩訶止觀 is a 20-fascicle text published in 594 (T 46: #1911), based on lectures given by Zhiyi, founder of the Tiantai school, as compiled and edited by Zhiyi's disciple Guanding 灌頂 (561–632). The text is centrally concerned with the theory and practice of Tiantai meditation 止觀, the "complete and immediate meditation of the Mahayana." Tiantai meditation combines śamatha 止 (stillness and focus of mind) and vipaśyanā 觀 (perception of the true nature of mind). The *Great Calming and Contemplation* is one of the central texts of the Tiantai school, discussing important Tiantai doctrines such as "one thought-moment, three thousand realms" 一念三千 (the teaching that the three thousand realms constituting the entire universe are immanent in each instant of thought).

214. The *Great Perfection of Wisdom Sutra* 摩訶般若波羅蜜經 is a 27-fascicle sutra translated into Chinese by Kumārajīva (350–409) in 404 (T 8: #223). The teaching of the sutra centers on the ideal of the bodhisattva, who remains in the world of samsara working to liberate all sentient beings while continuing to strive for ultimate enlightenment. Bodhisattva practice is based on insight into the nature of śūnyatā, the essential emptiness of all that exists, as well as on the use of upāya, "skillful means," by which the bodhisattva employs various devices to help free sentient beings from delusion.

215. *Tengu* 天狗 are Japanese supernatural beings, originally represented as fierce birds of prey but from medieval times assuming a more human-like form with wings, sharp eyes, and a very elongated nose. *Tengu* were reputed to be enemies of Buddhism, carrying off monks and attempting to lead them astray. Later they came to be associated with the mountain ascetics known as *yamabushi* 山伏 and were regarded as guardian spirits of the mountains and forests.

216. Ānanda, one of the Buddha's ten great disciples, was a cousin of the Buddha who served as his personal attendant. Because of his extraordinary memory as well as his proximity to the Buddha, Ānanda is said to have remembered more of the Buddha's teachings

than any other disciple, and thus he was the central figure in the compilation of the Buddhist sutras at the First Buddhist Council, held just after the Buddha's passing. Zen legend has it that he failed to reach enlightenment during the Buddha's lifetime, but he was finally awakened under Mahākāśyapa, the first Indian Zen patriarch.

217. This episode is found in the *Nirvana Sutra*, fascicle 40, chapter 13, part 2 (T 12: 597–603). The episode begins on p. 600b.

218. The relevant passage from the *Sutra on Purifying Karmic Hindrances* 佛説淨業障經 can be found at T 24: 1097b.

219. Source unknown. The quote probably conflates statements from separate works. Karaki Junzō identifies the first half as influenced by the *Record of Linji* and the second half as influenced by Liehzi 列子, "Tang wan" 湯問 chapter. Karaki Junzō 唐木順三, *Zenke goroku shū* 禪家語錄集 (Tokyo: Chikuma Shobō, 1969), 113.

220. The Ultimate Tathāgata of Self-Nature 自性天眞の如來 is the Dharmakāya as equivalent to the essential nature of all existence.

221. The three bodies 三身 of a buddha are: (1) the Dharmakāya 法身, buddha as the eternal, absolute truth; (2) the Saṃbhogakāya 報身, the "reward" body, received by a buddha in reward for fulfilling his bodhisattva vows; (3) the Nirmaṇākāya 應身, the body assumed by a buddha when he appears in the world to work for the liberation of sentient beings. The four wisdoms 四智 are: (1) the great perfect mirror wisdom 大圓鏡智, the wisdom associated with the eighth consciousness, which reflects all things as they are; (2) the universal nature wisdom 平等性智, the wisdom associated with the seventh consciousness, which perceives the essential equality of all things; (3) the marvelous observing wisdom 妙觀册智, the wisdom associated with the sixth consciousness, which perceives the distinctive particularity of all things; and (4) the perfecting-of-acting wisdom 成所作智, the wisdom associated with the first five consciousnesses, which perceive how best to guide sentient beings.

222. Daoshu 道樹 (J., Dōju; d. 825) became a monk around the age of fifty and practiced under Huiwen 惠文 (n.d.) of Mount Mingyue 明月. Later he lived on Mount Sanfeng 三峰 in Shouzhou 壽州.

223. The passage is from the *Two Entrances* 二種入, T 48: 370a.

224. Huangbo Xiyun 黄檗希運 (J., Ōbaku Kiun; d. 850) was a native of Fuzhou 福州 in present Fujian 福建 and studied Zen under Baizhang Huaihai. After succeeding to Baizhang's Dharma he resided at Da'an si 大安寺 in the city of Hongzhou 洪州 and then at a monastery on Mount Huangbo 黄檗 built for him by the governor, Pei Xiu 裴休 (J., Hai Kyū; 797–870). His most important disciple was Linji Yixuan 臨濟義玄 (J., Rinzai Gigen; d. 866), founder of the Linji school.

225. The five skandhas (aggregates) are form, sensation, perception, mental formations, and consciousness; the four (great) elements are earth, water, fire, and wind.

226. T 48: 381c. Translation based on *The Essentials of the Transmission of Mind* 傳心法要, trans. John McRae, in *Zen Texts*, ed. Numata Center for Buddhist Translation and Research, (Berkeley: Numata Center for Buddhist Translation and Research, 2005) 24–25. The *Essentials of the Transmission of Mind* is a collection of sermons attributed to Huangbo, as recorded and edited by his lay disciple Pei Xiu.

227. From the *Treatise on the Great Perfection of Wisdom* 大智度論 8; T 25: 118a.

228. Source unknown.

229. T 17: 916c.

230. The stage of nonretrogression 不退轉地 is the stage of practice in which the bodhisattva is assured of attaining complete enlightenment without retrogressing on the path.

231. See note 106, p. 386.

232. See note 97, p. 385.

233. Marvelous Enlightenment 妙覺 is the last of the fifty-two stages of bodhisattvahood, at which the full enlightenment of a buddha is realized.

234. The quote is from Huangbo's *Essentials of the Transmission of Mind*, T 48: 381c. For the Phantom City, see note 105, p. 386.

235. T 9: 30a. Translation based on *The Lotus Sutra*, trans. Burton Watson, 156.

236. T 19: 106c.

237. T 17: 920a.

238. I have not been able to locate this passage in the *Laṅkāvatāra Sutra*.

239. For the six pāramitās, see note 204, p. 393.

240. T 17: 917b.

241. "Activity-consciousness" translates 業識, the initial functioning of the unenlightened mind as activated through ignorance.

242. "Vacuity" translates 無記, indicating a lack of content or function. Other possible translations include "oblivion" and "blankness." Nanquan's statement is taken from Case 19 of the *Wumenguan*:

    Zhaozhou Congshen asked Nanquan Puyuan, "What is the Way?" Nanquan said, "Ordinary mind is the Way." Zhaozhou asked, "Can we deliberately strive toward this?" Nanquan said, "To strive toward it is to turn away." Zhaozhou said, "Without striving, how can we know the Way?" Nanquan said, "The Way has nothing to do with knowing or not-knowing. 'Knowing' is delusion, 'not-knowing' is vacuity. If you really attain the Way-without-doubt, it is vast and boundless like open space. How can you speak of affirmation and negation?" At these words Zhaozhou was deeply enlightened.

243. *Nyogenchi* 如幻智. The translation is provisional, as the meaning of the term is unclear.

244. Nirvana wisdom 無生智 (lit., "no-birth wisdom"), the highest of the ten wisdoms and the final understanding attained by the arhat, is the understanding that one is liberated from the realm of samsara.

245. Diamond Samādhi 金剛喩定 (金剛三昧) is the highest level of bodhisattva meditation, in which the final remaining defilements are purified.

246. From the *Song of Enlightenment* 證道歌, attributed to Yongjia Xuanjue 永嘉玄覺 (663–713), a disciple of the Sixth Patriarch Huineng 慧能 (638–713); T 48: 396a. The translation is from *The Poetry of Enlightenment*, Sheng-yen (Elmhurst: Dharma Drum Publications, 1987), 53.

247. T 9: 449c.

248. Transformational samsara 變易生死, according to the *Discourse on the Establishment of Consciousness Only* 成唯識論, is the type of samsara experienced by enlightened beings

such as arhats, pratyekabuddhas, and bodhisattvas, who are free from rebirth in the deluded realms of desire, form, and formlessness.

249. T 9: 449c.

250. The true form of the Middle Way is that the true nature of all things is characterized neither by the extreme of existence nor by the extreme of nonexistence.

251. T 51: 257a. Fenzhou Wuye 汾州無業 (J., Funshū Mugō; 760–821), a successor of Mazu Daoyi (see note 29, p. 377), taught at Kaiyuan si 開元寺 in Xihe 西河.

252. Musō appears to be combining two separate statements from Zhiyi's introduction to the *Great Calming and Contemplation* 摩訶止觀. The first part of the quote is located at T 46: 1b; the second part at T 46: 1a. Nanyue Huisi 南嶽慧思 (515–577) is honored as the second patriarch of the Tiantai school and the teacher of Zhiyi, although Zhiyi is considered the true founder of the tradition.

253. The text mentioned by Musō is the *Commentary on the Mahāvairocana-abhisaṃbodhi Sutra* 大毘盧遮那成佛經疏. The passage can be found at T 39: 587c.

254. The source appears to be a nearly identical statement attributed to Yunmen in the *Blue Cliff Record*, Case 9, Commentary (T 48: 149b); I have not been able to find the statement in Yunmen's records.

　　Yunmen Wenyan 雲門文偃 (J., Unmon Bun'en; 864–949) was the founder of the Yunmen school of Zen. He began his Zen practice under Muzhou Daoming 睦州道明 (780–877), then continued under Xuefeng Yicun 雪峰義存 (822–908), whose Dharma heir he eventually became. He later founded the temple Guangtai Chanyuan 光泰禪院 on Mount Yunmen 雲門. Yunmen is known for his terse responses to questions, many of which came to be known as Yunmen's "one-word barriers."

255. T 17: 920b–c. "The fault of allowing things to be as they are" is the second of the four faults discussed in the sutra:

> The second is the fault of allowing things to be as they are. If a man says: "I neither wish to sever birth and death nor seek nirvana. There are no conceptions of samsara and nirvana as truly arising or perishing. I allow everything to take its course with the various natures of dharmas in my quest for Complete Enlightenment," this is a fault, because the nature of Complete Enlightenment does not come about through accepting things as they are. (Ch'an Master Sheng-yen, *Complete Enlightenment* [Elmhurst, New York: Dharma Drum Publications, 1997], 57, 274)

256. Karaki Junzō identifies this as based on Dahui's letter to Chen Shaoqing 陳少卿 (T 47: 922c–24c). Karaki Junzō 唐木順三, *Zenke goroku shū* 禪家語錄集 (Tokyo: Chikuma Shobō, 1969) 126.

257. T 47: 785a.

258. The five tastes 五味 are either those associated with milk and its refined forms (milk, cream, curdled milk, butter, ghee) or the first five of the six flavors. The six flavors 六味 are: (1) bitter, (2) sweet, (3) sour, (4) spicy, (5) salty, and (6) delicious.

259. "The flavor of the Dharma" and "the taste of the doctrine" are, respectively, 法味 (understanding the truth of the Dharma) and 義味 (understanding the meaning of the scriptural texts).

260. For the four great elements, see note 225, p. 395.

261. Each of the four elements is thought in Chinese medical theory to have 101 associated ailments, so that the number of ailments associated with all four elements is 404.

262. From the *Treatise on the Great Perfection of Wisdom* 大智度論 (T 25: 361c).

263. I was unable to find the source of this quote.

264. T 47: 893b. The ancient master is Dahui Zonggao.

265. T 47: 720b.

266. T 47: 720b.

267. From the commentary to the main case, *Blue Cliff Record* 100. T 48: 223b.

268. x 67: 594b. The phrase is from Dahui Zonggao.

269. x 67: 594b.

270. *Kōjō* 向上, "directed upwards": efforts directed "upward," that is, toward the attainment of enlightenment; *kōge* 向下, "directed downward": efforts directed "downward," that is, toward the salvation of sentient beings.

   Nahen 那邊, "there": the essential nature of reality; *shahen* 這邊, "here": phenomenal reality.

   Hajū 把住, "taking in," "holding firm": in Zen, that which involves strictness, discipline, or restraint; *hōgyō* 放行, "letting go," "releasing": that which involves free expression, relaxation, etc.

   Kinjū 擒縱, "holding on to and stopping": similar to *hajū*; *sakkatsu* 殺活, "taking life and giving life": a method of training in Zen in which the master first deprives the student of every position the student holds, then turns the student loose in complete freedom.

   Sangen 三玄, "three mysteries"; *sanyō* 三要, "three essentials": these are two terms from the *Record of Linji*. The meaning is uncertain, but they refer, in general, to: (1) truth in its absolute state, (2) truth as wisdom and function; and (3) truth as manifested in the phenomenal world.

   Goi 五位, "five ranks": a system devised by the Chinese Caodong master Dongshan Liangjie, in which the Five Ranks are (1) the Apparent within the Real, (2) the Real within the Apparent, (3) the Coming from within the Real, (4) the Arrival at Mutual Integration, (5) Unity Attained (Isshu Miura and Ruth Fuller Sasaki, *Zen Dust* [Kyoto: The First Zen Institute of America in Japan 1966], 67–71). *Kunshin* 君臣, "lord and vassal": a way of interpreting the Five Ranks in which the lord represents the Real and the vassal represents the Apparent.

271. *Yokuyō* 抑揚 means "pushing down" 抑 and "raising up" 揚; *hōhen* 襃貶 means "to praise" 襃 and "to censure" 貶. Both are methods in which the master, depending upon the circumstances, guides the student by either tightening or loosening discipline.

272. T 47: 883a. The "ancient master" is Dahui; the passage is from the *Recorded Sayings of Meditation Master Dahui Pujue*.

273. x 65: 141a. The "man of old" is Luoshan Daoxian 羅山道閑 (J., Rozan Dōkan; n.d).

274. The five cardinal virtues of Confucianism are benevolence 仁, righteousness 義, propriety 禮, wisdom 智, and sincerity 信.

275. That is, the concept of the Dharma as something with a fixed essence.

276. Source unknown. Budai 布袋 (J., Hotei; n.d.) was a semilegendary Chinese Zen monk, ca. the tenth century. He lived outdoors, sleeping under bridges when it rained, and

kept his possessions in a large sack (the word *budai* means "cloth bag"). Later he was regarded as an incarnation of Maitreya, the buddha of the future.

277. Bodhicitta 菩提心 is the mind that seeks enlightenment and endeavors to save all sentient beings.

278. Source unknown. For Nāgārjuna, see note 40, p. 378.

279. Musō's comments are based on a legend found in the *Historical Records* 史記 and other Chinese classics. Emperor Yao 堯, the fourth of the legendary Five Emperors of ancient China, was revered as a sage-ruler. When the time came to find a successor, he disregarded his own son, whom he considered unworthy, and offered the throne to the virtuous official Xu Yu 許由. Xu rejected the offer, going so far as to wash out his ears in the River Ying to cleanse them of the defilement of the emperor's worldly offer. Xu's friend, Chao Fu 巢父, a man of equal virtue and detachment, heard of Xu's act and would not allow his ox to drink from the river in which Xu had washed out his ears.

280. This passage in the *All Dharmas Are without Actions Sutra* 諸法無行經 is found at T 15: 760a.

281. See the *Sutra of Bodhisattva Stages* 菩薩地持經 1. T 30: 888a–890c.

282. I was unable to find this passage in the *Nirvana Sutra*.

283. T 9: 767a.

284. T 18: 1c.

285. T 39: 587b. The text is the *Commentary on the Mahāvairocana-abhisaṃbodhi Sutra*.

286. "Directly investigate what *is*" translates 直下に參究. 直下 literally means "directly under," the implication being that one should be directly aware of what is right under one's feet, right here, right now.

287. The first sentence is found at T 15: 751b; the second is found at T 15: 760b.

288. "Sahā" literally means "endure" and is commonly used to indicate the ordinary secular world, in which living beings must endure various types of suffering and want.

289. Vimalakīrti, the legendary protagonist of the *Vimalakīrti Sutra*, was a wealthy and deeply enlightened householder who lived at the same time as Śākyamuni Buddha. He represents the ideal lay Buddhist, who follows the śūnyatā-based life of the bodhisattva in the midst of the ordinary world. In the *Vimalakīrti Sutra* he is ill at home, having brought on his infirmity as an opportunity to expound the Dharma to his numerous visitors. At the urging of the Buddha, the entire assembly of the Buddha's disciples, numbering in the tens of thousands, calls upon the sick layman. Owing to Vimalakīrti's miraculous powers, all are accommodated in his ten-foot-square room, and the layman proceeds to describe the practice of the bodhisattva.

Translations in this book are from the *Vimalakīrti Sutra*, trans. Burton Watson. (New York: Columbia University Press, 1997).

290. The four evil paths are those of the asuras, the animals, the hungry spirits, and the hell-dwellers.

291. The eight types of human suffering are the sufferings associated with: (1) birth, (2) old age, (3) sickness, (4) death, (5) separation from those one loves, (6) meeting those one dislikes, (7) not getting what one seeks, (8) attachment to the five elements that make up one's existence.

292. The Chinese Zen master Zhongfeng Mingben 中峰明本 (J., Chūhō Myōhon; 1263–1323) was a contemporary of Musō's whom he admired greatly, and whom he mentions several times in *Dialogues in a Dream*. Zhongfeng was a native of Jiantang 錢塘 in Hangzhou 杭州 who succeeded to the Dharma of Gaofeng Yuanmiao 高峰原妙 (J., Kōhō Genmyō; 1238–1295) of Mount Tianmu 天目, then commenced an itinerant lifestyle that was in many ways similar to Musō's during the latter's wandering years. Zhongfeng maintained no fixed residence, living instead in hermitages, huts, or boats. He referred to himself by the sobriquet Huanzhu 幻住, "Phantom Resident." Despite his peripatetic existence he became an influential teacher with many students, including a number from Japan.

293. x 68: 113a. The "ancient" is Yunmen Wenyan.

294. See note 118, p 387. Uttarakuru, located to the north of Mount Sumeru, is said to be inhabited by beings who live in better circumstances than those on the other continents. They have life spans of a thousand years and are always happy.

295. T 17: 919b.

296. T 8: 749b.

297. Musō appears to be saying that in order to avoid the danger of quietistic resting in the void, inherent in the third practice of nonseeking, Bodhidharma taught practice in accordance with the Dharma—that is, the selfless practice of the six pāramitās.

298. I have not been able to determine what "mysterious illusion" 不思議玄 signifies.

299. The annihilationist position is that there is a soul that is completely destroyed after death. The eternalist view is that there is a soul that exists eternally.

300. The term "Middle Way" refers here to the mean between the two extreme views of substance and void.

301. See T 18: 3c. The "Types of Mind" chapter 住心品 is the first chapter of the *Mahāvairocana Sutra*.

302. For the pertinent passage in *Sutra of Complete Enlightenment*, see T 17: 914a. I was unable to locate any similar passages in the *Laṅkāvatāra Sutra*.

303. Musō is apparently referring to the three methods of contemplation—śamatha, samāpatti, and dhyāna—in the *Sutra of Complete Enlightenment*, T 17: 917b–18a. The passage on samāpatti is as follows:

> If, after awakening to pure Complete Enlightenment, bodhisattvas with pure enlightened minds realize the nature of mind and realize that the six sense faculties and sense objects are illusory projections, they will then generate illusion as a means to eliminate illusion. Causing transformations and manifestations among illusions, they will enlighten illusory sentient beings. By generating illusions, they will experience lightness and ease in great compassion. All bodhisattvas who practice in such a manner will advance gradually. That which contemplates illusion is different from illusion itself. Nevertheless, contemplating illusion is itself an illusion. When all illusions are permanently left behind, the wondrous cultivation completed by such bodhisattvas may be compared to the sprouting of seeds from soil. This expedient is called *samāpatti*. (Ch'an Master Sheng-yen, *Complete Enlightenment* [Elmhurst, New York: Dharma Drum Publications, 1997], 240)

304. *On Believing in Mind* 信心銘; T 48: 376c. Translation from the *Poetry of Enlightenment*,

by Sheng-yen (Elmhurst, New York: Dharma Drum Publications, 1987) 28. Sengcan 僧璨 (J., Sōsan; d. 606) is traditionally honored as the third patriarch of Chinese Zen. Little is known of his life. He is said to have been a layman when he first met Huike, the second patriarch, and that after receiving ordination and Dharma transmission he resided on Mount Sikong 司空 in present-day Anhui 安徽. During the Buddhist suppression by Emperor Wu in 574 he secluded himself on Mount Huangong 皖公 for more than ten years. After transmitting the Dharma to Daoxin 道信 (580–651) he retired to Mount Luofu 羅浮, in present Guangdong 廣東, where, it is said, he died standing up, grasping the branch of a tree.

305. The "ancient master" is Dahui Zonggao. The first passage is from the *Recorded Sayings of Meditation Master Dahui Pujue*, T 47: 865a; the second is from the same text, T 47: 890c; the third is from the *Essential Sayings of Meditation Master Zonggao Dahui Pujue* 宗杲大慧普覺禪師語要; x 83: 765b.

306. The passage is from the *Two Entrances* 二種入, T 48: 370a.

307. This appears to be a paraphrase of a passage found in the *Letters of Dahui* 大慧書 (T 47: 998a–b).

308. T 48: 377a.

309. T 12: 1035c. From the *Comprehensive Sutra Explaining the Descent of the Bodhisattva's Spirit from Tuṣita Heaven into His Mother's Womb* 菩薩從兜術天降神母胎説廣普經.

310. T 17: 913b. The six sense objects 六塵, lit., "six dusts," are colors, sounds, smells, tastes, textures, and phenomena.

311. Nanyue Huairang 南嶽懷讓 (J., Nangaku Ejō; 677–744) was one of the most important successors of Huineng, the Sixth Patriarch.

312. T 51: 240c. The original Chinese can also be translated as "Explanations are close, but they miss the mark."

313. T 47: 549c. The quote, from Yunmen Wenyan, literally reads, "Above, nowhere to climb; below, self is cut off."

314. Maitreya is the buddha of the future. The belief is that when he appears in the world 5,670,000,000 years in the future he will save all sentient beings.

315. This is described in the *Compendium of the Five Lamps* 五燈會元 3; x 80: 73a.

316. For Eminent Scholar Liang, see Introduction, pp. 12–13.

317. For Mazu Daoyi, see note 29, p. 377.

318. T 47: 949a.

319. The first half of this quote appears in numerous texts and records, e.g., the *Record of Xutang* 虛堂錄 x 67: 370a. The second half is a paraphrase of a line in the *Essentials of the Transmission of Mind* 傳心法要, T 48: 379c.

320. *On Believing in Mind*; T 48: 376b.

321. For "One Great Matter" see note 13, pp. 386–87.

322. The word translated as "practice," *kunshū* 熏修, literally means "perfuming practice," that is, continuous practice that imbues the mind with its merits, just as objects are imbued with fragrance by the constant burning of incense.

323. This statement is found in several Tendai texts, such as the *Annotations on Calming and Contemplation* 止觀輔行傳弘決 (T #1912). T 46: 167a.

324. That is, it differs according to whether or not it leads to liberation from deluded desires and views.

325. The sixteen contemplations are sixteen meditation practices that are believed in the Pure Land tradition to lead to rebirth in the Pure Land of Amitābha. In the contemplations the meditator focuses on various realms of existence, on the features of the Pure Land, on the buddha Amitābha, and on the bodhisattvas Avalokiteśvara and Mahāsthāmaprāpta.

326. Huiyuan 慧遠 (J., Eon; 334–416), one of the most important figures of early Chinese Buddhism, was a student of the Buddhist scholar and contemplative Daoan 道安 (J., Dōan; 312–385), under whom he studied the prajñāpāramitā sutras using Taoist concepts as an aid to understanding. From 381 till his death in 416 he lived on Mount Lu 廬, which he helped make into an important Buddhist monastic center. Huiyuan carried on an extensive correspondence with Kumārajīva (344–413) to clarify basic Buddhist concepts like "Dharmakāya" and "bodhisattva." With a group of his disciples he formed the White Lotus Society 白蓮社, dedicated to rebirth in the Pure Land of Amitābha; for this reason Huiyuan is regarded as a founder of the Pure Land school.

327. For example, the *Heart Sutra* 摩訶般若波羅蜜多心經; T 8: 848c.

328. The passage is found in fascicle 2 of the *Great Collection Sutra* 大方等大集經 (usually abbreviated to 大集經); T 13: 12a.

329. 般舟三昧經. T 13: 908b–c.

330. The six sense organs 六根 are the eye, ear, nose, tongue, feeling body, and thinking mind.

331. T 19: 123b. Aniruddha was one of the ten great disciples of the Buddha. After falling asleep once in the presence of the Buddha he vowed never to sleep again, causing him to eventually lose his eyesight. Subsequently he acquired the supernatural power of deva vision. Upānanda is one of the eight dragon kings mentioned in the *Lotus Sutra*. Gavāmpatī was an arhat said to have been afflicted with a condition in which his mouth moved constantly, owing to his having insulted a monk in a previous life. Mahākāśyapa was another of the ten great disciples of Śākyamuni, renowned for asceticism. Following the demise of the Buddha he became leader of the Sangha, and he is honored as the first Indian patriarch of Zen.

332. The doctrine of the three truths 三諦 is the Tiantai view of the nature of reality. The three truths are the truth of nonsubstantiality, the truth of provisionality, and the truth of the middle. The truth of nonsubstantiality is that phenomena have no permanent essence or independent existence and are thus empty. The truth of provisionality is that phenomena, though empty, have an apparent, temporary existence produced by causes and conditions. The truth of the middle is that the ultimate truth of all phenomena lies in neither their nonsubstantiality nor their provisionality but in a synthesis of the two in which the absolute abides in the phenomenal.

333. The three mystic practices are the three esoteric practices associated with the body, mouth, and mind, based on the view that the body, mouth, and mind of the practicer are one with and manifestations of the body, mouth, and mind of the Tathāgata. The mystic practice of the body is the formation of mudras with the hands; the mystic practice of the mouth is the recitation of mantras; and the mystic practice of the mind is the contemplation of mandalas. See also the note on the "three mysteries" (note 181, p. 392).

334. *On Believing in Mind* 信心銘; T 48: 376c.

335. This appears to be a conflation of several statements. The phrase "here is where all buddhas strive" 諸佛用心處 is found in passages attributed to Fenzhou Wuye (e.g., the *Compendium of the Five Lamps* 3; x 80: 82a). A passage containing the phrase "where there is no striving" 無用心處 and basically similar to Musō's statement can be found in words attributed to Haklenayaśas, the twenty-third Indian patriarch, in the *Compendium of the Five Lamps* 1 (x 80: 38b–c).

336. Musō may be paraphrasing Mazu, who, when asked, "What is the cultivation of the Way?" answered, "The Way is unrelated to cultivation. If you speak of gain through cultivation, then what is gained can be lost. That is the same as the śrāvakas. If you speak of no need for cultivation, that is the same as the common person." (x 2: 23.2.80b). Translation from *The Record of Linji*, trans. Ruth Fuller Sasaki (Honolulu: University of Hawaii Press, 2009), p. 179.

337. In the Japanese literary tradition, classical poems were commonly composed on assigned themes.

338. "Word-head" 話頭 is a term that can be used synonymously with "koan," but that often indicates a key point, word, or phrase in a koan upon which the student focuses his or her inquiry when using the koan during meditation.

339. "Face-to-face guidance" is an attempt to translate *tekimen teiji* 覿面提持, in which 覿面 means "direct" or "face-to-face" and 提持 means to clamp down, to disabuse a student of false views so that a deeper understanding may be reached.

340. This passage appears in the *Essential Teachings of Meditation Master Foguo Yuanwu Zhenjue* 2 (x 69: 473b).

341. A monk asked Zhaozhou Congshen, "Does a dog have Buddha-nature?" Zhaozhou answered, "*Wu*!" [No!]

342. The statement by Zhongfeng, which forms Case 52 of the koan collection *Zen School Koan Collection* 宗門葛藤集, is as follows: "Zhongfeng Mingben asked, 'What was the reason that Zhaozhou said "*Wu*"?' This is called 'The eight-word question of Zhongfeng' or 'The question of why he said what he did.'"

343. This saying is attributed to several masters, including Baizhang Huaihai (x 63: 510c) and, principally, Dahui Zonggao (T 47: 886a).

344. 大慧普覺禪師語錄 4. T 47: 825c.

345. *Kufū* 工夫 indicates an active and creative engagement in the process of Zen practice, whether seated or active.

346. I have been unable to find a specific source for this exact statement, but it is fully in line with standard Zen teachings. See, e.g., chapter 62, p. 267.

347. x 68: 227b. The master was Foyan Qingyuan 佛眼清遠 (J., Butsugen Seion; 1067–1120).

348. T 47: 667c. The master was Wuzu Fayan. See note 442, p. 408.

349. This statement is found in a number of sources, e.g., the *Recorded Sayings of Meditation Master Shishuang Chuyuan* 石霜楚圓禪師語錄; x 69: 191c.

350. King Śuddhodana had opposed his son Gautama's leaving the world to become a monk, but after Gautama's enlightenment he became a follower of his son's teachings and encouraged members of the Śākya clan to join the renunciant community.

351. T 25: 47b–c.

352. Bai Letian 白樂天 (J., Haku Rakuten; 772–846) was one of China's great poets.

353. Karaki identifies this as an expression from the "Tales of Mountain Travels" 遊巖傳 of the *Chronicles of the Tang* 唐書 (Karaki Junzō 唐木順三, *Zenke goroku shū* 禪家語錄集 [Tokyo: Chikuma Shobō, 1969], 154, note). The expression refers to people who cannot resist the allure of natural beauty.

354. Lu Tong 盧同 (7–8 c.) was a Tang-dynasty poet-scholar known for his love of drinking tea and for a famous poem that he wrote on the subject.

355. Lu Yu 陸羽 (d. 804) is said to have been raised in a temple but later fled to become a clown. An official who noticed his ability gave him books to educate himself. He later lived as a hermit and is known as the author of the *Tea Classic* 茶經.

356. The Saint of Toga no O 栂の尾 was Myōe Kōben 明惠高辨 (1173–1232), a Japanese monk honored for his maintenance of the precepts and his restoration of the Japanese Kegon school. Myōe studied the Kegon teachings at Tōdai-ji in Nara and Mount Shirakami on the Kii Peninsula. In 1206 he was granted land in the Toga no O area near Kyoto and there established Kōzan-ji 高山寺 as a Kegon training temple.

357. "The founder of Kennin-ji" refers to Myōan Eisai. See note 1, p. 373.

358. X 83: 765b. The ancient master is Dahui Zonggao.

359. The ancient master is most likely the Sixth Patriarch. See, e.g., T 48: 360a.

360. T 48: 376c. The master is Sengcan. See note 304, p. 400.

361. 畢竟空 and 獨空, respectively.

362. T 47: 829c. The ancient master is Dahui Zonggao.

363. The three knowledges 三明 are: (1) knowledge of past lives; (2) knowledge of future lives; (3) knowledge of the nature of suffering and how to eradicate the causes of suffering. The six supernatural powers 六通 are explained in the next paragraph of the text.

364. I was unable to locate a source for this quote. It may be Musō's play on the passage "A sage with five powers said to the Buddha, 'The Buddha has six powers. I have five. What is your extra power?',", which occurs in several Zen texts (e.g., the *Recorded Sayings of Meditation Master Dahui Pujue*, T 47: 896a). Musō is emphasizing that the true "extra" supernatural power is Original Nature.

365. X 69: 131a.

366. See also Linji's famous statement: "Followers of the Way, mind is without form and pervades the ten directions. In the eye it is called seeing, in the ear it is called hearing, in the nose it smells, in the mouth it talks, in the hands it grasps and holds, in the feet it runs and carries. Fundamentally it is one pure radiance; divided it becomes the six harmoniously united spheres of sense. If the mind is void, wherever you are, you are emancipated." (T 47: 497c) (Sasaki, *The Record of Linji*, 165).

367. T 17: 913a.

368. The bodily light is the aura emitted by a buddha's body; the wisdom light is the light of the buddha's wisdom; and the supernatural light is the light emitted by a buddha at the time of enlightenment and other special occasions.

369. Śarira (holy relics) are remains left behind when a buddha or sage is cremated, usually said to consist of indestructible, gem-like substances.

370. For the Trāyastrimśa Heaven, see note 123, p. 387.

371. "Enduring power" translates 薰力, an abbreviation for 薰習力, lit., "the force or power of fragrance-practice." Here the effects of practice are likened to that of incense, the fragrance of which imbues clothes that are in contact with the smoke and remains long after the incense has disappeared. Similarly, sustained practice imbues the consciousness of the practicer and has lasting beneficial effects.

372. A story from the "Devadatta" chapter of the *Lotus Sutra* (T 9: 35b). As the daughter of a dragon she was an animal, yet she was able to attain enlightenment quickly by practicing the teachings of the *Lotus Sutra*.

373. Vipaśyin was the first of the Seven Buddhas of the Past. The others are Śikhin, Viśvabhū, Krakucchanda, Kanakamuni, Kāśyapa, and Śākyamuni.

374. Similar statements are found in several texts, among them Baizhang Huaihai's *Pure Rules for the Zen Community* 禪林清規 (T 48: 1143a).

375. I was unable to find an explanation of the eighteen mysterious manifestations.

376. According to the traditional biographies, several masters died violent deaths such as execution by the government (e.g., the Second Patriarch, Huike) and murder at the hands of bandits (e.g., Yantou Quanhuo 巖頭全奯 [828–887]).

377. I was unable to locate this passage in the *Great Treasure Collection Sutra*.

378. See note 39, p. 378.

379. The doctrine of the tathāgata-garbha 如來藏 (tathāgata-womb) is the Mahayana teaching that all sentient beings possess the "womb" of Buddha-nature, which gives them the inherent potential to attain Buddhahood.

380. The ancient master is Yongjia Xuanjue; the quote is from the *Song of Enlightenment* (T 48: 396b).

381. T 8: 749b.

382. T 17: 913b. For the six perfections, see note 204, p. 393.

383. x 2: 882a. The Thirty-seven Honored Ones 三十七尊 are buddhas and bodhisattvas that represent various virtues or practices in the Diamond Realm Mandala. The Diamond Realm 金剛界 represents the wisdom of Mahāvairocana, the buddha who symbolizes Dharmakāya. The castle of the mind 心城 represents samādhi.

384. Karmic consciousness 業識 is the unawakened, deluded consciousness that arises through the workings of fundamental ignorance.

385. T 17: 913b.

386. T 19: 138b.

387. In Japanese the same character, 心, is used for what are in English the separate concepts of "mind" and "heart."

388. In the *Record of the Source Mirror* 宗鏡錄 the term is found at T 48: 434c.7.

389. Transliterated in this case as 矣栗陀. *Hṛdaya* has the same Indo-European linguistic root as the Greek word *kardia* and the English word "heart."

390. The Mind King 心王 is the cognitive or directive function of the consciousness, as opposed to its functions or qualities 心所.

391. T 16: 483b. The gloss that appears in the *Taishō* text is 肝栗大, not 乾栗馱.

392. A paraphrase of a line found at T 48: 434c.

393. T 39: 585b. The text is the *Commentary on the Mahāvairocana-abhisaṃbodhi Sutra*.

394. The quoted passage appears to be a much abbreviated and paraphrased version of an exchange found in the *Transmission of the Lamp* 28 (T 51: 437c–39b).

395. Feng Jichuan 馮濟川 (n.d.).

396. Laozi 老子 (sixth c. BCE?) and Zhuangzi 莊子 (fourth c. BCE) are the traditional founders of Taoist philosophy.

397. The maṇi jewel is the wish-fulfilling jewel.

398. T 17: 914c. Translation based on *Complete Enlightenment*, by Ch'an Master Sheng-yen (Elmhurst, New York: Dharma Drum Publications, 1997, pp. 128–129). The final line of the passage actually reads, "For this reason they are unable to depart from illusion."

399. T 48: 396b. From the *Song of Enlightenment*.

400. I was unable to locate the source of this quote. Changsha Jingcen 長沙景岑 (J., Chōsa Keishin; ninth c.) was an heir of Nanquan Puyuan. After leaving Nanquan he founded the temple Luyuan yuan 鹿苑院 in present Hunan. He subsequently taught the Dharma in the district of Changsha 長沙 in the same province.

401. T 17: 919c.

402. The concept that "the three realms are just one mind" 三界唯一心 is found in numerous texts, notably the *Avataṃsaka Sutra* 華嚴經 (T 10: 288c). The earliest mention of a statement close to Musō's, "The three realms are just one mind; outside of mind there is nothing" 三界唯一心 心外無別法, appears to be from the *Notes on the Discourse on the Establishment of Consciousness Only* 成唯識論述記 (T 43: 320c).

403. The six consciousnesses 六識 are the six types of consciousness that occur when the six sense organs make contact with their objects of perception. The six consciousnesses are: (1) sight, (2) hearing, (3) smell, (4) taste, (5) touch, and (6) conscious thought.

404. The seventh consciousness, the mano-vijñāna, is the level of consciousness that is aware of consciousness itself and that is formed by the sense of self. The eighth consciousness, the ālaya-vijñāna (storehouse consciousness), is the basic consciousness in which the impressions resulting from an individual's karmic activities are stored and out of which the other seven levels arise to produce all samsaric existence.

405. The ninth level of consciousness, the amala-vijñāna, is the level of pure consciousness. It is free of all karmic defilements and is in many ways equivalent to Buddha-nature. The concept of this ninth level of consciousness is taught in the Huayan school, the Tiantai school, and the Shelun school (which taught Yogācāra doctrine).

406. T 17:913c.

407. The long quote that follows is a paraphrase of passages found in the *Śūraṅgama Sutra*, fascicle 1 (T 19: 108b and below). The simile of the rice and sand is from fascicle 6 of the *Śūraṅgama Sutra* (T 19: 131c).

408. Nanyue Huisi 南嶽慧思 (J., Nangaku Eshi; 515–577) was the teacher of Zhiyi, the great priest who founded the Tiantai school.

409. The 大乘止觀法門 (T 46: #1924). Musō calls it *On Śamatha and Vipaśyanā According to the One Vehicle* 一乘止觀.

410. I have not been able to locate the full quote. For the first part, see T 46: 654a.

411. T 39: 600a. The commentary is the *Commentary on the Mahāvairocana-abhisaṃbodhi Sutra*.

412. The *Sutra on Divining the Effects of Karma* 占察業報經 (2 fascicles; T 17: #839) is said to have been translated into Chinese by Putideng 菩提燈 (ca 6–7 c.), but is now believed to be a Chinese apocryph. In it the bodhisattva Kṣitigarbha explains the true Buddhadharma, shows sentient beings in the Latter Age how to divine the effects of karma through the use of tree rings, and teaches two methods of meditation.

413. T 17: 907b.

414. Fire is one of the four essential elements (earth, water, fire, and wind). The fire that arises in conjunction with the other elements is known as "phenomenal fire" 事火; the fire element itself, independent of the other elements, is known as "essential fire" or "fire-nature" 性火. Fire-nature forms an inherent part of all material dharmas.

415. For transformational samsara, see note 248, pp. 396–97.

416. Musō may be referring to the passage in the *Sutra of Complete Enlightenment* at T 17: 914c. The discussion in the *Śūraṅgama Sutra* is found at T 19: 117c–119b.

417. "Objects and knowledge" translates 境智, the objective world and the subjective knowledge that recognizes the objective world.

418. T 17: 914c.

419. T 51: 438a.

420. I was unable to locate the source of this quote.

421. This appears to be from an argument developed in the *Laṅkāvatāra Sutra* 3; e.g., T 16: 504b.

422. T 14: 541a.

423. For the six objects of sensation, see note 310, p. 401.

424. See note 405, p. 406.

425. The true Dharma-realm 眞法界 is the realm separate from temporality, arising, and destruction. Some *Muchū Mondō* texts have 一眞法界, the Dharma-realm of the bhūta-tathatā, the one reality or essential suchness.

426. "The essential substance of phenomena" translates 法體, which can mean either the essential substance of a phenomenon or phenomena, or the essential elements that constitute the universe.

427. A chiliocosm (J., *sanzen sekai* 三千世界) consists of a billion world systems, with each world system consisting of a Mount Sumeru with its surrounding continents, seas, mountains, and celestial objects, and including the six realms from the hells up to the heavens of desire and the first of the heavens of form.

428. T 12: 397b.

429. T 46: 289b; the text cited is the *Annotations on Calming and Contemplation* 止觀輔行傳弘決. The "four eyes" referred to are the first four of the five eyes discussed above; the "two wisdoms" are the first two of the "three wisdoms": (1) the wisdom of the śrāvakas and pratyekabuddhas that sees the nonsubstantiality of all phenomena (一切智), (2) the wisdom of the bodhisattvas that sees the particularity of all phenomena (道種智), and (3) the wisdom of the buddhas that sees both the aspect of emptiness and the aspect of particularity (一切種智).

430. This is a paraphrase of passages found in the "Medicinal Herbs" 藥草 chapter of the *Lotus Sutra* (T 9: 19b).

431. The first sentence of the passage is found at T 17: 916b; the remainder is at T 17: 917a.

432. 佛說像法決疑經 (T 85: #2870); the passage is found at T 85: 1338a–b.

433. A paraphrase of a statement in the *Laṅkāvatāra Sutra* at T 16: 498c. The Deer Park is where Śākyamuni, after his enlightenment, preached his first sermon. The River Hiraṇyavatī is near the place where Śākyamuni passed away under the sāla trees. Neither is mentioned in the *Laṅkāvatāra Sutra*, which says instead, "From the time of my true enlightenment until my entry into nirvana I have spoken not a single word."

434. I was unable to locate this quote in the *Avataṃsaka Sutra*.

435. 不二摩訶衍論 (T #1668); T 32: 601c.

436. Probably a reference to chapter 14 of the *Diamond Sutra*.

437. See, e.g., the *Record of Xutang* 虛堂錄 (x 67: 370a) and the *Essentials of the Transmission of Mind* 傳心法要 (T 48: 379c).

438. Lit., "the transmission *of* mind, *with* mind" 以心傳心.

439. The three major kleśa, or impurities: attachment, aversion, and delusion.

440. The ancient master is Dahui Zonggao. The quote is from the *Recorded Sayings of Meditation Master Dahui Pujue* 14; T 47: 867c.

441. The quote is from the *Treasury of the True Dharma Eye* 正法眼藏 6 (x 67: 629c).

442. Wuzu Fayan 五祖法演 (J., Goso Hōen; 1024?–1104) was born in Mianzhou 綿州 in Sichuan 四川. He became a monk at the age of thirty-five and studied the Yogācāra ("Consciousness Only") teachings before turning to Zen. After studying under several masters, including Yuanjian Fayuan 圓鑑法遠 (J., Enkan Hōon; 991–1067), he eventually received the sanction of Baiyun Shouduan 白雲守端 (J., Haku'un Shutan; 1025–1072). He later settled on Mount Huangmei 黃梅, also called Mount Wuzu 五祖 (Fifth Patriarch Mountain) because the Fifth Patriarch, Hongren, had lived there. One of Fayan's heirs was Yuanwu Keqin, from whom all modern Japanese Rinzai masters descend.

443. The quote is based on a passage in the *Zen Arsenal of Meditation Master Dahui Pujue* 大慧普覺禪師宗門武庫 (T 47: 946a).

444. T 48: 396b.

445. "Individual beings and their environments" translates 依正, a term combining 依報, the body and mind of a sentient being gained on the basis of past karma, and 正報, the environment and circumstances in which that being lives. 依報 and 正報 are considered to be aspects of the same reality, since every being with its subjective existence lives in a unique objective environment, and both are the karmic expressions of the being's past actions.

446. 起世經. A paraphrase of a passage found in T 1: 348b–c.

447. T 14: 538a.

448. T 85: 1337a.

449. The master is Yuanwu Keqin; the quote is a paraphrase of a passage in the *Essential Teachings of Meditation Master Foguo Yuanwu Zhenjue* 1 (x 69: 456a).

450. Fayan Wenyi 法眼文益 (J., Hōgen Mon'eki; 885–958), a native of Zhejiang 浙江, entered temple life at the age of seven and studied the Confucian classics and Buddhist sutras, especially the *Avataṃsaka Sutra*. He later studied Zen under Changqing Huileng 長慶

慧稜 (854–932) and Luohan Guichen 羅漢桂琛 (869–928). After becoming Luohan's Dharma heir he served as abbot of several temples and produced sixty-three successors. Fayan is recognized as the founder of the Fayan school of Zen.

451. T 49: 666a. This is a reference to one of Zhaozhou's most famous koans:

> A monk once asked Zhaozhou Congshen, "What was the meaning of Bodhidharma's coming from the West?" Zhaozhou answered, "The juniper tree in the garden." The monk replied, "Master, don't teach me using external objects." Zhaozhou said, "I'm not teaching you using external objects." The monk asked, "What was the meaning of Bodhidharma's coming from the West?" Zhaozhou answered, "The juniper tree in the garden."

Following the exchange between Fayan and Juetiezui mentioned in the text, Fayan is said to have praised Juetiezui with the words, "The true child of a lion gives a good lion's roar!"

452. "The Original Vow of Other Power" refers to the eighteenth of the forty-eight vows made by Amitābha Buddha when he was still practicing as the bodhisattva Dharmākara. In this vow Dharmākara pledged that if, when he attained Buddhahood, all beings who heard his name rejoiced, sincerely entrusted themselves to him, and called his name even just ten times should not attain rebirth in his pure land, then he would not attain Supreme Enlightenment.

453. T 17: 915b.

454. See chapter 60, p. 258, and note 372, p. 405.

455. Ajātaśatru was a prince who, at the instigation of Devadatta, murdered his father, King Bimbisāra, and usurped the throne of the Indian kingdom of Magadha.

According to the account given in the *Nirvana Sutra*, King Bimbisāra, concerned that he had no son, consulted a diviner and learned of a hermit in the mountains who was to be reborn as his heir. In order to hasten the process the king had the hermit killed, but after the royal birth he was warned by the diviner that the new prince, Ajātaśatru, was destined to harm him. The king therefore threw the prince off the top of a tower, but the infant suffered nothing more than a broken finger. As foretold by the prophecy, upon reaching adulthood Ajātaśatru murdered his father and usurped the throne. Years later, however, he came to be tormented by guilt, causing virulent sores to break out all over his body. On the advice of his minister Jīvaka he visited Śākyamuni, who taught him the doctrines of the *Nirvana Sutra*. Ajātaśatru recovered his health and his evil karma was erased. The story of Ajātaśatru is found in fascicle 20 of the Northern Text of the *Nirvana Sutra* (T #374) and fascicle 18 of the Southern Text (T #375).

456. Vipaśyin Buddha was the first of the Seven Buddhas of the Past.

457. A paraphrase of a passage found at T 12: 728b–c.

458. I was unable to locate the source of this quote.

459. From the *Recorded Sayings of Meditation Master Gulin Qingmao* 古林清茂禪師語錄 3 (X 71: 243c).

460. The three Pure Land sutras are the *Sutra on Eternal Life* 無量壽經, the *Sutra on the Contemplation of Eternal Life* 觀無量壽經, and the *Amitābha Sutra* 阿彌陀經.

461. See, for example, T 12: 401b–402c (*Nirvana Sutra* 5); T 12: 642b–643b (*Nirvana Sutra* 6); and T 11: 304b–c (*Sutra of the Great Treasure Collection* 52).

462. According to the Pure Land teachings, aspirants to the Amitābha's Pure Land are divided into three classes: those of the highest class, those of the middle class, and those of the lowest class. Each of these classes is in turn divided into three categories: highest birth, middle birth, lowest birth. The Pure Land has nine grades, corresponding to the nine respective types of class and birth.

463. A great kalpa comprises four medium kalpas or eighty small kalpas. A small kalpa is a period during which the human life span increases one year every century from ten years to eighty-four thousand years, then decreases one year a century from eighty-four thousand years to ten years.

464. See note 104, p. 386.

465. T 12: 346a.

466. The *Samādhi of Beholding the Buddhas Sutra* 般舟三昧經 (T #416, #417, #418, and #419), an early Mahayana sutra that is one of the first to mention the Buddha Amitābha, teaches meditations that enable the practicer to perceive Amitābha and all the other buddhas as though they were standing directly before one.

467. T 12: 485a; T 12: 728a.

468. See note 93, p. 384.

469. Kṣitigarbha is the bodhisattva who was charged by the Buddha with liberating sentient beings between the time of the Buddha's death and the appearance of Maitreya, the buddha of the future.

470. 思益梵天所問經 (T 15: #586).

471. The quote is a paraphrase of a passage found at T 15: 37a.

472. T 17: 914b.

473. T 9: 50c. The original text does not mention "celestial demons, non-Buddhists, evil people, and good people," but only monks, nuns, laymen, and laywomen.

474. T 17: 919c.

475. I have not been able to locate this passage in the *Nirvana Sutra*.

476. T 85: 1337a.

477. Emperor Ming 明 (28–75) was the second ruler of the Eastern or Later Han 後漢 dynasty (25–220).

478. Another title for Baizhang Huaihai. See note 41, p. 378.

479. The original has 持犯開遮 (a term for the various circumstances in which those things that are normally forbidden by the precepts are allowed, and in which those things that are normally allowed by the precepts are forbidden) and 五篇七聚 (an overall term for the various categories of precepts).

480. I have been unable to find the source of this quote.

481. The realms of pure form and formlessness are the second and third realms of the three-fold world, above the realm of desire. See note 121 on p. 387 and the corresponding sections of chapter 6.

482. The four meditations 四禪 are four stages of meditation that enable practicers to over-come desire and illusion and attain rebirth in the four meditation heavens of the realm of pure form. These four meditations plus the four meditations associated with the four heavens of the realm of formlessness comprise the eight samādhis 八定.

483. See T 16: 492a.

484. That is, the reality that posits neither existence nor nonexistence.

485. Uncaused universal wisdom translates 自覺聖智, which is wisdom as the fundamental nature of the universe 法界體性智, a characteristic of the Dharmakāya (buddha as absolute truth).

486. E.g., x 64: 293c.

487. The discussion of the three contemplations in the *Sutra of Complete Enlightenment* is found in the chapter "The Bodhisattva of Sound Discernment" 辯音菩薩, at T 17: 918a–19a. The terms actually used in the *Sutra of Complete Enlightenment* are not samādhi 定 and wisdom 慧 but rather śamatha 奢摩他 and samāpatti 三摩鉢提. In the context of the discussion the significance is the same, however.

488. Guifeng Zongmi 圭峰宗密 (J., Keihō Shūmitsu; 780–841) was the fifth patriarch of the Heze 荷澤 school of Zen and also the fifth and final patriarch of the philosophical Huayan 華嚴 school.

489. "Contemplation of the absolute mind" translates 絕待靈心觀. This term appears in several of Guifeng's works, such as the *Subcommentary on the Sutra of Complete Enlightenment* 大方廣圓覺修多羅了義經略疏 (T 39: 557c).

490. The *Anthology of Essential Writings on the Origins of Zen* 禪源諸詮集 is a nonextant collection of writings related to early Zen history and thought.

491. T 9: 19c. Translation from *The Lotus Sutra,* trans. Burton Watson, 100.

492. The ancient master is Yuanwu Keqin. See, e.g., the *Recorded Sayings of Meditation Master Foguo Yuanwu Zhenjue* 10 (T 47: 757a).

493. T 16: 498c. See note 433, pp. 408.

494. T 85: 1337a.

495. T 17: 917a.

496. "Abolish verbal explanations to express the tenet," 廢詮 or, more fully, 廢詮談旨, reflects the Hossō view that ultimate reality is ineffable. "Sacred silence" 聖默 expresses the Sanron position that only silence is appropriate when one attains Nāgārjuna's Middle Way of the eightfold negation, where the paths of speech are severed and the activities of thought transcended. "Subtle tenets" 妙旨 refers to such abstruse Tendai teachings as "the three contemplations in a single thought" 一心三觀 and "the three thousand realms in a single thought-moment" 一念三千. The ineffability of the buddha-fruit of enlightenment is expressed in Kegon in the term 果分 or, more properly, 果分不可説. The Shingon "absolute words" translates 如義言説.

497. The sutra is the *Sutra of the Pavilion of Vajra Peak and All Its Practicers* 金剛峰 樓閣一切瑜伽瑜祇經. The passage is found at T 18: 269c.

498. 大日經疏指示鈔 1 (T 59: 576b).

499. See note 148, p. 389.

500. The *Commentary on the Principle of Wisdom Sutra* 理趣釋 (T 19: #1003) is a commentary on the esoteric *Principle of Wisdom Sutra* 大樂金剛不空眞實三昧耶經 (usually abbreviated as 理趣經), which teaches the essential purity of all desires and the attainment of that purity through the realization of prajñā.

501. The *Lineages of the Innerly Realized Buddhadharma* 内證佛法相承血脈譜, written in 819,

lists the lineages of the various traditions in which Dengyō Daishi received transmission during his sojourn in Tang-dynasty China. The traditions are: the perfect teachings 圓教, esoteric teachings 密教, Zen 禪, and vinaya 律.

502. The 達磨大師付法相承師々の血脈一首, the 天台法華宗の相承師々の血脈一首, the 天台の圓頓菩薩戒の相承師々の血脈一首, and the 胎藏金剛兩曼茶羅の相承師々の血脈一首, respectively.

503. Emperor Saga 嵯峨 (786–842) is traditionally counted as the fifty-second emperor of Japan.

504. Egaku 慧萼 (n.d.).

505. Yanguan Jian 塩官齊安 (J., Enkan Saian; 750?–842), a successor of the great Chinese Zen master Mazu Daoyi, was the abbot of the temple Lingchi si 靈池寺 in Hangzhou 杭州.

506. Yikong 義空 (J., Gikū; n.d.).

507. Danrin-ji 檀林寺.

508. Empress Danrin 檀林皇后 was Tachibana Kachiko 橘 嘉智子 (786–850), the consort of Emperor Saga.

509. Qiyuan 契元 (J., Keigen; n.d.); Kaiyuan si 開元寺.

510. Jikaku Daishi 慈覺大師 (794–864), commonly known by his name Ennin 圓仁, studied under Dengyō Daishi at Mount Hiei from the year 808; in 838 he journeyed to China, where he studied Sanskrit, esoteric Buddhism, and the doctrines of the Tiantai school. In 847 he returned to Japan and took the position of chief abbot (Zasu 座主) at Mount Hiei. He promoted Tendai esotericism (Taimitsu 台密), as distinguished from Shingon esotericism (Tōmitsu 東密).

511. 教祖同異集.

512. Chishō Daishi 智證大師 (814–891), commonly known by his name Enchin 圓珍, studied under the second Tendai Zasu, Gishin 義眞 (781–833). In 853 Chishō traveled to China, where he practiced Tiantai meditation and deepened his knowledge of the esoteric doctrines. He returned to Japan in 858, and in 868 he became the fifth Tendai Zasu. He is honored as the founder of the Jimon 寺門 school of Tendai.

513. 教時諍論. T 75: 2395A.

514. Annen 安然 (841–889/98) was a Tendai priest born in present-day Shiga Prefecture. He studied under Ennin and Henshō 遍昭 (815–890), and was particularly active in systematizing the Tendai esoteric doctrines.

515. For Prince Shōtoku, see note 159, p. 390; for Nanyue, see note 311, p. 401. The legend does not account for the fact that Prince Shōtoku (574–622) predates Nanyue (677–744) by over a century.

516. Ikaruga is another name for Prince Shōtoku, derived from the fact that his palace, built in 601, was named Ikaruga no Miya.

517. Gedatsu Shōnin 解脱上人 (1155–1213) is the popular name of Jōkei 貞慶, a Hossō school priest. Jōkei studied at the great Nara temple Kōfuku-ji 興福寺 and at a young age ascended to the prestigious position of lecturer. He later served as abbot of the remote temples Kasagi-dera 笠置寺 and Kaijūzan-ji 海住山寺. He was a prolific writer and is remembered for his many treatises on Hossō doctrine, his promotion of the precepts, and his criticism of Hōnen's *nenbutsu* movement.

518. 説法明眼論.

519. 十住心論. A treatise by Kōbō Daishi written about 830, outlining the ten stages in the development of religious consciousness.

520. Zhijue Dashi 智覺大師 is the title of Yongming Yanshou 永明延壽 (J., Yōmei Enju; 904–975). Yongming became a monk at the age of twenty-eight, after serving as a government official for a number of years. He received transmission from the Fayan school master Tiantai Deshao 天台德韶 (J., Tendai Tokushō; 891–972) and became the third patriarch of the school. He wrote a number of works, notably the *Record of the Source Mirror* 宗鏡錄, and is known for advocating the use of the *nenbutsu* as part of Zen practice.

521. I have not been able to locate the source of this quote.

522. Tiantai Dashi 天台大師 is the title of Zhiyi; see note 201, p. 393. "Word-and-letter Dharma teachers" 文字法師 and "dark-enlightenment meditation masters" 暗證禪師 are mentioned in the Tiantai lineage text *Annals of the Lineage of Buddhas and Patriarchs* 佛祖統紀 50 (T 49: #2035).

523. In the *Record of the Source Mirror* (T 48: 418c).

524. The instant students understand the meaning behind the teacher's words, they are separated from the experience itself. Who the ancient master was is unknown.

525. For Kosen Ingen, see note 66, pp. 381–82.

526. "General of the Left" (Sabuei Shōgun 左武衞將軍) was a title of Ashikaga Tadayoshi; Kozan 古山 was his Buddhist lay name.

527. Ōtaka Shigenari 太高重成 (?–1362) was a military commander under Ashikaga Tadayoshi.

528. A passage from the *Lotus Sutra*; T 9: 8a. The full passage reads: "In the Buddha lands of the ten directions there is only the Law of the one vehicle, there are not two, there are not three, except when the Buddha preaches so as an expedient means, merely employing provisional names and terms in order to conduct and guide living beings and preach to them the Buddha wisdom" (*The Lotus Sutra*, trans. Burton Watson, 35). Zhuxian Fanxian appears to be playing on words, since the characters for *kana* 假名 and the characters for "provisional names" 假名 are the same.

529. "[Earlier or later,] the principle is the same" 其揆一耳 is a quote from Mencius 孟子, Li Lau 離婁 2.

530. The passage is from the *Recorded Sayings of Meditation Master Dahui Pujue* 25 (T 47: 919a).

531. The original has "...with the characters 鳥 (bird) and 焉 (here) becoming 馬 (horse)."

532. Wakasa 若狹 Province was an important district just north of Kyoto, corresponding to the southern section of present-day Fukui Prefecture.

About the Translator

Thomas Yūhō Kirchner was born in Baltimore, Maryland, in 1949. He went to Japan in 1969 to attend Waseda University in Tokyo for a year, after which he remained in Japan to study Buddhism. He spent three years training under Yamada Mumon as a lay monk at Shōfuku-ji before receiving ordination in 1974. Following ordination he practiced under Minato Sodō Roshi at Kencho-ji in Kamakura and Kennin-ji in Kyoto. Following graduate studies in Buddhism at Otani University he worked at the Nanzan Institute for Religion and Culture in Nagoya and subsequently at the Hanazono University International Research Institute for Zen Buddhism. He presently lives at Tenryū-ji in Arashiyama, Kyoto. Among his publications are the *Record of Linji* and *Entangling Vines*.

About Wisdom

Wisdom Publications is the leading publisher of classic and contemporary Buddhist books and practical works on mindfulness. Publishing books from all major Buddhist traditions, Wisdom is a nonprofit charitable organization dedicated to cultivating Buddhist voices the world over, advancing critical scholarship, and preserving and sharing Buddhist literary culture.

To learn more about us or to explore our other books, please visit our website at www.wisdompubs.org. You can subscribe to our eNewsletter, request a print catalog, and find out how you can help support Wisdom's mission either online or by writing to:

Wisdom Publications
199 Elm Street
Somerville, Massachusetts 02144 USA

You can also contact us at 617-776-7416 or info@wisdompubs.org.

Wisdom is a 501(c)(3) organization, and donations in support of our mission are tax deductible.

Wisdom Publications is affiliated with the Foundation for the Preservation of the Mahayana Tradition (FPMT).

More Books from Wisdom Publications

Entangling Vines
A Classic Collection of Zen Koans
Translated by Thomas Yūhō Kirchner
Foreword by Nelson Foster

"A masterpiece. It will be our inspiration for 10,000 years."
—Robert Aitken, author of *Taking the Path of Zen*

The Book of Equanimity
Illuminating Classic Zen Koans
Gerry Shishin Wick

"Every student of Zen would do well to read this fine book."
—Robert Jinsen Kennedy, author of *Zen Spirit, Christian Spirit*

Sitting with Koans
Essential Writings on Zen Koan Introspection
Edited by John Daido Loori
Introduced by Thomas Yūhō Kirchner

"Required reading for those interested in how koans are used in Zen practice."
—*Shambhala Sun*

Inside the Grass Hut
Living Shitou's Classic Zen Poem
Ben Connelly
Foreword by Taigen Dan Leighton

"The very essence of Zen."
—Mike O'Connor, translator of *When I Find You Again, It Will Be in Mountains*

The Ceasing of Notions
An Early Zen Text from the Dunhuang Caves with Selected Comments
Sōkō Morinaga
Introduced by Martin Collcutt

"This powerful little book is a jewel of Zen Buddhism. Roshi Soko Morinaga goes right to the point of practice and realization."
—Joan Halifax, founding abbot, Upaya Zen Center

The Zen Teaching of Homeless Kodo
Kosho Uchiyama and Shohaku Okumura

"Kodo Sawaki was straight-to-the-point, irreverent, and deeply insightful—and one of the most influential Zen teachers for us in the West. I'm very happy to see this book."
—Brad Warner, author of *Hardcore Zen*